NYERERE OF TANZANIA

by

WILLIAM EDGETT SMITH

NAIROBI
TRANSAFRICA PUBLISHERS
1974

First published in February 1973
by Victor Gollancz Ltd., London
and first published in Africa
by Transafrica Publishers Ltd.,
P.O. Box 42990, Nairobi, Kenya
This book has been published in the United States
by Random House, Inc., New York, under the title,
We Must Run While They Walk: A Portrait of Africa's Julius Nyerere. A substantial portion of the book
appeared originally in *The New Yorker*, in somewhat
different form.

For my mother and father

Printed photolitho by General Printers Ltd.,
Dar es Salaam Road, P.O. Box 18001, Nairobi

ACKNOWLEDGMENTS

I SHOULD LIKE TO THANK President Nyerere for permission to quote from several of his essays and speeches that are included in his books *Freedom and Unity* and *Freedom and Socialism*, published by the Oxford University Press. More important to the writing of this book, however, were the many interviews that the President kindly granted me over a period of several years. He is in no sense responsible for the book's conclusions; yet it could not have been written without his unfailing courtesy and patience. I should also like to thank all the other persons, some named and some unnamed, who helped so much.

W. E. S.

New York, October 1972

I

JULIUS KAMBARAGE NYERERE, the President of the United Republic of Tanzania, is forever reminding his countrymen that they cannot go to the moon. "Our tools are as old as Mohammed, we live in houses from the time of Moses," he may cry, as he once did to a group of Chagga tribesmen, who grow coffee on the slopes of Mount Kilimanjaro. "The Americans are going to the moon! The Russians are going to the moon! *We* can't go to the moon!" Or he may lament gently, "While the Americans and the Russians are going to the moon, we Africans are dancing," or shout angrily, "Our friends are using their brains while ours sleep and grow fungus, they are sending rockets into outer space while we are eating wild roots!" One might have supposed that the thirteen million citizens of the United Republic of Tanzania scarcely needed to be reminded of these facts, but Nyerere, who is known to his countrymen as *Mwalimu*, the teacher, harps on them relentlessly nonetheless. "I should have been a preacher in a pulpit instead of the President of a republic," he once remarked to a friend, and indeed his talks in the interior, where he travels as much as half the time, are less like political speeches than stern adjurations or even haranguing sermons: he never seems to tell his listeners exactly what they want to hear. "Look," he once shouted, in his staccato Swahili, to the peasant farmers of a new tobacco settlement, "in the United States they get twenty-four hundred pounds of tobacco to the acre. And here you get six hundred. But over in Urambo, not many miles from here, they are already getting fifteen hundred pounds to the acre. This is something we can do! It's not like going to the moon. We can't go to the moon! But *this we can do* . . ."

Nyerere has been preoccupied with such comparisons since long before his country became independent in 1961. At that time it was known as Tanganyika, the name it had borne for forty-one years as a British mandate and later trusteeship territory. In April 1964 Tanganyika formed a union with the tiny offshore island republic of Zanzibar, and the new nation became known a few months later as the United Republic of Tanzania.

"The problem was overwhelming," Nyerere remarked one day in

early 1964, a short time after an army mutiny had nearly destroyed his government, "and I still see it. You do not just say 'independence'. It must mean many other things. And it is not good if the people become over-interested. The problem becomes *formidable* if they see it too quickly. Do you see? It's 1964 for everybody in the world, *including* the Masai," those tall, lean, spear-carrying warriors of the East African plains, "and the pressure for all to live in 1964, including the Masai, is fantastic. People tell me, 'The Masai are completely happy.' I tell them, 'It's not a question of whether they are happy. That's a philosophical question. I'm not trying to make them *happy*!' But"—chopping his words hard—"there is a difference between clean water and dirty water. My problem is to get that woman clean water. My problem is to get her a healthy child. Happy! I'm not involving myself in that." He gave a sort of ironic shudder. "I don't know if my own family right here in State House is any happier than the Masai. The question is, What kind of water are the Masai drinking in 1964?"

He was sitting on the veranda of State House in Dar es Salaam looking down across a yellow-green lawn toward the glistening turquoise Indian Ocean, a slight, wiry man with a high forehead and a toothbrush moustache. In those years he still looked far more like an earnest graduate student than a *baba wa taifa*, the father of a nation. He wore khaki slacks, a bright sports shirt and leather sandals. "In the twelfth century," he continued, "this problem perhaps would not have been formidable. But today the standard of living in the United States of America is part of Tanganyika. Sometimes I wish I could put Tanganyika on another planet. Then we could give it a hundred years to catch up. But we can't do that, we can't isolate ourselves. The Masai *know* that these things are possible—milk for children, clean water, good houses: these things are objective, desirable, necessary. But the Masai don't easily accept the disciplines required. Clean water requires piping. That pond must be drained. Work! But it requires knowledge, technical know-how. Germany was virtually razed, and Japan, but they had the necessary attitudes and skills for reconstruction. So I have to build these attitudes. But I can't wait. I can't wait to train Masai vets and doctors. So I have to borrow skills. But borrowing is difficult because"—very slowly again—"certain attitudes of resistance have been created. That same fellow who wants clean water piped to his village would say, 'Hey! Why are you getting an Englishman to do it?' And if I tell him, 'Because there isn't a Masai engineer,' he will ask"—mock astonishment—" 'Why not?'" At which Nyerere burst out laughing, apparently as much at the stubbornness of the Masai as at the ridiculousness of the situation. "You see?"

One cool April morning in 1966, in the season that passes for autumn in Dar es Salaam, Nyerere set off for a four-day tour of one of mainland Tanzania's seventeen regions, Tabora, which lies deep in the interior along the ancient trade and slave route that once ran from Bagamoyo, on the coast opposite Zanzibar Island, to Lake Victoria and Lake Tanganyika. His grey Mercedes-Benz sedan arrived at the airport at seven-forty-five, preceded by a single police car with flashing blue light, and Nyerere, waving his ebony hand stick, jumped out and began to shake hands and trade quips with the handful of government officials who had come to see him off. His hair had turned quite grey in the preceding two or three years. He was wearing a collarless, coat-style shirt and matching trousers of a Japanese drip-dry fabric. Such uniforms had come to be known as "Tanzanian suits," since practically every man of influence in Dar es Salaam had followed the President's lead and begun to wear them. Many Europeans and Americans in East Africa, already uneasy about Nyerere's growing friendship with China, had seized on the introduction of the uniforms as yet another indication that Nyerere was "going Chinese". The Tanzanians, exceedingly sensitive to such talk, were going to great pains to point out that Nyerere had first seen such a suit on Zanzibar and admired it for its simplicity, and that Chinese Premier Chou En-lai himself, during his state visit to Tanzania, had remarked that the suit was not heavy enough for the Chinese climate.

Nyerere also wore an Arab cap from Zanzibar, a *kofia*, and it was this novelty that caught his colleagues' fancy. "Ah, you like it?" he said to the chief justice. "Perhaps you would like one? No?" Then he climbed into the government's twin-engine Aero Commander, taking the seat beside his British pilot. He was followed by his Minister of State, Bhoke Munanka, his aide-de-camp and two young security men. A moment later the little plane took off and immediately disappeared into lush green bush country, thereby revealing a fact generally obscured by the pleasures and intrigues of life in the capital: that the wilderness of Tanganyika begins at the far end of the Dar es Salaam runway.

The first day. Amid signs of KARIBU BABA WA TAIFA (Welcome, Father of the Nation), Nyerere was spirited off to Tabora's new community hall for a lunch of chicken, Indian pasties, tea and cakes. Then, in the hot midday sun, he handed out one hundred and eight literacy certificates to adults who had learned to read and write during the preceding year. One young mother, who set her baby at the President's feet as she accepted her certificate and bowed, was so flustered that she forgot the infant until after she had returned to her seat. Later, on the veranda of the regional commissioner's house, Nyerere chatted with the local elders of the Tanganyika African National Union (TANU), the political party of mainland Tanzania. "Why do you wear that?" one elder chided him. "It's a Zanzibar cap." "No," said Nyerere, "it's a Tanzanian cap," and they all laughed because the concept of Tanzanian union still seemed unreal. Hashim Mbita, the President's young press secretary, said the cap was an expensive one, worth eighty shillings at least. "You seem to know a lot about them," Nyerere said. "Have you been making them on the side?" For a while they argued about the merits of the bride-price tradition, which involves the payment of cows or other wealth by the prospective bridegroom to the father of the bride. One elder defended the practice and added slyly, "Besides, I have four daughters." "But *I*, brother," Nyerere shot back, "have two daughters and five sons, so I must pay." The talk turned to a recent rash of cattle thefts, and Bhoke Munanka, a huge, good-natured man who serves sometimes as the butt of the President's jokes, spoke at length of the various methods of marking cattle illegally. "He is an expert," Nyerere said. A moment later, in great good spirits, he told in Swahili a long story about his childhood—"about the hairs of a goat's head," Hashim whispered—and, whatever he said, it caused the men to howl with laughter.

In the afternoon, the party drove forty-eight miles south to the Moravian leprosarium at Sikonge, where Nyerere dedicated a new clinic. The patients gave him a drum, and he responded by buying a second one. On the dusty road back to Tabora, Hashim, who had spent his childhood in a nearby village, spoke of how the rural life was changing. "We used to think the European was selfish because he looked out only for himself," he said. "We would say scornfully, 'He behaves like a European.' If a man had three or four hundred goats, he would slaughter one at the weekend, and everybody would be welcome. It was a terrible insult to have someone leave your house hungry. But now the people are so dependent on the cash economy, they buy for themselves only. If a guest arrives after a meal is over, there is nothing left for him."

The second day. North of Tabora on the Mwanza road, thirty women waved as Nyerere drove past. "This is Kazima," Hashim said. "We will stop here on the return. *Mwalimu* always stops here." At Isikizya, Nyerere urged the tobacco farmers to increase their yields per acre, inspected a new baling station, and called for his Polaroid camera so that he could take a picture of four women carrying water jugs. "This is a first-class picture," he said. "Not bad for an amateur, eh?" The women were too shy to reply. At Nzega, he cut a red ribbon to open a new cattle dip, but the cattle were frightened and refused to pass through it. "Too many people," Nyerere said. "Give them way." At the Maria Nyerere Maternity Clinic, named in honour of his wife, Nyerere was presented with a trayful of gifts, and the party sat down to tea. Here, as at Tabora, a gigantic woman, the local chairman of the national women's organization, stood before his table, urging him to eat more chicken and corn-bread, and waving her handkerchief as a fan. She pointed through the window at an old mud hut, and Nyerere smiled. "She is explaining," he told a visitor, "why she seated me here. She wanted me to see the old clinic we inherited from the Empire. Also, she says she can now read and write her name. In colonial times she knew nothing, she says, she had to use her thumb print for her name." The new clinic had been built under the national self-help programme, Nyerere said, under which villagers donated a day's work a week to a community task; the clinic had cost over £3,000 for materials, but was said to be worth at least twice as much. "One of the troubles we had with self-help in the beginning was that, when a building like this was finished, there might be no one to run it. But under our five-year plan, a midwife will be provided."

At Bukene, Nyerere thanked the people for their work but warned them, "There is a Swahili saying, 'A brewer whose brew is praised is likely to dilute it.' Don't do that. If you do that, you will bring shame to us." Then he made his main point: "Nzega district has a higher cattle population than any other district in the country. Cattle is our wealth, and you must use your wealth. Every year you must sell some cattle to get money for your children's schooling, and for better houses. Look at the Chagga. The Chagga have become rich on their coffee. You must use your cattle to make you rich too."

In late afternoon, as Hashim had predicted, Nyerere stopped to see the women of Kazima. Mostly widows, with a few children and grandchildren, they had moved to this open land a few years earlier from Tabora, six miles away, after Nyerere had urged people to leave the towns and go out and cultivate the soil. The women served boiled peanuts and corn to the President, and then they told him their troubles. Their rice had dried up for lack of rain, they said, but they had earned 300 shillings on their tomatoes. "If you had grown three times as many, you'd have made nine hundred shillings," Nyerere said, and one woman replied, "It is true, *Babu*, it was our folly." She complained bitterly about the red tape involved in getting water from the nearby dam; vouchers were now required, she said. Nyerere wheeled around to the area commissioner, the official in charge of that part of Tabora region, who replied, a bit defensively, "It is to prevent unauthorized people from spoiling the water." Nyerere told the woman not to worry; he had a plan for piping water from the dam to the village, and he would tell them about it soon. As he prepared to leave, the women sang for him: "*Nyerere has called the people to go to the country, he wants to see those who took hold of the soil*," followed by a local tribal song, which Hashim translated: "*The child of the lion is a lion/You have finished the night/Now put on the fire and cook.*"

The third day. "Look at me," Nyerere said to a group of children. "If you weren't so shy, this picture would be beautiful." Instead it was fuzzy. "Ah," said Nyerere, in mock dismay, "the camera let me down." Then he tried a picture of a young farmer, his wife and suckling baby, but the Polaroid was out of film. The aide-de-camp ran for more. "I'm trying my best for the 1970 elections, you are my witnesses," Nyerere said. When a farmer boasted that he had made 82,000 shillings—almost £4,300—on his tobacco the previous year, Nyerere expressed surprise. "That's twenty thousand shillings more than *my* salary," he said. "I should move to Urambo. I'd save my hair from turning grey."

To a foreign visitor he shouted, "Look at this hoe, this *jembe*." He was pointing to a single-stroke hoe with a three-foot handle, the basic farming tool in Tanzania. "You see? No matter how hard a man works, even if he works twenty-four hours a day, he cannot achieve very much." Later, at the Urambo Farmer Training Centre, he discussed the oxen plough as an alternative to the *jembe*. "I'm sure the oxen plough is the answer," he told the British principal. "I'm a very big oxen-plough man."

When Nyerere asked a farmer how much tobacco he had grown the year before, the man shrugged and said he didn't know. "Aha," said Nyerere jubilantly, "maybe you don't want to say, for fear we will assess the personal tax." The man laughed timidly. As Nyerere toured a small tobacco field recently planted by the local TANU youth league chapter, the Tabora Member of Parliament, an Indian, criticized the youth league's effort as uneconomic. "What do you mean?" demanded Nyerere. "We're getting into the third year of our five-year plan, and Tabora hasn't planned *anything* yet, but you criticize those who have started something. Why is that?"

On the regional commissioner's veranda that evening, Nyerere listened on his portable radio to the British Broadcasting Corporation's short-wave news broadcast, followed by a panel discussion on the political situation in Rhodesia. When one panel member suggested that African members of the Commonwealth might "secede" if Britain did not adopt a more active policy, Nyerere burst out laughing. "Secede!" he said. "They think we are still part of the Empire."

The fourth day. For two hours Nyerere presided over a Tabora town meeting. The questions, all of which dealt with local problems, were delivered with surprising gusto and at considerable length. Nyerere answered each question slowly, reasoning as he talked, but his voice changed constantly; one moment it was shrill and animated, then whispering, then fast and imploring, then sputtering with laughter.

Exactly who, he was asked, should be required to pay the business tax to the local council? Nyerere gave some examples. "A woman who makes *vitumbua*"—rice fritters—"and sells them in her home so that she can buy soap and matches, she should not be required to pay the tax. A man who sells cigarettes or textiles in his van, that's different. He should pay the tax, I would say, not because his business is mobile, but because it renders a profit."

What about people who sold milk and coffee? Should they be licenced? "Milk can be dangerous if it is not treated hygienically," Nyerere said. "Therefore those who sell it should be known, and it is easier to know them if they have licences. As for coffee, I think your council should include it in the same category as work done by womenfolk at home. There is not much profit in it unless it is sold on a very large scale." An argument broke out over whether milk merchants should be taxed if they sold only from their own homes. "I recommend that they be licenced," Nyerere said. "But it is up to the council."

"The council prays," said a TANU elder in a flowing white *kanzu*, "that industries be established in Tabora, such as a shoe factory, a leather factory and a tobacco factory." Nyerere referred the first two examples to the MPs from Tabora, and dwelt at length on the third. "I once asked a leader of the tobacco industry why a tobacco factory was not going to be built at Tabora or at Iringa, where tobacco is grown in abundance, and why Morogoro was selected as the site of a factory instead. I wanted him to convince me. The answer I got was this. At present, tobacco is grown mainly in two areas, Tabora and Iringa. Iringa has a small factory already, but it is not large enough to take in all the tobacco grown in Tanzania. We could expand it. But the problem is transport. Tobacco from Tabora to Iringa must be loaded and unloaded twice before it would reach Iringa. You see? If Tabora were to have the factory, it would be the same. So Morogoro was selected. The tobacco from both Tabora and Iringa can go straight to Morogoro without being unloaded. Secondly, there is the problem of moisture. There is more moisture at Tabora than at Iringa or Morogoro. So Tabora was dropped.

"And thirdly, there should be a focal point where all our tobacco would be auctioned. For example, in Salisbury there is a place where all Rhodesian tobacco is auctioned, and buyers from all over the world go there and buy the tobacco. Morogoro will be a suitable place for our tobacco auction. Buyers will be able to go to Morogoro to buy our tobacco and then return to Dar es Salaam the same day. I do not think they would like to go from place to place in our country just to buy small amounts of tobacco. In the future, when the crop is larger, we will surely have a factory at Tabora. But meanwhile, the factory at Morogoro will be built, and we will expand it four times until it can take forty million pounds of tobacco a year."

By the time the meeting was over, it was very hot. "This is what I am trying to do," Nyerere explained to a foreign visitor. "The other day, at Urambo, you saw the old style, where I would talk for an hour or two. This way is much better. It gives me a chance to hear *them*.

"Tabora is a second home to me," he continued. "I spent six years here as a schoolboy, and three as a teacher. But Tabora is a problem. We are on the old slave route here, you know. The people are the sons of slave sellers. They like to argue too much."

One evening that week, Nyerere stood on the regional commissioner's veranda chatting with townspeople who had come to see him, including a young man and woman whom he greeted warmly, and an old woman who seemed to be very worried. As the visitors and the TANU elders began to drift away, Nyerere sat down and switched to English.

The man and woman, he said, he had known in Tabora fifteen years before. "I used to teach them English in the evenings. Once, during Ramadan, they all stayed at home. I was very angry. I said— I shouldn't have got so angry—I said, 'If you don't come, all right, I have other things to do.' " He laughed. And the old woman? "This was her problem. She is a poor woman, I don't know how old— sixty, at least. But her mother is still alive. Her problem is to support her mother and herself. She was very keen to get hold of me. I told her yesterday morning, 'Come to the regional commissioner's house in the evening.' But she was afraid she might get lost in the confusion. So she went with us to Sikonge and back, and today to Nzega and back. Well, at Bukene, her town, we forgot to deal with the problem while we were there, so I didn't have a chance to tell her what we have done. I asked the area commissioner if he could find her a job that would cover her needs, and he said yes, it was possible."

He was asked if he would repeat in English the story he had told the elders about the goat's hair. "Ah, that," he said, with a despairing laugh. "I don't think that story can be told in English. But, very well, I will try.

"When I was about ten, my father sent me one day to accompany his first wife—one of my stepmothers—to another village, eight or ten miles away, where one of her relatives had died. As we were about to leave this village, to return home, she was given a goat by her relatives. Well, since I was a boy, it was my function to lead the goat by a rope. But the goat refused to budge. And as I was struggling with it, one of her relatives said, 'Don't worry, I'll make it easy for you.' Well! He took some hairs from my head and some hairs from the goat's head, and mixed them with some roots, and chewed them together, and fed them to the goat. He said, 'The goat will follow you now,' and the goat followed me, all the way home." He laughed with glee. "Yes, very tame. It followed me like a dog."

He was asked if he felt it was difficult for an African leader to bridge the gap between tribal life and the modern world. "I don't believe it is as hard as one might think," he said. "I was twelve when I went away to school. In tribal society, a boy gets to be practically an undergraduate by the age of twelve. Yes! You know a lot of life at twelve. You know as much as there is to know of open society.

You're kept apart from the elders' secrets, of course. But you know a lot. When I go home now, my people are always surprised at how much I know of tribal life.

"In a sense, if you have become satisfied with one form of life, the question is, How do you make the jump? Almost by what the Christian calls revelation. If you have lived one life and have matured in that life, it is very difficult to make such a leap from Hinduism to Christianity—even, I think, from Protestantism to Catholicism. My confirmation in tribal life was never wiped out. As a boy of twelve, I already had beliefs I had accepted. I had to be convinced before I could accept a different kind of faith, a faith in a defined God.

"The Christian rejects tribal ideas. Yet he has less reason to do so than many others, because he too believes in things that cannot be explained scientifically. All I know is, the goat followed. The maximum I can say is: I don't know.

"The tribe of this man"—he pointed to Hashim Mbita—"had a vaccination against snakebite for ages past. You could *see* the Nyamwezi be bitten, and not fall down. If anybody had said to me, 'Other tribes fall down from snakebite, but not the Nyamwezi,' I would have said, 'Rubbish!' But that would have been based on ignorance. In any case, I'm tolerant of the beliefs of my own people, and of science, too."

By that time it was dark, and all but two or three of the elders had gone. Nyerere was asked if he would describe his impressions of China, which he had visited the previous year.

"Well," he said, "I wish the Cold War were not a complicating factor here. I wish we could just speak simple facts. If you take me to see General Motors, I will marvel. If you take me to London, I will say, 'How wonderful.' Last year I visited Holland, a small country but a very advanced country, and"—his voice high in wonder—"they are spending hundreds of millions of pounds to *push back the sea!* Well! All I can say is: 'Wonderful!' But it is irrelevant to what we can do in Tanzania. The assembly plants in America and Europe are irrelevant. Oh, the time will come—but not yet.

"That water, that little dam you saw today. That cost fifteen hundred pounds. That we can do. And if we could make dams like that everywhere, and give everybody water, it would be a revolution.

"China is different. China is a backward country trying to pull itself up. But it is two steps ahead of us. No—three steps in some places, two in others, *one* in others. You can see the steps, and you say, 'Boy! Why didn't we think of that? We should do that!' I should send many people to see these things. But it has nothing to do with the Cold War. It is a question of what we are capable of.

"I've been telling my own people, 'We've got to change, we must mechanize, we must have better tools.' But what are better tools? Not the combine harvester. If I were given enough combine harvesters for every family in Tanzania, what would I do with them? No mechanics, no spare parts . . ." A shudder at the thought. "It would be a very serious problem—unless, of course, I sell them for hard cash. But we still have to give the people better tools, tools they can handle, and can pay for. Americans, when they speak of better tools, are talking about something quite different. We are using hoes. If two million farmers in Tanzania could jump from the hoe to the oxen plough, it would be a revolution. It would double our living standard, triple our product! This is the kind of thing China is doing. An ancient people, dealing with the difficulties of feeding seven hundred million people. The *stage* of their development is relevant to us. I wish I could state this as true, observed fact, and nothing more. But when I say, 'From China we can learn,' they say we are going Red."

He remained silent for a moment. "But also," he said slowly, "there is a problem of attitude. I don't know quite how to put this. There is a difference between Eastern and Western countries, and between poor and rich countries. Let me try to illustrate this. We have a medical school in Dar es Salaam. The other day the students went on strike. They wanted better conditions. Some are doing medical studies, and others are in the health-inspection course. They all wanted better conditions. And, in addition, the medical students didn't want to eat together with the health-inspection students. Yes! I said—I was joking, of course—'What is this, Alabama in Dar es Salaam? They want separate facilities!'

"Well, all but two students went on strike. Of those two, we discovered, one had returned from studying in Russia, and the other from East Germany. Now, I suspect—I may be wrong—but I suspect they didn't go on strike for two reasons. In the first place, they may have compared the facilities we were offering with those in East Germany and Russia, and decided ours didn't compare too badly. But it was also, I suspect, a difference in attitude. The West" —he broke off and remained silent for a moment—"is just too individualistic. All the textbooks of Western countries talk about rights, rights, rights, and no duties. The Charter of the United Nations is a charter of rights. Very good. This is very good. You couldn't state it better. Schools, churches talk about rights all the time. And duty is usually defined as 'obey the law'. The minimum! And a large number of crooks *do* obey the law.

"In the Eastern countries, there has been a reaction to this. A reaction, I think, that works like a pendulum; to strike a balance, you must swing each way. When human society has exaggerated something very much, I think the opposite must be established before a balance can be reached. And the Eastern countries have something Africa needs: a stress on duty. The West looks at this as privation of freedom. They would say, 'Duty! They regiment the people.' Yet I feel that for our type of world, where it is so easy for a man to make himself comfortable at the expense of the many—especially those in power and those with an education—we must look at the other side of the coin. One of the biggest dangers now is corruption at the top. This is the *silent* scramble for Africa. Make yourself rich as quickly as possible! And if that is questioned, you are questioning the people's freedom.

"One thing I have in common with the West is Christianity. I am Christian. I think it curious that we should learn these things from the East. Christianity is a revolutionary creed, but something went wrong somewhere. Africa, I know, I know, if we don't learn anything else from the East, we must learn to despise private property a little. But the big scramble for personal wealth in Africa is not going to help. There is not enough wealth on this continent. It will all be at the top, and the people will be left with nothing."

II

"Those who receive this privilege of education have a duty to return the sacrifice which others have made. They are like the man who has been given all the food available in a starving village in order that he might have the strength to bring supplies back from a distant place. If he takes this food and does not bring help to his brothers, he is a traitor."

"YOU HAVE TAKEN me to that big German house and I have had a good sleep there," Nyerere told a crowd in Dar es Salaam in December 1962, soon after he was sworn in as President of Tanganyika. "I eat well, so I may forget about doing work. But it is your job to come to me and urge me to work with you. Don't complain. Just come and remind me to work."

State House is not, strictly speaking, an old German house. The Government House of German colonial times had been destroyed by Royal Naval gunfire in 1914. The present structure, a pleasant two-storey ramble of whitewashed Moorish walls surrounded by palms, frangipani and bougainvillaea, was built by the British after the First World War. It served as the official residence of the British governors from 1922 to 1961, when Tanganyika was a British mandate and later a trusteeship territory. Nyerere had never liked the place, and referred to it privately as "my prison". "He never wanted to live there, never," his brother Joseph has said. "People would say, 'There's the big Government House, where we've always seen the governor. Now we want to see our own man there.' He would say, 'So what? I don't actually have to live there.'" But he endured it as a combined residence and office for three and a half years. It has remained his office and official residence, but since 1966 he has lived elsewhere.

A visitor to State House is often surprised to find it so peaceful. A Thomson's gazelle and a peacock wander aimlessly on the lawn. A dhow, arriving on the monsoon from the Arabian peninsula, can be seen gliding along the horizon toward the narrow mouth of Dar es Salaam harbour. A servant clad in a white suit walks noiselessly down an open corridor carrying two mangoes.

In Nyerere's second-floor office, the same stillness prevails. A ringing telephone rarely interrupts him during appointments; his closest colleagues, including his Vice-President, Rashidi Kawawa, are more likely to drop by to see him than to telephone. As Second Vice-President of the United Republic, Kawawa was long known, in State House shorthand, as "the V.P. Two." Sheikh Abeid Karume, who served as First Vice-President from the time of the union, in April 1964, until his assassination, in Zanzibar, in April 1972, always lived on Zanzibar but occasionally flew over to Dar es Salaam for weekly Cabinet meetings.

In the early sixties, Nyerere maintained private telephone lines to the offices of the other East African Presidents, Jomo Kenyatta of Kenya and A. Milton Obote of Uganda (who was overthrown in an army coup in January 1971), but these were eliminated a few years ago to save money. At the time of the Rhodesian unilateral declaration of independence, in November 1965, Nyerere often conferred by telephone with his friend Kenneth Kaunda, the President of Zambia; but the only connection available at that time—a reminder of Africa's vulnerability—ran from Dar es Salaam to Lusaka, the Zambian capital, by way of London and Salisbury, the capital of Rhodesia. A direct line was later installed. Even today, if Nyerere should wish to telephone another neighbour, the President of Burundi, his call would pass through London and Brussels.

"He jokes about everything," Joseph Namata, who served as Nyerere's principal secretary for three years, once said. "He never shouted at me, but he can shout if he is angry. He may say, 'Why did you *do* this? You can't do such a thing!' Once, a regional commissioner locked up a European for a fortnight, and we didn't know about it until we received a complaint from an ambassador. The President called the regional commissioner to Dar es Salaam—yes, a great distance, more than four hundred miles—and ordered the European released immediately. The regional commissioner is no longer a regional commissioner. But that happened months later—so you could not connect the incident with him."

During his mornings at State House, Nyerere reads a stack of reports and memorandums, which he initials "J.K.", his first two initials. Most of his staff members address him as "*Mzee*" (literally, "old man"), although a few say "*Mwalimu*". Soon after independence, Nyerere declared that he didn't wish to be called "Dr Nyerere" or "Your Excellency", and he periodically reissues directives reminding his countrymen that his official title, to be used only in "very formal references", is "The President of the United Republic of Tanzania, *Mwalimu* Julius K. Nyerere," and that his wife should never be referred to as "Lady", or her assistants as "ladies-in-waiting". "A worshipping secretary had begun to refer to Maria as 'Lady Nyerere'," a family friend has said. "Well, he wasn't having any of that. He said, 'She *is* the First Lady. But she is Mrs Nyerere.' "

One of his most famous sermons, first published as a memorandum in 1963 and later included in his book *Freedom and Unity*, was a blistering letter to his colleagues asking their help in "stamping out the disease of pomposity." "The growing tendency to confuse dignity with sheer pomposity must be checked," he wrote in 1963, "or it will destroy the dignity of the Republic . . . Nothing could be more disrespectful to our National Anthem than to treat it as a popular song hit, to be plugged the moment any member of the government appears on the scene. Yet we sing it on the most unsuitable and unlikely occasions, and if some unfortunate passer-by does not happen to notice us, we take offence and start shouting about 'insults to the Republic' . . . It is not customary in other countries to play their National Anthem without warning just because some government official happens to have landed at an airstrip on a visit to his mother-in-law . . . It is the same with police escorts. Hitherto, whenever I have questioned the value of all this very undemocratic pomposity, I have been assured that the people like it. But this is highly doubtful. Do they really love being shouted at to get off the road because the President or a minister or a regional commissioner is taking an afternoon drive? We should stop deceiving ourselves. This sort of pomposity has nothing to do with the people, for it is the very reverse of democratic. We must stop it!"

Nyerere's friends believe his instinctive dislike of living in State House was reinforced by the army mutiny of January 1964, during which the President was forced to flee from the official residence and go into hiding. In any case, two years later he built a seafront house at Msasani Bay, a few miles north of Dar es Salaam. For security reasons, the area around the house was cleared of trees, and a barbed-wire fence, a system of floodlights and a guardhouse were erected; and for a while it appeared that Nyerere might change his mind and never move in. "We insisted he should have guards at the Msasani house for the sake of security," Joseph Namata has recalled. "The barbed wire and the lights, we put those in. Well! He refused the house! He said, 'This is my private house, I'm not afraid, why don't you leave me at peace in my house?' And at first he refused to occupy it. Finally he changed his mind because his wife persuaded him, not because we in government prevailed upon him. All the furniture in it is his own. I had bought a radiogram from public funds, as I would do for State House, to entertain our visitors. He refused to take it, so I sent it back to the shop. He wanted this house to be pure."

In the same manner, Nyerere has tried to protect the sanctity of his family life. His wife, Maria Gabriel, is a shy, handsome woman who has borne seven children and has stoically endured her husband's public career. "I know, I know, he doesn't belong to me," she has occasionally complained to friends, "he belongs to Tanzania." She rejoiced in the move to Msasani Bay and soon was saying, "We are living a family life again." Her friends regard her as a woman of strong will, a devout Catholic who, when Julius returned from three years of study at Edinburgh, delayed their long-planned wedding until she was certain that he had not changed. They also recall that it was she who persuaded her husband to flee from State House on the morning of the mutiny, just as she later convinced him that they should move to Msasani, even if the house were not to be as private a refuge as he would have liked.

"He doesn't want to dictate to anybody, not even to his wife and children," a family friend has observed, "but he has a certain way. Well, the other night, for instance, his wife—she's a cinema fan—took the children to a film, Elvis Presley or Cliff Richard or somebody. Julius said afterwards, 'You know, one time years ago when I was in the States, a radio interviewer said to me, "Mr Nyerere, do you like rock and roll?" I said, "Well . . . it's not exactly like African rhythms, I suppose I enjoy it, I don't know how to do it myself." Then he asked, "How about Elvis Presley?" So I replied, "What about Elvis Presley? What is Elvis Presley?" Well! That was the end of the interview. And the interviewer said to me afterwards, "You know, by that reply of yours, you have made many friends and many enemies." '

"Well," the family friend continued, "he recited this in front of his wife, as a cue to her. Then he said to her, 'If Elvis Presley comes here, he can stay over there'—he shuddered, like this—'I don't want him too close. I don't think I'd have too much to say to him.' "

In October 1966, a few months after Nyerere's trip to Tabora, a group of four hundred students, most of them from the Dar es Salaam University College, marched to State House. They were protesting against a new law requiring that they serve in the National Service, a system under which young Tanzanians were obliged to devote two years to various "nation-building activities". During this period, university graduates were to be paid only about forty per cent of what they would earn in civilian life. The students were especially angry at Second Vice-President Rashidi Kawawa, the minister in charge of the National Service programme, and carried signs bearing such messages as To HELL WITH KAWAWA AND HIS SCHEME and—the ultimate insult—LIFE DURING COLONIAL DAYS WAS BETTER.

At the steps of State House, they were met by Nyerere, Kawawa and most members of the Cabinet, and a spokesman for the students, speaking in English, proceeded to deliver their "ultimatum" in a high-pitched twang. The government, he declared, was trying to throw "the burden of financing this extensive scheme on the shoulders of young and helpless students", and he offered a compromise: "Either we be paid our full rights of earning, or else all those in the high-income brackets should also be in that category which could be interpreted as a form of sacrifice rather than a form of exploitation." In other words, if university graduates were expected to spend two years in the National Service at forty per cent of their civilian pay, government officials should make sacrifices too. "Therefore, Your Excellency, unless the terms of reference and the attitude of our leaders towards students change, we shall not accept National Service in spirit. Let our bodies go, but our souls will remain outside the scheme"— wild applause—"and the battle between the political elite and the educated elite will perpetually continue. Thank you."

Nyerere began to speak in a calm, almost perfunctory manner. "I did, I have understood your protest. It is not really addressed to the Second Vice-President, it is addressed to the government, we have got your message. I understand it, I want to see if I can explain a little, I want to be absolutely clear that what we have said to your leaders has got to you.

"This matter did not start yesterday. It is the intention of the government that National Service should not merely be for ex-primary [school leavers] or for unemployeds; it is *national* service. It should include secondary [school leavers], and university graduates, and all others. We asked, 'At what point in the life of a youth, at what particular point, do we ask him to enter National Service? Do we take him before he finishes his education, or after?'

"So we decided *no*"—his voice cracking a bit now—"you don't cut his education, you don't interfere with it, you wait until he has completed his education. We made that decision. I think it was an extremely considerate decision on the part of government. Very considerate. Very considerate. But it had some definite implications. If you wait until a student has finished his education, his training as a teacher, then he has certain expectations. If he is trained to be a teacher, his salary will be—what is it? Seven hundred and sixteen pounds a year? Ah, seven hundred and sixteen plus seventy-six. This is his salary, seven hundred and ninety-two pounds. This teacher, he has in mind: 'At the end of my education, I get seven hundred and ninety-two pounds.' This is his expectation. So. If you wait until he completes his training as a teacher, you have allowed him to think, 'Seven hundred and ninety-two pounds is my right.' As your spokesman said, 'my full right'." He rolled the *r*. "My full rrrright.

"We made other mistakes. We said, 'Treat them differently. Count as National Service the work they do as teachers or doctors or engineers. A student has been trained as a teacher; very well, let him go into the classroom. If he is a doctor, let him go to the ward, let him go to Muhimbili hospital, count that as National Service.'

"Obviously, if we had taken you people and said, 'OK, don't let them finish their education yet, let them complete their National Service first,' then you would not be talking to us, or to the Vice-President, asking him to resign. You would not be talking about forty per cent. Forty per cent of what? You would have no salaries. I mean, really the easiest way to get out of this damned forty-per-cent rubbish is to ask you people to do National Service before you go to university. That's all.

"Now, I explained this forty-per-cent business ages ago. Since then we have changed it. We've changed the damned thing. We have said, 'We guarantee a minimum wage—the government minimum wage in Dar es Salaam; no National Service person will be getting less than one hundred and eight pounds a year.' In terms of the teacher, you knock off one hundred and eight pounds from the seven hundred and ninety-two pounds, and then take forty per cent of the rest, and you add that together, and I am told this comes to three hundred and eighty-one pounds. Did you also say, Mr Vice-President, 'Free housing'? And were you also saying, 'No direct taxation'? Were you really saying this? That on an income of three hundred and eighty-one pounds, no taxation? This is rubbish, when we are talking about National Service. The nation says to its youth, 'We want your service.' And the youth does not then turn to the nation and say, 'For how much?' The youth simply says, 'Where? What to do?' This is the meaning of National Service."

Calmly, again: "Now, I've accepted your ultimatum. And I can assure you I'm going to force nobody. You are right, your bodies would be there, your spirit wouldn't be there, you are right. I take *nobody* into the National Service whose spirit is not in it. Nobody! Absolutely nobody!" Hesitant applause.

"It's not a prison, you know. I'm not going to get anybody there who thinks it is a prison camp, no one! But nevertheless it will remain compulsory for everybody who is going to enter government service. So you make your choice. I'm not going to spend public money to educate anybody who says, 'National Service is a prison camp.' No"—very quietly now—"I won't have this. I have accepted your ultimatum."

After a long pause he began again, chopping out every word in fury. "You are right when you talk about salaries. Our salaries are too high. You want me to cut them?" Fairly strong applause. "Two years? I'm not talking about two years. I'm not building this country for *two years*. I'm willing to slash salaries. Do you want me to start with my salary? Yes! I'll slash mine." Cries of "No!" could be heard. "I'll slash the damned salaries in this country. Mine, I slash by twenty per cent, as from this hour. Twenty per cent. I slash my salary. This damned country! The salaries are too high! Too high for Tanzania!

"My salary! Do you know what my salary is? Five thousand damned shillings a month! Five thousand damned shillings in a poor country! The poor man who gets two hundred shillings a month—do you know how long it's going to take him to earn my damned salary? Twenty-five years! It's going to take the poor man in this country, who earns two hundred shillings a month, twenty-five years to earn what I earn in a year.

"The damned salaries! These are the salaries which build this kind of attitude in the educated people, all of them! All of them! Me and you! We belong to a class of exploiters! I belong to your class! Where I think three hundred and eighty pounds a year is a prison camp! Is forced labour! We belong to this damned exploiting class on top. Is this what the country fought for? Is this what we worked for? In order to maintain a class of exploiters on top?

"I agree with you! We are paying too much! Everybody in this damned country is paid too much—except the poor peasant. I'll slash the salaries! I agree with you! I'm glad you're so concerned about this country! Forced labour? Where do we get this language? The day I can give every worker in Tanzania three hundred and eighty pounds, we will have worked a revolution that has not been worked anywhere in Africa. The day that I succeed in giving everybody in this damned country three hundred pounds, we shall have worked a terrific revolution; we could stand, all of us, on top of Kilimanjaro and proclaim the Tanzanian revolution!

"Forced labour! Go, go in the classroom, go and don't teach. This we shall count as National Service for three hundred and eighty pounds a year. You are right, salaries are too high. Everybody in this country is demanding a pound of flesh. Everybody except the poor peasant. How can he demand it? He doesn't know the language. Even in his own language he can't speak of forced labour. *What kind of country are we building?*" He fairly screeched the words.

"I have accepted what you said. And I am going to revise salaries permanently. And as for you, I am asking you to go home. I'm asking all of you to go home. Rashid! You are responsible to see that they go home."

There was mild applause, presumably from those students who didn't realize what had happened. He had expelled them, three hundred and ninety-three in all, and sent them home.

Sir Richard Turnbull, the last governor of Tanganyika: "He has rather a Gandhian streak, you know. He doesn't lack courage, but he will never grasp the nettle. He was very slow to realize that, when you rule, you hurt people's feelings; every act will benefit some and bring disadvantage to others. He has a tremendous adherence to principle. As Shaw said in his *Prefaces*, the man who would 'sell all and follow me' would create absolute chaos. Well, Julius would sell all and give it to the poor and rather enjoy the ensuing chaos. There's a shadow of a death wish in him. He likes to follow a principle to its logical end rather than its realistic end. But he's a bigger man than that suggests. He once told me how he would go to endless lengths to avoid quarrels. Only once or twice, he said, had he let it happen; he feared the humiliation of shouting and getting red in the face, and how ashamed he felt afterwards. The great thing about Julius was: he didn't want the spoils of leadership; he just didn't care about possessions. At one time, as I recall, he was smoking one hundred cigarettes a day; and when he found it was affecting his work, he cut it, just like that."

One of his staff assistants: "The staggering thing is how little he has changed. At Mwanza, there is a Nyerere Street. He says, 'It's named for my father.' The Dar City Council thought of taking down the Askari Monument and putting up a statue of the President. He said no. He doesn't like the personality cult. He doesn't believe in one-man government, he believes in consensus government. His way is to try to bring people around, as in the TANU National Executive committee meetings. They argue and argue and argue. He usually gets his way—because he argues. They could have a dictator here as easily as anywhere else; democracy is stronger here because the President is preaching it."

One of his ministers: "He starts by trusting a person. Then he lets you prove it. Or prove otherwise. He starts by showing interest in a human being. He absolutely believes the human being to start with. Then maybe he will discover you are a fool or a rascal; or maybe he will discover you're somebody he could get on with. Some people say, 'He likes to give you a long rope.' "

His friend Father Richard Walsh: "The last thing Julius Nyerere believes in is mandarins. He has a tremendous confidence in the innate goodness of people. I used to tell him, 'There's only one Nyerere in Africa,' and he didn't always believe it."

Colin Legum, the Commonwealth Correspondent of The Observer: "He was never afraid of losing his leadership in a cause he knew was right. He was prepared to stake his leadership on causes that were important. On questions of race and dignity, his immediate reaction, always, is emotional—sharp, stinging. And this creates problems for the diplomats who have to deal with him immediately afterwards, because he is already deeply committed to the emotional position. And then always there is the second phase; the rational man takes over. And essentially he is a rational man."

His former colleague Oscar Kambona (a few months before he broke with Nyerere and went into exile in 1967): "He had two qualities, and he has them still, and I believe, if he keeps them, he will become a very great leader of Africa. One is his simplicity, his understanding of the other man's point of view. The other is his not caring about wealth. He has no idea of wealth. The first time he went to the United Nations, he had old rotten suitcases. Clothes he doesn't worry about."

Oscar Kambona (a few months after he fled from Tanzania): "I can accuse the President and substantiate that he is hiding behind the façade of democracy, while quietly building himself into a dictator. This is the mind of a man enmeshed in a web of wickedness."

A Western diplomat (formerly assigned to an embassy in Kenya): "He should be in a university. He has to keep proving he's non-aligned, having so long been the darling of the British and the Americans. With Jomo Kenyatta, if you accuse him of being pro-British, he can say, 'After nine years of imprisonment by the British, I can judge that for myself.' But with Julius it's more difficult."

A Western diplomat (formerly assigned to an embassy in Tanzania): "There are many bridge players in this world who can take a good hand and get good results. There are few hands as poor as his."

Julius Nyerere (soon after he had broken diplomatic relations with the British government over Britain's Rhodesian policy, in 1965): "I have not changed, I was considered a moderate in the past because I stuck stubbornly to certain principles—two in particular. One was our method of winning independence. It was very clear in my mind that, because of the nature of the Trust Territory under the British, it was possible to win independence without violence. I stuck to it. I'm not non-violent in the sense of Mohandas Gandhi. But I feel violence is an evil with which one cannot become associated unless it is absolutely necessary. And so, in Western circles, they said, 'Julius is very good.' I don't think the communists thought I was so good. They accused me of being a stooge of the British, I think. Secondly, I said that racialism must never be a part of our campaign for independence. I put my foot down. Some of my colleagues were not happy about this 'purity'. But I stuck to it, and the West said 'Julius is very good'. So I earned a good reputation —fine until independence. But the same principle applies to Rhodesia. I wanted six words out of Harold Wilson: independence 'on the basis of majority rule'. And I suddenly became an extremist for sticking to my non-racialism. Now I am an embarrassment to Britain on Rhodesia, and I'm a bad fellow. My reputation in the West is very bad just now. But sticking to principles is not a mistake. Do they want me to say now, 'Racialism is all right; let my people oppose the Indians who live here'? No!"

In his spare time Nyerere has translated two Shakespeare plays, *Julius Caesar* and *The Merchant of Venice*, into Swahili. He received so many suggestions and corrections from friends and Swahili scholars after publishing the *Caesar* translation that he later revised it. Occasionally he has exchanged poems, in the Swahili manner, with local writers. Most of these poems are said to have patriotic themes, but Nyerere has rarely discussed them; he once said, "after some careful thought", that he did not think it useful to make them public.

Most of his writing has dealt specifically with Tanzanian affairs, and has ranged from the 1967 Arusha Declaration to a privately circulated memorandum to Tanzanian foreign service officers entitled "Argue, Don't Shout", a gentle effort to soften the tone of diplomatic oratory. Two volumes of his speeches and papers have been published. While assembling the material for the second volume, *Freedom and Socialism*, he decided to omit any passages from the extemporaneous speech to the complaining students in 1966. "I was too angry," he said.

In April 1967, he asked the parents of the expelled students to write letters to their regional commissioners stating that they were satisfied that "the student will be of benefit to the nation if he resumes his studies". Nyerere permitted most of them to return to university, saying he felt they had come to believe that Tanzania could only be built "through the religion of socialism and self-reliance".

III

"When the Christian missionaries tried to convert my father, he would listen to them and, after they had finished, he would preach to them, and then they would go away for good. When they said to the old man, 'Love your brother', he would say, 'I agree with you.' The only thing the British had against him was his twenty-two wives."

"WE ZANAKI have two reputations among our neighbours," Nyerere has said of his tribesmen. "One, of being cunning, and the other, which follows the first, of being untrustworthy. People will say, 'A Zanaki friend will kill you' ·which is not true. I don't know how we got that reputation. But certainly we are very independent-minded. As is usual in such small communities, the people are very conscious of themselves, very proud of themselves."

The Zanaki are one of the smallest of Tanzania's one hundred and twenty-six tribes, numbering no more than thirty-five or forty thousand out of the country's thirteen million. Their homeland lies in hill country to the southeast of Lake Victoria and to the west of the Serengeti Plain, a starkly beautiful landscape of granite outcroppings, brooding skies and the magnificent colours of tropical Africa. The Zanaki raise cassavas, millet, corn, cotton, chickens, and, here and there, a few cattle. The soil is poor and the rains irregular, but, as Nyerere says, "The Zanaki know no famine."

"They are much more aggressive than most tribes, and noted for making mischief," says the Reverend Arthur Wille, an American Maryknoll priest who in the early nineteen-fifties founded a Roman Catholic mission in Busegwe, near Butiama, the village where Nyerere was born some three decades before. "They love court cases. There are more killings out there in Zanaki"—or Zanaki-land, the tribal area—"than elsewhere. The police in Musoma," the capital of a region occupied by several tribes, including the Zanaki, "used to have a map with pins showing murders, thefts and other serious crimes. Zanaki was always a cluster of murder pins." The Zanaki have demonstrated their stubbornness to the Catholic priests by their resistance to Christian teachings; after more than fifteen years of missionary activity, only three or four hundred Zanaki have been converted to Christianity. To the British colonial administrators, the Zanaki proved their truculence by their frequent quarrels with neighbours, and, specifically, by a riot they staged in 1952 in support of Ihunyo, their chief and rainmaker, whom the British were seeking to depose. "I don't think many other tribes would have dared," Father Wille has said, "or even thought of such a thing, at that time."

Unlike most African tribes, the Zanaki never had a chief until the Germans came in the late nineteenth century. Instead they had a *mwami*, or "rich one", whose function was to make rain. It is this rainmaking tradition, in part, that has led tribal historians to trace Zanaki origins to Buhaya, west of the Lake, where the rainmaker played an important role in tribal life. Indeed, there is a legend in Buhaya of a rainmaker who long ago was driven away for failing to make rain; and a similar story in Zanaki lore of a rainmaker who came from the west. Or it may simply be that the Zanaki migrated eastwards a thousand years or so ago in search of food. The name Bazanaki—with the tribal prefix added—means, "Those who came with what?" The story is told of a stranger who drifted long ago into a village on Majita Bay southwest of Butiama. The local chieftain asked, "*Baza na ki?*" ("What does he bring with him?") When told that the stranger had come with nothing, the chief hustled him on his way, to settle in what was to become Zanaki.

Some authorities believe that, in addition to his duties as rainmaker, the *mwami* of the Zanaki performed certain secular functions; in time of war, for instance, he would order the warriors to the defence of the tribe, and in victory he would collect a share of the spoils. By tradition, anyone who had killed a man could find sanctuary, pending judicial proceedings, if he fled to the rainmaker's village. But the *mwami*'s executive powers were not extensive. "There was no chief," Father Wille has said. "The government was in the hands of the warrior class, the *erikura*. This group ran the tribe. Within it were the speakers, the *abagambi*—literally, 'those who speak'. When an important decision was to be made, there would be a meeting of the *erikura*. Various speakers would present their opinions. These people had a special status, but they had no power other than the ability to persuade. After his advocacy, a speaker would revert to being an ordinary member of the *erikura*."

All this changed when the Germans arrived and colonized the region in the late nineteenth century, establishing the colony they called German East Africa. In the Zanaki region, the Germans wanted chiefs to run the tribe and control its members, and instead of appointing one chief over all the Zanaki, they named eight chiefs to conduct the affairs of the various Zanaki villages. "The natural candidate," said Father Wille, "was the *omugambi*,"* the local speaker. In the village of Butiama, the Germans picked a man named Buhoro, but he was quickly succeeded by a cousin, Nyerere Burito, who later became Julius Nyerere's father. The name Nyerere, which means "caterpillar" in Ki-Zanaki, the tribal language, commemorates the fact that a plague of caterpillars attacked the Zanaki countryside in 1860, the year Nyerere Burito was born. The name is pronounced Nyuh-*reh-reh* by the Zanaki and most other Tanzanians, and Nyuh-*reh*-ree by most foreigners in Tanzania today.

The subtleties of Zanaki traditional government were utterly lost on the Germans. When they first reached Zanaki country, the *mwami*, a rainmaker named Monge, sent a messenger to greet them. The messenger was a wily fellow named Fundi Kenyeka, and he was the *omugambi* of Busegwe village. Eventually Kenyeka managed to convince the Germans that his son Kitara was chief of all the Zanaki. So Kitara became the chief, even though he was regarded as a pretender by the Zanaki, and he retained the post until after the Germans were driven out of Tanganyika during the First World War. A paper in the library of the Catholic mission—unsigned, undated, but apparently written years later by an educated young Zanaki—describes the tribe's plight at the time of the British arrival. "All this happened while Monge was still alive, for he died in 1918. My elders explained that they themselves remembered these happenings, but no one dared at the time to complain, even Monge himself, because no one knew the new masters, and everyone was afraid."

The intrigues continued. Kitara's brother Isomba became chief, and Monge's son Ihunyo became *mwami*, and the two clashed. For six years, Ihunyo lived in exile on Kurukuba Island in Lake Victoria, having been convicted of trying to make rain by obtaining a human sacrifice. In 1926 he was allowed to return to Busegwe and two years later, following Isomba's overthrow, Ihunyo became the chief. In 1930 the post was abolished, and Ihunyo reverted to being merely the *omugambi* of Busegwe. His political status was no different from that of Nyerere Burito of Butiama village and the other *abagambi* of Zanaki. But Ihunyo alone remained the rainmaker.

Throughout the period of British colonial rule, the most numerous

* The singular form of *abagambi*.

and complicated cases of inheritance to reach the courts in Musoma were the ones from Zanaki. This excerpt from the same unsigned paper gives an indication of what the British district commissioners at Musoma were occasionally faced with.

"The age of the (deceased) person was important. If the deceased had not passed through the first stage of *nyangi*, which made him an elder entitled to carry the *kiraburu*, the black oxtail, his heir would have been his father. There was an exception, not uncommon in Zanaki: if the father had disowned his son, perhaps because the son had turned cattle thief and the father had had to pay for his delinquencies, and the son turned to his *wajomba* (his maternal uncles) and they assisted him—especially if they bought him a wife—then they became his potential heirs. But once the man had passed *nyangi*, his senior heir, in the majority of cases, became his maternal uncle and the second heir his brother by the same mother, the latter becoming the senior heir if by chance he was older in years than the maternal uncle. . . ."

In today's market, the price of a Zanaki bride averages about twenty cows, although it varies by location and circumstances. "In some places it's as high as thirty-five or forty cows," Father Wille has said. "And if you're talking about an old man who already has a lot of wives, then you're going to be up in the high forties." It is not uncommon for a man to pay a dowry for a five- or six-year-old girl, perhaps making a deposit of five cows at that time. When she is nine or ten, the child may move to her husband's village, and at fifteen or sixteen will be formally married. "Polygamy," a long-time Musoma resident has said, "is the ideal of the Zanaki man. He looks forward to it, whether he can afford it or not." Julius Nyerere's half-brother Edward Wanzagi has eleven wives. "Julius used to kid him about his wives," a friend has recalled. "Edward would say, 'But I need them for work.' Julius would say, 'Buy a tractor'. But Edward treats them with a great deal of affection. To one he granted a divorce."

"Once," said Father Wille, "one of the television companies was up here, and they were in front of Edward's cluster of houses, where each wife has her own hut. A reporter asked Julius if he would explain why there were so many houses. Julius said, 'Well, they are for my brother's wives. He has eleven, I think.' They asked him what he thought of polygamy, and he said something like this: 'Ah, well, it is a popular custom in Zanaki. But it will pass, for economic reasons.'"

Chief Nyerere Burito died in 1942, at the age of eighty-two, and was succeeded by Edward Wanzagi, his eldest son. "If my father had followed tradition," Julius Nyerere has said, "a nephew would have succeeded him. It would have been a sister's son, if he had had one. Since he didn't, another nephew—sons of his maternal cousins, these we call nephews—might have succeeded him. But he decided not to be traditional in this matter of succession. He was practically retired before his death, and he appointed my brother Edward to represent him everywhere. He also tried to leave some of his property to his sons, but the tribe rejected this."

In the late nineteen-forties, the British decided to reunite the Zanaki under a single chief. "For years," Nyerere has said, "a number of educated people in the tribe had advocated amalgamation of the Zanaki, for we still had eight so-called chiefs. Ridiculous! Even now, there are not more than forty thousand Zanaki, so there were probably fewer then. If we had one chief, I argued, it would be better for the tribe. But the problem was the person. The obvious choice was my brother Edward—but they didn't like him. Well, I couldn't press my brother. They asked me, 'Why don't you do it yourself?' I said, 'No, no, I can't be chief.' "

But in the early nineteen-fifties, at a time when Julius Nyerere was studying abroad, the Zanaki held a tribal convention, and the amalgamation took place. "And I think they did the right thing. They picked an innocuous chief—Ihunyo, who was believed to be the rainmaker. This was his one qualification, but it was accepted by all the Zanaki. So, good. And they named two others as his assistants: my brother was to be his administrative assistant, and another young man his judicial assistant.

"Well, the chief's work was being done by my brother. My brother is no nationalist, but he was pushing progress. The chief was useless. I mean—a rainmaker!" Ihunyo, moreover, was suspected of taking bribes; and so in 1952, the local British authorities decided to get rid of him and make Edward Wanzagi the chief.

The British district commissioner and his assistant called a meeting in a field near Busegwe, Ihunyo's village. "They were warned that there might be trouble," Father Wille has recalled, "and so they took a few police with them. And sure enough, a crowd of Ihunyo supporters gathered, and most of them were carrying walking sticks. There was also a smaller group from Butiama and Buhemba, and they were supporting Edward Wanzagi. The commissioner could see it was a hostile group—people were waving their sticks—and he told Ihunyo to say, 'I won't start the meeting until you all put your sticks in front of the table.' Instead, Ihunyo said, in Ki-Zanaki, which the commissioner couldn't understand, 'Let's go!' and they attacked.

"The police shot over their heads, but that didn't stop them. The commissioner and his party managed to get to their cars. Edward Wanzagi was badly beaten. From Musoma, the commissioner wired the police mobile unit at Mwanza, and the assistant district commissioner and Edward spent the night helping the police round up the Busegwe leaders. About a hundred were later convicted, and Ihunyo himself died in jail. It's amazing how many chiefs died in jail. They just couldn't stand the confinement."

The incident occurred in October 1952, two days before Julius Nyerere returned to Zanaki after spending three years at the University of Edinburgh, where he earned a master of arts degree. On his return he had lingered a few days at Dar es Salaam, then taken the thirty-six-hour train ride to Mwanza. The riot took place while he was waiting at Mwanza to catch the lake steamer to Musoma. "It was a completely tribal incident," Nyerere has recalled. "It happened on a Friday, and I arrived on a Sunday. My brother and our friends were all bandaged when they came to meet me at the boat. And so the chief was deposed. Before this, I had said we must have an elected chief; we couldn't have this rainmaker rubbish. It was my first election campaign, and we got our first elected chief, our first and last." Was Ihunyo deposed for corruption? "For uselessness," Nyerere snapped, betraying a touch of the young Zanaki reformer's zeal. "He was useless and corrupt."

Edward Wanzagi thus became the chief of the Zanaki in 1952. He held the post until a few months after Tanganyikan independence, when all the tribal chiefs were relieved of their political powers. They were allowed to retain their titles, however, and some were given local jobs. Chief Edward became a regional official in Zanaki, and has since continued to perform many of his old chores—collecting taxes, carrying out development projects and pressing the stubborn Zanaki to work for progress.

For generations before his time, the Zanaki had hunted and waged war with bow and arrow, the arrow points needle-sharp and dipped in a black syrupy poison made from bark. Now that the larger plains animals the Zanaki traditionally hunted for food—the impala, the zebra, the wildebeeste—are disappearing from the region, Chief Edward urges and cajoles his tribesmen, who have always raised cassavas, millet and corn for their own use, to grow cash crops, such as cotton, sisal and peanuts, as well. A few years ago he took part in the building of a self-help dam on a government-sponsored resettlement scheme nearby. A curiosity of contemporary Tanzanian life is that Chief Edward, who had never previously been outside East Africa, was taken on a two-week trip to China a few years ago to observe agricultural methods there. "Edward is a driver for work," a friend has observed. "He will say, 'Everyone is eating, but no one is working, so eventually we will all starve.' Sometimes he despairs and says, 'I can't do anything.' But he keeps at it just the same. He may schedule a meeting for nine, and nobody will turn up except him." No matter how hard he has worked in Zanaki, however, Edward Wanzagi has made little progress in winning over the people of Busegwe village, the home of Marwa the rainmaker, the son of Ihunyo. There the villagers still say, "Wanzagi is not our chief. Marwa is."

Because it was raining so hard on the day of his birth, in March 1922, Julius Nyerere was named Kambarage, after an ancestral spirit who lived in the rain. The name Julius he took at the age of twenty, when he was baptized a Catholic. When he was already sixty-one years old, Nyerere Burito had taken a fifth wife, Mugaya, who was fifteen. Julius was the second of the four sons and four daughters she bore him, of whom six survived. By the time of his death, Chief Nyerere had taken twenty-two wives, most of them toward the end of his life, and left twenty-six sons and daughters. "There were many more," Nyerere's younger brother Joseph has remarked, "but many died." It is often said that Nyerere's character is similar to that of his eldest half-brother, Edward Wanzagi. But, according to Joseph, "there was only one of our brothers who was like Julius, and that was Burito. He was a little older than Julius, and they were great friends." Burito was a private in the British army in the Second World War. His family is not certain where he was killed. Joseph thinks Burito died in Burma, and Julius has the impression it was somewhere in Africa.

The cluster of hillside huts where Julius Nyerere spent his childhood lies in ruins today, returned to nature. A cement memorial, surrounded by tall grass, bears the words in Ki-Zanaki: "Deceased Chief Nyerere Burito, ruled from 1912, died 1942, aged eighty-two." The old chief was, in the absolute judgment of his sons and their friends, the most important influence in the shaping of Julius Nyerere's character. "His father was very slow, very careful, before acting," Julius' childhood friend Oswald Marwa* once said. "We

* No relation to the rainmaker.

thought this was the foundation of Nyerere." And Chief Edward Wanzagi has said of his father, "He always insisted on giving people their rights." The eight Zanaki chiefs would take turns presiding over the tribal court. "But people would not go to court if they knew another chief was presiding. If they knew he was presiding, there would be a long queue because they knew that from him they would get justice."

Julius Nyerere is especially fond of recalling the occasional confrontations between his father and the Christian missionaries. "To the extent that I have some humanity, I took it from my father. He would talk to the missionaries about never seeking revenge. He was a chief under the Germans, and when the British soldiers came down to Musoma from Kenya, his enemies tried to overthrow him. One man brought the soldiers to my father's house, and they beat him almost to death. Years later, somebody slipped into my father's tent late at night for asylum, and it was this man, his enemy. The man had committed a crime, and the British were after *him* now. And the district commissioner was only a few yards away! But the old man fed him and hid him and next morning took him out several miles from the camp and said *kwaheri*, goodbye.

"To the extent that a man can be an upright human being, he was one. And"—jubilantly—"he couldn't see why having so many wives and children was sin."

It is sometimes said by family friends that Julius' mother Mugaya, was his father's favourite. "No," Nyerere has said carefully. "She was not far from that. But no, it is not true. She was one of the more liked ones. Another, who died recently, was clearly the favourite, and perhaps my mother came next.

"The women all knew this, and accepted it. The position of the eldest is accepted, the position of the favoured one is accepted. Oh, there are frictions, of course. He is a patriarch. It is difficult to explain to someone from a monogamous society, who thinks of women's jealousy as a natural thing. But in a tribal society, the women accept their position. In my own tribe, jealousy is something to be ashamed of. It's one of the biggest insults to say a wife is jealous, that she doesn't want her husband to have a big family and many children. It's like saying she dominates him. It's a terrible thing."

In certain tribes, it is customary for each wife to come forward with food, taste it and retire. "In our tribe, the wives bring food, and he will accept it and pick, pick, pick. Sometimes he will eat with the children and one of the younger women, and the other women will eat together. They would know he prefers a certain woman's food because she cooks very well. What they do not accept is the rejection of food. That is a terrible thing."

Although Nyerere's father was a chief, his pay was only sixty shillings a month and his family lived meagrely. One of Nyerere's sharpest memories is of his mother's endless attempts to repair the roof of the mud hut in which he grew up, which leaked on rainy nights. In later years, the cry for good houses with good roofs became one of his political refrains. "At least," he has often said, "we always had milk."

His childhood was thoroughly tribal. His teeth were filed in the Zanaki manner. Until he was twelve, he rarely saw a "European" or an "Asian", the East African terms for whites and Indians. Occasionally the Zanaki still fought with their neighbours, notably the dreaded Masai. The Zanaki, who defended themselves with their bows and arrows, were hardly a match for the spear-carrying Masai, but at long last they hit on a plan for avenging themselves. "When they first attack, we'll shoot in the air," a tribesman suggested. "The Masai will raise their shields to protect their heads. The second time we'll fire at the lower part of their bodies." The strategy proved to be devastatingly effective.

"Julius always tells of the time," Father Wille has said, "when the Zanaki were attacked by the Nguruimi, who had disguised themselves as Masai by painting their bodies red with ochre and by carrying spears. The Zanaki were terrified and fled. But later the Nguruimi made the mistake of boasting too much, and the Zanaki said in disgust, 'Ah, it's only the Nguruimi,' and beat them up."

"Under the British, hunting was regarded as poaching," Nyerere has said. "Well, we didn't like this, of course, so we hunted anyway. Once I went out with the elders to part of what is now the Serengeti National Park. A boy of my own age and I, and one or two others, were left in the camp to look after the meat. And one afternoon I saw a car coming toward us. I thought, 'It must be the game warden! We are finished!' And we rushed out of camp. But it was only a gold miner who was poaching too.

"And I remember another time, when I must have been about eleven. As I told you, a tribal boy of eleven is much more grown-up than an urban boy of the same age. But still he is only eleven. Well, another boy and I had gone off into the bush alone. And then we started back toward camp. Tribal youths are very good about directions—much better than Boy Scouts. Then suddenly we heard a voice calling my name, 'Kambarage, Kambarage'. I remember it vividly! As I opened my mouth, this boy put his hand over it and said, 'Don't answer. Your father is a chief. You don't know if this man is calling you to kill you. Let's go quietly until we find out if he is a friend or enemy." So they crept along until they recognized a friend of Julius' father's. "Imagine," Nyerere said, "a boy of eleven."

At twelve, Julius was sent to school in Musoma, twenty-six miles away. "It was really my brother Edward who was responsible," Nyerere has said. "Ihunyo himself said I should go. There is a Bantu game, *bao*. It's a clever game, the best tribal game, I think. Well, Ihunyo was very clever at it. My father was good at it, but not good enough for Ihunyo. One reason my father and mother got on so well was that she was the only one of the wives who played *bao*. And I was very good too. Well, one time when Ihunyo visited our house, I played him. I don't think I defeated him, but it was clear to him that I had some brains, and he told my father, 'This boy is very clever. He should be sent to school.' But my father had sent his first two sons already, and didn't see much point in sending any more. The problem was, Which should he pick and which should he leave out?

"Well, Edward had married the daughter of a neighbouring chief, and this girl got to know me very well. I was small, and was liked by my sister-in-law. So when Edward came home from Ikoma, where he was working for another chief, he also got to know me well—better than he knew the other younger brothers. Eventually he adopted his wife's sister's son, Wambura Wanzagi, who was my own age. This boy had already learned to read and write, and he tried to teach me, but it was no good. He spoke Swahili, and I was completely tribal. One day the district commissioner came and met the boy. The boy was very clever, and was not afraid of Europeans. So the commissioner ordered my brother to send the boy to school. And my brother went to my father and said, 'I suggest you send Kambarage too.' So I was really chosen to accompany this boy. I was delighted. And right away, the next day, I left." What happened to Wambura Wanzagi? "He has disappeared, abandoned his wife and children. I don't know where he is."

Not long after Julius went away to school, his old father bought him a bride. This insured that, in case of the chief's death, Julius would still have been able to marry. Under the Zanaki system, he could have been left with no cows or other wealth; but no one else could inherit his bride. "Of my father's four bigger sons, two were already married, the third could have married at any time, and I was the fourth. So I was the only one who wasn't provided for. And my father was worried about his health. Besides this, my mother had had three daughters, and I was my mother's eldest son, and there is a tribal obligation to allocate the bride-price of a mother's daughters to her sons." Otherwise this money, like the rest of the chief's estate, would have gone to a brother or nephew. "I'd have been inherited by a nephew or an uncle," Nyerere has said, "and it takes a very long time before an inherited son is able to get married. He will be by-passed. The stepfather gives brides to his own sons first." As it turned out, Nyerere never married the girl his father bought for him. He sold his equity in his child bride when, years later, he became engaged to Maria Gabriel.

The year Nyerere returned from Edinburgh, he and Father Wille were driving to Chief Edward's *shamba* one day, when Nyerere yelled at a woman on the road. Then he explained to Father Wille, laughing, "She's my wife. My father paid cows for her."

IV

"THERE WASN'T ENOUGH TO LEARN," Nyerere said years later, recalling his first days at the Mwisenge School in Musoma. He began to study Swahili at twelve and English at fifteen; he came top in the territorial examination of 1936 and advanced to the Tabora Government School. "The British were trying to build a public school, which of course is anything but public," Nyerere once explained. "Originally Tabora was built for the sons of chiefs; it was as close to Eton as it could have been in Africa—fagging, sportsmanship, fair play, all that. If you went through it for six years, and succeeded, that was really something. When I took the examination at Musoma—it was Standard Four exam, to get into Standard Five—there were only two Standard Fives in what was then the Lake Province. One was at Mwanza, but it was a blind alley. If you went there, you were stuck. The other Standard Five was at Tabora, and this led to Standard Ten. It was not a blind alley."

Nyerere's training as a Catholic began at Musoma and continued at Tabora. "It was an accident," Nyerere has said, "in human terms, at least. I was a completely tribal boy. But at Musoma, on Tuesdays and Thursdays, religious instruction was given to those boys who wanted it. It was a good practice; we still have it. Well, I was the friend of a neighbouring chief's son, who said, 'Why don't you come with me to my class?' So I went. But I used to protest to him about this peculiar teaching. I told him I couldn't believe in this bearded man, and I felt we should only worship the gods we knew.

"But I wasn't baptized until several years later. The church thought I might succeed my father as chief—which was most unlikely." The assumption, apparently, was that a man could not be both a chief—at least not a polygamous chief—and a Christian. So the baptism did not take place until after Nyerere's father died in 1942. It was then that he took the name Julius. "It's silly that you have to take a name other than a tribal name when you are baptized. Later I investigated and found that the name didn't stand for a very good saint. Well, I mean, all saints are good, of course, but it didn't stand for a particularly well-known saint."

Nyerere's schoolmates at Tabora remember him as an ambitious, competitive boy, thin and wiry and small for his age. "If he didn't finish first, he could be very unhappy," a classmate has said. Nyerere thinks of himself as having been a rebel during his six years at Tabora; certainly he was a reformer. He was deeply offended by the special privileges accorded the prefects. "One of my biggest humiliations was trying to defend one of the boys in my house. A prefect, I felt, had mistreated the boy by tying his hands. I took exception to this, I went to the headmaster, I said this was not justified. So the headmaster asked me to call them in. The prefect explained, the boy explained, and the headmaster took the side of the prefect—the side of the system. A prefect could do no wrong. The boy got four strokes with the cane, and I was to do it. I did cane him, but I wasn't too enthusiastic.

"I had already been in trouble with the prefects. They had decided the only way to save me was to make me a prefect too. But I never became head prefect. The teachers recommended me, but the headmaster vetoed it. He felt I was too kind for the job."

"We used to talk a lot about our homes," a classmate, Emanuel Kibira, has recalled. "Once, I remember, those of us who were from Bukoba told him we had eight chiefdoms in Bukoba. He said, 'You're lucky. Bukoba is very big. Eight is all right. But in our small tribe, which is the size of one chiefdom, we have eight chiefs. That's too many. Something must be done!' " Once the debating club, which Nyerere had founded, held a debate on the question of brideprice. "He didn't approve of it," Kibira has said, "but he was very interested in it because he had a wife already; his father had *paid*."

After completing his Standard Ten studies at Tabora in 1943, Nyerere entered Makerere College in Uganda. Since most students entered Makerere after completing Standard Twelve, the Tabora graduates usually had a difficult time at first. "Tabora was very good in biology," Nyerere has said, "and at Makerere we could compete with any boy in biology. I was very keen on it. And English I was all right in. But my real interest was—nct politics exactly, but philosophical subjects—ideas, thought, John Stuart Mill's essays on representative government and on the subjection of women—these had a terrific influence on me. Twice I entered the East African literary competition and won first prize, and the second time I wrote on the subjection of women and applied Mill's ideas to tribal society." With friends he organized a campus chapter of the Tanganyika African Association, an organization that had been established in Dar es Salaam in 1929 as a social group for African civil servants; but Nyerere, already concerned about the special privileges enjoyed by Europeans in East Africa, used the campus branch as a club for studying political issues. He completed his studies at Makerere in 1945, with a diploma in education, and spent that summer building a house in Zanaki for his mother, who had been staying with an uncle since her husband, Chief Nyerere, had died three years earlier.

Nyerere received two teaching offers that year, one from the Tabora Government School, the other from a new Catholic secondary school, St Mary's College, which was also located in Tabora. The Reverend Richard Walsh, who was the first director of St Mary's, has recalled that the headmaster of the Government School told him, "You won't get Nyerere. He's coming straight to Tabora." "So," said Father Walsh years later, "we bet five bob." Nyerere accepted Father Walsh's offer at the urging of his friend Andrew Tibandebage, who was already teaching at St Mary's. The government, as Father Walsh remembers it, then advised Nyerere by letter that "at a mission school, you won't get the same salary or pension, and if later you should transfer to a government school, you won't be able to count the years in the mission school toward your pension rights." Nyerere was furious and replied, "If ever I hesitated, your letter has settled the matter. The mission teachers are doing as much for Tanganyika as the government teachers are."

He taught biology and history at St Mary's, and his salary was £6 5s a month. In his spare time, he helped organize a co-operative store, an effort aimed at breaking the monopoly of the Indian merchants in Tabora, but the store was badly run and closed down a few years later. In the evenings he taught English to the townspeople. He shared a house with Tibandebage and at night, with a group of friends that included Chief Harum Lugusha, talked endlessly about Tanganyikan affairs. Joseph Nyerere, who was twelve when his brother brought him to Tabora to begin his schooling, has recalled, "I used to listen to them talking politics. They talked for hours and hours—till four in the morning, sometimes."

As secretary of the local Tanganyika African Association branch, and therefore a young man of influence, Nyerere was asked by the government to serve as a price inspector. "It was after the war, and goods were in short supply. The government wanted prices to be regularized, and so there was a price-control department. I used to go around the shops inspecting—not so much for overcharging, because it was very difficult to catch them on this, but to see that their price labels were displayed properly. My job was to report them to the authorities. But the shopkeepers would say to me, 'You can do what you like, but you'll get nowhere.' And in fact, when I reported a violation, nothing happened. So I lost interest." His friend Oswald Marwa, who was visiting him at the time, has added, "He caught one merchant, but the case was dropped by the government. He was so angry he sent back his uniform: 'I'm not going to do it if justice is not done.' "

Through the African Association, Nyerere was beginning to take an interest in territorial politics. In April 1946 he went to Dar es Salaam for the first time to attend a general conference of the association; the meeting had been called to oppose a British Colonial Office proposal for the creation of a Central Assembly for East Africa. The Africans of Tanganyika feared that such a step would lead to an East African federation dominated by the white settlers of Kenya.

Rashidi Kawawa, who years later was to become Nyerere's deputy in power, entered the Tabora Government School in 1948, and soon afterward saw Nyerere for the first time. "He came to our school to participate in a debate," Kawawa has said. "It was a competition between secondary schools, Tabora and St Mary's, and he was so convincing that he converted us all—we all voted for his side. The subject was 'Wealth Is Better Than Education,' and he was against that, of course. He said, 'I chose the teaching profession in order to make people *understand*; and once you understand, then you are a happy man. Not because you are wealthy; you can be a wealthy man but not a happy man. . . .' But I didn't meet him that day. I was only eighteen."

For several years Nyerere had wanted to continue his studies abroad, but he had been reluctant to leave Tanganyika because his mother and younger brothers needed to be cared for. He had also been the victim of some subtle political pressure; a local British official, according to Oswald Marwa, had written to the Governor advising him that Nyerere should not be allowed to study overseas because he was politically minded and might be dangerous when he returned. Finally, in 1949, Nyerere's friend Father Walsh helped to arrange a government scholarship as well as a grant from St Mary's for the support of Nyerere's family and his fiancée. A few months earlier, Nyerere had become formally engaged to Maria Gabriel, whom he had met in Musoma.

He reached London in April 1949. "The idea was that I should take a degree in biology," he once recalled. "I liked biology, and my boys at St Mary's were doing well in it. It was my strongest exam subject, but not my strongest interest. So I had a debate with the Colonial Office, and they were kind enough to let me do as I wanted. At Edinburgh, my degree was in history and economics; my strongest subject was philosophy. I read a great deal. I had plenty of time to think. My ideas of politics were formed completely. It was my own evolution, but it was complete."

In an essay entitled "The Race Problem in East Africa,"* Nyerere wrote at the time: "There is too much hypocrisy in East Africa today. The European official and the European settler rule and maintain their prestige mainly by hypocrisy; their inner motives would hardly stand examination; the Indian trader makes his living by downright dishonesty or at best by sheer cunning, which is hypocrisy; the African clerk or labourer often disregards fulfilling his part of a contract and even a very educated African will pretend to love the Europeans where his heart is nearly bursting with envy and hatred." Recalling an incident in which a British minister had walked out of a meeting after an East African settler had said he would sooner dine with swine than with an African, Nyerere continued: "The statement by the settler was regarded by the white community in Tanganyika and Kenya as unfortunate, but everywhere the Minister was blamed for doing what he thought was the only thing he could do under such circumstances.

"The expression of hatred is not on one side; an African friend of mine once referred to the Europeans in East Africa as *mbwa hawa*— 'these dogs'. Personally I welcome these outbursts; they show us the seriousness of the disease, they are like bubbles that fly off a boiling pot. . . .

"The African's capacity for bearing insult is not really limitless. . . [Africans] cannot bear insult for ever, and it is well to remember that a day may come when someone may want to incite them. How easy it is to inflame an insulted people! I really shudder when I think of the terrible possibility—but it will not be a mere possibility if our white neighbours insist on this vulgar doctrine of the Divine Right of Europeans. . . . A day comes when the people will prefer death to insult. . . . I hope and pray that such a day will never come. But the European holds the answer. He has only to will that such a day shall never come, and it will never come. . . . Africa is for the Africans, and the other races cannot be more than respected minorities. . . . Should

* Published years later in his book *Freedom and Unity*.

it come to a bitter choice between being perpetually dominated by a white or an Indian minority and between driving that minority out of East Africa, no thinking African would hesitate to make the latter choice."

Apparently Nyerere rarely discussed politics with his friends at Edinburgh. He obviously liked the British, and often remarked at how hard they worked, as compared with the British colonials of East Africa. He lived at the British Council residence, and on evenings and weekends often visited a friend, Walter Wilson, and Wilson's mother, a widow whose husband had been a medical missionary in the Belgian Congo and Angola. Mrs. Wilson has recalled that Nyerere delighted in the crossword puzzles in *The Scotsman* and loved to play canasta and Lexicon. "English was only his third language," she has said, "but he always seemed to win." Nine years later, he invited her to Tanganyika's independence celebration.

"I had had three years in which to think," Nyerere has said. "I had given up the politics of complaint, and was ready to tackle the roots of the problem of colonialism." Exactly when he fixed on the idea of working for independence he does not know. "No. There was no moment when it all clicked into place. It wasn't a sudden inspiration, I didn't suddenly see the light. It was not like the call of the Christians, 'I've been called!' At Edinburgh, I was certain I was coming back to get myself involved full-time in politics. I had made up my mind that my life would be political. I had been away three years; now I would give myself three years to look at the country before taking up politics fully. And I nearly did my three years. By 1953 it was quite clear to me: it must be the politics of independence.

"In 1953, Colin Legum and I went to a hotel in Dar es Salaam— I won't mention its name—and he asked me what I would have and I said beer. As I was about to drink it, the manager came running over. 'This is terrible,' he said, 'Africans are not supposed to drink here.' I was very angry! But it was very clear to me: it was absurd to talk about wanting to be able to enter hotels. This was not the point at all. This was a result of colonialism. I was refused a beer. So what? Not many Africans in this country cared about being served in hotels. It was just the problem of a minority that wanted to be accepted by the colonial club. Absurd! We had to distinguish between the issue of colonialism and the desires of Africans of my type to be accepted by their colonial masters. Should we have fought about being given a licence to drink European beer? Should this have been the peak of our achievement? This approach was ridiculous."

Nyerere flew home to Tanganyika in October 1952. He landed at Dar es Salaam and had a reunion with his fiancée, Maria, and then proceeded by train to Mwanza and lake steamer to Musoma. There he was met by his family, including his bandaged brother Edward, and together they went on to Zanaki. "We started to build a house for Julius and Maria," Nyerere's friend Oswald Marwa has recalled. "And when he began to make mud bricks, everybody started to laugh and ask, 'Why is he doing such work?' He said, 'I went for an education. Everybody who has an education must work.' And then we put on the thatched roof."

During Nyerere's years at Edinburgh, Maria had taken a domestic-science course at a school in Uganda and had later taught at a Lutheran school in Moshi; then, at the urging of Father Walsh, who felt she should receive more schooling in order to be a suitable wife for Nyerere, she studied English at St Joseph's Convent in Dar es Salaam. Friends recall that Maria refused to meet Nyerere at the Dar es Salaam airport on his return from Britain because, she said, "It is not a woman's place to run after a man." She also insisted that the wedding should not take place immediately. "We wait," she is said to have told him. "I want to know you better. I knew you before you went away, but I want to see if you have changed." "And so," Nyerere has told his friends, "I had to build our house first. I had to take off my Edinburgh suit and my shoes and with my bare feet mix the sand and cement, and not until I had built the house did I earn her respect." They were married at the Musoma mission on January 24, 1953, and soon after returned to Dar es Salaam.

Nyerere had already been hired to teach history at St Francis' College in Pugu, twelve miles from Dar es Salaam. At first he was paid £300 a year. "But after a little noise," he has said, "they raised it to four hundred and fifty pounds. I knew this was only three-fifths of what I would receive if I were a European expatriate. But I also knew it was more than I would have been paid for the same kind of work in England. It was more than Tanganyika could afford. And a thirty per cent 'cost of living' allowance besides! Salaries were too high. It was one of the crimes of the colonial administration."

Within three months, Nyerere was elected president of the Tanganyika African Association. "It had been dormant," he has said, "and I felt it was my job to try to revive it." Most observers of the new Africa formerly believed that political consciousness came late to Tanganyika—later than to Ghana or Nigeria or even to Kenya, where the Mau Mau rebellion broke out in the early nineteen-fifties. But the speed with which the independence movement developed following the founding of the Tanganyika African National Union in 1954 suggests otherwise. The clue to TANU's rapid growth lies partly in the homogeneity and stability of Tanganyikan society. The slave trade of the nineteenth century had caused considerable up-rooting of the population and resettlement along the main trade route from Bagamoyo on the coast, to Lake Victoria and Lake Tanganyika. Swahili, originally a language of the East African coastal peoples, was carried inland along the trade routes. In the days of German East Africa, the colonial government maintained a well-trained African civil service and transferred its employees throughout the territory. As a result of its history, both ancient and recent, Tanganyika as a candidate for nationhood had three distinct advantages over many of its neighbours. It had a large number of tribes, one hundred and twenty-six in all, of which none was dominant; it was thus spared the strife of two or three large rival tribes. Since it was neglected by the British in favour of Kenya, a Crown colony, the Trusteeship Territory of Tanganyika had only a small colony of white settlers to resist the rise of African national-ism. And it had Swahili, a genuine lingua franca. Only twice during the seven years he stumped the country working for independence, Nyerere has often recalled, was he unable to speak directly to the people.

In 1929 Sir Donald Cameron, a highly respected British governor, had established the Tanganyika African Association as a social organization for African civil servants. By the nineteen-forties, several of the TAA's stronger branches, including the one at Make-rere College that Nyerere helped to organize, were delving into political issues, or at least were talking about grievances connected with government service. In 1945 the TAA's leaders considered moving the organization's headquarters from Dar es Salaam to Dodoma, in the interior, because so many of their members were being transferred out of the capital. "If you had a big mouth, and talked too much," Chief Patrick Kunambi once explained, "the British moved you to a smaller place, and at that time quite a few of the members were concentrated at Dodoma." Rarely if ever did its members talk of independence in the early days. "Not of independence," one has said. "Of equality." By the time Nyerere reached Dar es Salaam in 1953, the TAA had once again become little more than a social group. "Nyerere couldn't see much point to an organization that merely gave tea parties for every European officer who went home on leave," Chief David Makwaia, of the Sukuma Tribe has said. "This didn't appeal to him. He thought, 'Why have it ?' "

Somehow Nyerere, a newcomer to Dar es Salaam, and a member of a small tribe from the interior at that, quickly assumed the leadership of the TAA. "He was one of the first university graduates in the Territory," Abbas Sykes, an early member of the Association, has said. "And he came at the right time. Usually, if a man went away to university, when he came back he would not be one of us, he would be very sophisticated. But here was a man who had the same kind of education, who was willing to be with his people. This humility— 'I'm willing to serve you'—made everyone forget that he was from the interior and that he wasn't a Moslem." There are almost as many Christians as Moslems in Tanganyika as a whole, but the coastal region is heavily Moslem.

The favourite African politician of the Governor, Sir Edward Twining, was Chief David Makwaia; and in Twining's eyes Nyerere soon became, as Colin Legum has put it, "the bad black because he wouldn't join the Twining club". Makwaia—whom Nyerere was later to call "our Hamlet" because, in Nyerere's view, Makwaia could never make up his mind whether or not to join the nationalists —had clashed with Nyerere and the other young TAA intellectuals as early as 1947. "He had it all," Abbas Sykes has said, "a black man with a white man's education. But he was so conceited. He would arrive by train from the interior, go straight to the Legislative Council [the parliamentary branch of the colonial government], and when the session was over, he would go straight back to his home in Shinyanga. We would go to see him and he would brush us aside; 'I have to go to the chief justice's party now,' he would say, trying to escape from us. Once, in a discussion, he said, 'Look, boys, if you want to have *your* voice,' as if he were not part of Africa's voice, 'you fellows have to organize yourselves.'

"But *now*, we thought, we have got a fellow of the same kind of education who is entirely different, who puts himself *below*, who discusses ordinary things with people." Later, when Nyerere was forced to resign his teaching job because of his political activities, his friends were even more impressed. "He showed he was prepared to sacrifice," Sykes said. "We said, 'Here's the man who has come to save us.' " In addition Nyerere, as a mission school teacher, was relatively free of government control, whereas most of the other TAA leaders were civil servants. And he was easily the best orator in the Territory.

"The fact that he came from an insignificant tribe," the former chief of a large tribe has said, "made him less identifiable to the big tribes, so there were no big blocs automatically set against him. It was also an advantage to have at the top a man who has the human touch, a man who can easily sell himself and his ideas." His leader-ship wasn't based on what he promised, as Chief Patrick Kunambi has said, "because Julius practically never promises anything". But he quickly transformed the organization. "The colonialists believed all we wanted was a square deal," Abbas Sykes' late brother Abdul once said. "Nyerere made us start to think: all we wanted was independence." With this goal in mind, Nyerere and his colleagues reorganized the TAA as a political party, TANU, on July 7, 1954—a day that has been celebrated ever since as *Saba Saba*, the seventh day of the seventh month. Nyerere, at thirty-two, was unanimously elected its president.

Among his earliest colleagues were the three sons of Kleist Sykes, who had been a corporal in the German signal corps during the First World War, and had learned typing, short-hand and accounting; later he became a co-founder of the TAA and, in the words of his son Abbas, "one of the two or three most highly paid Africans here". Other early TANU members were Dossa Aziz and John Rupia, eighteen years older than Nyerere, who was one of the territory's first African entrepreneurs. *Mzee* John had worked as a government clerk and tax collector; then he bought a lorry and became a trans-porter of building materials. By the time TANU was founded, he was the most prosperous African in Tanganyika, and he talked as eloquently of the virtues of hard work as any Western capitalist: "What I want is that they all work hard. Time is money! We can do big things in the world if people work hard." He was the first treasurer of TANU but, as he said, "There was no money. The treasury was our pocket." In the beginning, in fact, the treasury was *Mzee* John himself. When Nyerere and his TANU organizers started out in the morning on their political rounds, Rupia would ask them, "Do you have any power?" Then he would dig into his pockets for money.

The same year, the Governor decided to give Nyerere some parliamentary experience by appointing him to fill a temporary vacancy in the Legislative Council. The permanent member, David Makwaia, had been sent to London to serve on the Royal Commission for Land and Population Problems. "Julius was very serious about it," his brother Joseph, who was living with Julius and Maria at Pugu, has recalled. "He was teaching full time and working in politics full time, sometimes walking twelve miles into Dar es Salaam to attend meetings in the evening." His first Legco speech dealt with the need for more schools. "By 1956, we shall still have sixty-four per cent of our children of primary age outside schools", he said, addressing the Speaker of the Council. "I do not think, Sir, this gives us any cause for complacency." It was the period of the Mau Mau Emergency in Kenya, and Nyerere assured the council: "I am certain that every African wants to see this country peaceful, because it is only through peace that he can get the things he wants, and that is development." It would be a mistake, however, to assume that Nyerere disapproved of the Mau Mau in principle. He once said to Father Walsh, "How do you explain it? The Christian faith put fire in the bellies of the Africans in the eighteen-eighties. Now you're reduced to pulling them into church. You don't spark the dynamism. You're like the government: you thought we were people without ideals, and lived only for our bellies. But look at the Mau Mau up there: they're dying for their ideals. The British thought they would win us over by building roads and schools. But those things alone will not satisfy us." Nyerere's service in the Council ended abruptly a few months later, when he let it be known that he planned to oppose a government recommendation that civil service salaries be increased. Before the debate had begun, Makwaia was whisked back from London and Nyerere was automatically unseated.

In August 1954, a four-man United Nations mission visited Tanganyika and subsequently published a report recommending that the Territory be given a timetable for independence within twenty or twenty-five years. The territorial administrators were infuriated by the mission, and particularly by the pro-African views of an American member, Mason Sears. A few months later, TANU voted to send Nyerere to New York to address the U.N. Trusteeship Council on the subject of independence. Twining responded by dispatching a three-man delegation to support the government's position. He also urged Father Walsh (who by then had moved to Dar es Salaam) to refuse to allow Nyerere to be absent from his classes, implying that Nyerere's political activities verged on sedition. Walsh refused. "If it's sedition," he demanded, "why isn't Nyerere in jail?"

At the British government's request the United States government restricted Nyerere to an eight-block radius of the U.N. headquarters and limited his stay to within twenty-four hours of his appearance before the Trusteeship Council. Such gestures must have seemed foolish in the light of his reasoned appeal to the council on March 7, 1955. On behalf of his party, Nyerere said, he wanted to refute "the outrageous assertion . . . that the vast majority of the Territory's inhabitants were against the major political recommendations of that report"—that Tanganyika should be granted independence within twenty or twenty-five years. "What will satisfy my people is a categorical statement, both by this council and by the Administering Authority, that although Tanganyika is multi-racial in population, its future government shall be primarily African. Once we get that assurance, everything else becomes a detail."

Nyerere had had trouble raising the money for the trip. "I almost didn't go at all," he has said. But *Mzee* John contributed 5,000 shillings, and a little more was collected from other friends. Rupia has recalled that, on the night before his departure, Nyerere stayed at Rupia's house in Dar es Salaam. The next morning they were all so nervous that they couldn't remember where Julius had left his suitcase. Finally, after turning the house upside down, they found the suitcase in the car trunk, where Nyerere had put it the night before. They dashed to the airport, and Julius barely caught his plane.

Father Walsh, who had cleared the way for Nyerere's trip, told him before his departure, "I think we're coming to the end of the road; one day you'll have to give up your teaching job." The headmaster of St Francis' College, who was considerably less sympathetic than Father Walsh, told Maria during Julius' absence, "Your husband is causing our school to be threatened by the government. He had better decide whether he wants to be a teacher or a politician." A year earlier, the government had ruled that civil servants could not participate in TANU. By the time of Nyerere's trip to New York in 1955, the Governor had made it clear to the Catholic priests that he felt no teacher in their employ should be permitted to engage in political agitation. In 1966, a year before Twining died, in England, at the age of sixty-eight, he explained his action by saying, "Nyerere was in receipt of a salary paid by government. I said, 'We wouldn't allow civil servants to do this. Nyerere must choose between being a political leader and being a teacher paid by government. I can't have a man who is in receipt of a government salary, even if indirectly, being a political leader.' "

Nyerere resigned from his teaching post as soon as he returned, partly because he didn't want to get the missionaries in trouble. "But by then," he has said, "I was sure it would be absurd to go on teaching anyway. I really came back from the U.N. prepared to say to the headmaster that in June I would go to Makerere to find a trained Tanganyikan teacher to take my place. But before that, he gave me a choice."

In April 1955, Nyerere took his family back to his Zanaki homeland to the house he had built for Maria three years earlier. He had received job offers from a newspaper and from an oil company, but had turned them down. "I must be a free man," he said. In Musoma, he accepted a job as translator and tutor, at 700 shillings a month, from the Maryknoll Fathers, who were preparing to establish a mission in Zanaki. "I asked him if he would help me with the tribal language, Ki-Zanaki," Father Wille, who was to direct the new mission, has said, "and so he moved into Musoma; he stayed with Oswald Marwa, and he taught me every day. He translated some catechisms and a teachers' manual for the catechism. He offered to try to do a translation of the New Testament into Ki-Zanaki. No, there still isn't one. What he did translate was a reading from the Gospels for every Sunday in the year. And he taught me—oh, from nine until twelve-thirty, and from one to five. He used to exhaust me, he has tremendous intellectual energy. We were using the *Teach Yourself* book on Swahili as the basis for the Zanaki grammar. I think there are seven classes of verbs in Swahili, and he would say, 'My language has twelve classes—this class in Swahili is similar to this one in Zanaki,' and so on. I used to be amazed he could remember it so well, because he had left tribal life when he was twelve and had never really gone back to it. He might say, 'I'll have to ask my mother,' or Oswald.

"Then, after the lesson, we would have tea and talk about what he was going to do. He would say, 'There's no problem getting independence. The problem is preparing for it.' His greatest worry was what would happen afterwards. He once said, 'Those Baganda' "—the members of the largest tribal kingdom in neighbouring Uganda— " 'I'm sure Britain would give them independence tomorrow if Uganda were united. *I'd* get them united, and then I'd put on the brakes.' I'm sure if someone else had appeared to lead Tanganyika, Julius would gladly have gone back to his books. He was a scholar at heart. He would say to his friends, 'Why don't you go and read something?' Sometimes he would talk about the Masai. He had no sympathy for the way the British had romanticized the Masai, and he said the Masai would have to develop, like everybody else. 'They're going to have to fall in line.' He would say, 'My people—it's a vicious circle; not enough food to do a day's hard work, and not enough money to buy good food.' He said he knew that Tanganyika would have to build a strong Presidency into its constitution, and yet somehow protect the individual, a big problem."

In April 1955, a new Legislative Council had gone into session, this one based on Twining's multi-racial "parity" policy under which "Europeans", "Asians" and "Africans" had roughly equal representation among the unofficial members of the council. Despite the fact that the Tanganyikan population was more than ninety-eight per cent black African, Nyerere recognized the new formula as a modest advance. But he was infuriated a few months later when he learned that the Twining government proposed to divide certain funds gained from the confiscation of German properties during the Second World War in the same way—£711,000 for European education, and equal amounts for Asian and African schooling. Nyerere fired off a letter to members of the Legislative Council, charging that such a method of distribution was "inexplicable" in view of the Territory's racial make-up: 22,000 Europeans, 80,000 Asians and 8,000,000 Africans. "The advocates of parity have a duty," he wrote, "to see to it that its application does not make it look absurd and unjust." It would be far better, he said, to use the full amount to expand higher education without regard to race.

Occasionally, wearing a white shirt, khaki trousers and carrying a walking stick, he held TANU meetings. "He had a big meeting at Butiama," Father Wille has recalled, "and he brought up the point: 'If anybody tells you we will throw out the Europeans and the Asians after Uhuru—that is wrong. We all know Mr Patel, over there. And we all know Father Wille and the Mennonites. We respect them, we need them.' " The government, however, had been keeping a close eye on him. Oswald Marwa, who was an assistant district officer, had been asked to instruct Nyerere to report to him regularly—an easy matter, since the Nyereres were staying with Marwa. Once the provincial commissioner, the senior official in Musoma, asked Marwa, who was acting as TANU's local treasurer, to bring him the TANU books; but after inspecting them, he merely suggested a few book-keeping techniques. Occasionally the police asked Nyerere's old friend Emanuel Kibira, who by then was headmaster of the Musoma School, how much money Nyerere had.

"During those months at Musoma," Father Wille has said, "Julius was kind of lost, I think. This was a time to rethink his life. He was a great admirer of Gandhi; he wanted *no* bloodshed. He fully expec-ted to go to jail sooner or later. The house he had built Maria near Chief Edward's village had only a thatched roof, so I lent him the money—a thousand shillings, I think—for a corrugated-iron roof. He was concerned that, if he should be imprisoned, Maria might have difficulties; a grass roof requires repairs. He got Oswald, who was doing all kinds of construction work, to put it on for him. Well, I never pressed him for the money. But on his second trip to the U.S., a couple years later, he appeared on TV, and when he got home he gave me a cheque and apologized for taking so long to repay, but said, 'Really, Father, I haven't had any money, and I got this for my appearance on television.'"

He also tried to fight the corruption in the Musoma hospital. "He knew the African drug dispensers were forcing people to pay for the government medicine they were giving out—a widespread form of petty graft, even today. So he sent in a child with a marked twenty-shilling note, and arranged for a police officer to check the dispenser immediately afterwards. But the fellow was clever—he insisted the child change the bill and bring coins, so they didn't catch him."

When reminded of the incident many years later, Nyerere ex-claimed, "Yes, I failed. The fellow escaped." Then, in an aside to his secretary, he murmured, "It's not easy catching corrupt people."

In August 1955, Nyerere was visited by Oscar Kambona, a young colleague from TANU headquarters in Dar es Salaam. Kambona has recalled, "Julius had left us in April, and until August we never had a word from him. Not a word! So in August, the TANU Central Committee asked me to find out how he was, and to take him three hundred shillings. So when I got to Musoma, I found him sitting on the floor reading a book about Gandhi. I told him of our troubles and gave him the three hundred shillings and, to my astonishment, he gave it to his brother Joseph to buy a cow—to give to *me* for a feast! This made a tremendous impression on me. We began to talk, and we decided to hold a public meeting and try out the non-violent technique. The district commissioner refused us permission to hold the meeting, but we said we would hold it anyway, and two hours before the scheduled time they said it was all right."

During the visit, the two men talked about TANU's rapid growth in the preceding six months, and Nyerere told Kambona that he would return to Dar es Salaam in September or October. After leaving Musoma, Kambona took the lake steamer to Bukoba and then to Mwanza, where Paul Bomani, another close colleague, told him Nyerere wanted him to return to Musoma. But Kambona also received a telegram from Dar es Salaam advising him that the entire TANU Central Committee had threatened to resign. So he took the train to Dar es Salaam. As Kambona told the story years later, John Rupia, who was serving as committee chairman in the absence of Nyerere, had made the members angry. "John was very outspoken always, he would say, 'This is rubbish!' So I went to all the members and told them, 'Look, you can all write down your versions of the fight, and we'll settle it after independence.' Then I told them I had brought *money* from Bukoba—ten thousand shillings!—and that Julius would be coming back soon, and so they forgot about the fight."

The shy, brooding, emotional Kambona was born in 1928 in a corner of southern Tanganyika somewhere near the Mozambican border. His tribesmen, the Nyanja, were cousins of the Zulus of South Africa; they had wandered northward until their migration was checked by the Hehe of central Tanganyika. Unlike most of his contemporaries, Oscar was the son of educated parents. "My grand-father was a chief," Kambona has said, "and when the missionaries asked him for a boy to teach, my grandfather sent only a slave. Later, when he saw how the boy was benefiting, he sent his own son, my father. And my father became an Anglican priest. My mother, who also had been sent to school, was always arguing with my father's father. He wanted his grandchildren to look after the cattle, and he complained that school was making us tame. But my mother insisted. She read us stories about Booker T. Washington. She told us about all the big American Negroes.

"Our paramount chief had been given his chieftainship by the Germans. He ruled us for forty years against the intrigues of all the factions, including my grandfather's. He balanced the factions against each other, and the man he feared most was my grandfather. Late in his life, my grandfather became an Anglican priest too, and I always felt the chief encouraged him in this out of fear rather than love. He got the missionaries to move my grandfather out of the area.

"My grandmother was an exceptional woman. She almost came to rule. When my father was ready to be transferred to another post, his mother would go first to the new post to see the chiefs and make arrangements for her son's arrival. Sometimes she would sit in the courts, and sometimes she would veto the court proceedings. She was very powerful. She had enemies. And she was poisoned and died. Yes! When I was twelve or thirteen. A sub-chief did it. The tribe wanted to bury him alive, according to the custom of the time. But my father urged them not to do this." And so the man was simply deposed.

Kambona's pursuit of schooling, as he tells the story, was a seemingly endless series of rebuffs and misunderstandings. At the mission school, where classes were taught in the tribal language, he was punished for using English words, he has claimed. "Even in Standards Seven and Eight, we had only two periods of English a week. I wanted to go to an English school, but I was rejected because I was already in a vernacular 'stream'. The bishop wanted me to become an Anglican priest, but my father refused because I was the first son, and so I was to become a grade-two teacher, a vernacular teacher."

The story of Kambona's eventual transfer to an English-language school, as he describes it, reveals both the extent of his hunger for education and his youthful cunning. "I was determined to go to secondary school, but I was rejected by them all. A new one was being built at Dodoma, with Australian and New Zealand missionaries, and they agreed to take me. But the fees were very high: I was to pay three hundred shillings a year, and my father was earning thirty-five shillings a month, with a family of six. So I went to the bishop. I said, 'Look, Bishop, I know you've tried. If a school admitted me, would you help me to go?' He said of course he would, but he thought no school would do it. Then I gave him the letter I had received from Alliance School! Well, he was very cross, he prayed for me. But then he said that, since he had promised, he would help. He gave me the three hundred shillings."

After two years at Dodoma, Oscar moved on to Tabora, where he spent the most difficult and apparently the most painful years of his schooling. "Twice I was almost expelled. The first day I was at Tabora, the headmaster, Mr Blumer, said, 'Well, who is Oscar?' He saw me and said, 'I want you to cut off your hair by tomorrow morning, and cut it every two weeks thereafter.' He was one of the most *dictator* headmasters I ever met. At first he disliked me, but then we became friends. At Tabora I didn't do very well. I thought my English schoolmistress was against me. She didn't realize that my English was weak. At Dodoma, three of my teachers had been ill, and we didn't have the attention we needed. She said awful things to me. I began to take a keen interest in reading magazines, and she thought I spent too much time on them."

When he had finished at Tabora, Kambona became a teacher at the Dodoma school, transferred for a while to a nearby teacher training college but resigned because he decided the college authorities were not trying to help him get a scholarship to Britain or the United States.

Back at the Dodoma school, Kambona met Kanyama Chiume, a fellow teacher who was later to become a member of the government in neighbouring Malawi before fleeing into exile in Tanzania. Kambona has given this account of how the two young men became interested in politics: "Every Saturday we went up the hill to a cave, the two of us. Chiume would stand up and address the audience, and the audience was me. Then we would break for tea. And then I would address the crowd, and my audience was Chiume. We would discuss how to organize a youth league, how to draft a constitution.

"Well, this was during Mau Mau in Kenya. One Saturday the Bishop"—the one who had sent him to school years before—"and the district commissioner and the headmaster came to the cave. Unfortunately it was I who was speaking. And Chiume said, 'Go on, go on,' and I went on, 'The British government must leave this country,' and so on, and Chiume was clapping. The bishop said, 'Let us pray'—for us to renounce hate. We joined in the prayer—for them to see our cause. They were angry, yes; they banned us from further preaching; all the teachers had taken turns preaching. But the bishop had great understanding." As he told the story twelve years later, Kambona added, "Just yesterday, someone told me his grave is in Dar es Salaam, and it needs attention."

Then, leaving his teaching career behind, Kambona moved to Dar es Salaam. He arrived soon after the founding of TANU and became a full-time party organizer. "I used many tricks," he has recalled with great enthusiasm. "I'd ride the buses, and talk to people at the stops, and then jump back in. I'd get a leader of a tribal group or a social group to buy memberships for all his members or friends." And by August 1955, he concluded, leaving the impression that the extraordinary rise of TANU had been largely a one-man feat, "we had one hundred thousand members!"

V

"We've never accepted the arguments of 'readiness for independence'—that people were not ready to govern themselves. That is like saying to an individual, 'You are not ready to live.' How do you say to a nation, to a people, 'You're not ready to be human'? It's part of humanness that people should govern themselves. It is incompatible with our being human beings that we be governed against our will."

"I THINK I REMAINED much more philosophical than political," Nyerere has said. "I wouldn't tackle things like discrimination. I just said, 'It is wrong for one people to govern another,' and everything else fell into place. So they called me a moderate. I believe I was a big extremist—that we must jolly well be independent! But probably this philosophical way removed the bitterness from the campaigns. I was not saying, 'Today a man was refused beer,' but just, 'We must govern ourselves.' Well, politically, this is the wrong way. In the Lake Region, the colonial government was saying, 'There are too many cattle.' I said, 'We can't campaign against cattle de-stocking because we may have to de-stock when *we* come to power.' There was one TANU man in Iringa who campaigned against cattle dipping.* He made dipping *extremely* unpopular. I was very angry with him! But politically, of course, you exploit every grievance."

Nyerere returned to Dar es Salaam from Musoma in October 1955. During the next six years until independence in December 1961, he toured the interior of Tanganyika almost continuously. TANU's Land-Rover, with number plates DSK 750, became a familiar sight throughout the Territory. "When he came to Bukoba," Miss Barbro Johansson, a Swedish missionary who campaigned with TANU, has said, "he and I would ride in the TANU Land-Rover, and the police would be in another. We had an understanding. If we had a puncture, they would stop to help; if they did, we would."

On his first trip to Mbeya, Nyerere found the police primed as if for a riot. "What are they expecting?" Nyerere asked his friends in

* Immersing them in a trough filled with a parasite-killing solution.

astonishment. He went to the police station himself, and was given permission to hold a meeting for TANU members only. Then the TANU party went to a local mission to borrow a loudspeaker, but the missionary couldn't decide whether it would be politic to lend them one. "It's up to you," the district commissioner told him. "So to play it safe," recalled Joan Wicken, then the Assistant Commonwealth Officer of the Labour Party, who was visiting Tanganyika on a research fellowship, "the missionary said no. Eventually the police lent the TANU chaps their own loud hailers. And then, to my surprise, the police, including the inspector, saluted him. In his speech, he said, 'We are fighting against colonialism, not against the whites.' "

On a tour of the Usambara mountains, Nyerere drove eighteen miles in a rainstorm to speak to the people of Kimweri village, only to discover that the local chief had sabotaged his visit. "We were not welcome," Bibi Titi Mohamed, the early leader of the national women's organization, has said. "The chief was a stooge of the British. He had made them all drunk with *pombe*"—the local brew, usually made from corn or bananas. "So we drove back to Korogwe for the night." The women of Kimweri were furious with the chief for wrecking the meeting and particularly for getting their men drunk, and they refused to cook the evening meal. "We are on strike," they said. "Why don't you go and eat at the chief's house?" So the villagers sent a delegation to Korogwe and, over Mrs Mohamed's objections, Nyerere agreed to return. "Listen, we must be patient," he told her, "we can't mind too much if we are chased away." So they drove back to Kimweri and, Mrs Mohamed reported later, "this time the *Mtemi* did nothing."

In Bukoba, Nyerere first met Miss Johansson when his throng of followers accidentally trampled the hedges and flowerbeds of her school. In the beginning, she has recalled, Nyerere complained of his sudden notoriety: " 'We must stop this, this singing of Nyerere songs.' " She told him, "You have to take this as a sacrifice for the sake of your work." The following year, there were great banners on the road to greet him. "I said to him, 'What do you think when you see your name in letters as big as a man?' He said, 'I beg your pardon?' I repeated my question and he said, 'Oh, I don't even see it.' "

Often, in the years after 1958, Nyerere rested at the Iringa home of Marion the Lady Chesham, the American-born widow of a British farmer. "There was no red-carpet stuff, no nonsense," Lady

Chesham has said. "Such an easy visitor. I'd just tell the servants, '*Baba* Julius is coming.' He read the U.S. Constitution in my home. He said, 'Ha! They were the same average age as we—and people say we are too young!' " In that period, Lady Chesham performed an invaluable service for Nyerere and his colleagues; she served as their liaison with the Governor, Sir Edward Twining. "He *had* to see me," Lady Chesham has said, "because I was the widow of a peer of the realm."

TANU continued to grow at a remarkable rate: from one hundred thousand members in 1955 to half a million by 1957. "In a sense," Nyerere has said, "we had won the battle by 1957." Although he opposed TANU, the Governor was painstakingly even-handed in the way he treated it; he occasionally punished individual TANU branches for breaking territorial laws, but at no time did he ban the entire movement. So Nyerere was always free to speak in one region if not another; at one point he was banned for several months from addressing public gatherings, but TANU meetings were not affected.

"When he first spoke in Iringa, there were fifty people," Lady Chesham has said. "By 1958 there were six thousand." A British friend who, a few years earlier, had taken Nyerere to Labour party meetings in London at which forty party members might dutifully show up, was embarrassed to discover that Nyerere's own meetings in Dar oo Salaam were drawing as many as thirty thousand by 1957. Miss Mary Hancock, a peppery little Englishwoman who had come to Tanganyika in 1940 "to help the black people, as we called them then," has recalled, "Oh, that man, how he thinks! The civil servants in Musoma couldn't see why I remained his friend after he declared for *Uhuru*. We civil servants had to be careful, you know— we couldn't attend political meetings. I would say, 'He's my friend. If you can't differentiate, I *can*.' Well! You should have seen the civil servants change when it became clear that he was winning. They would ask me to invite them for tea with him, when he was visiting Musoma, and I'd say, 'Why should I? You wouldn't even talk to him before.' "

Yet TANU's transformation to a national movement came none too soon, for the politics of Africa were changing more rapidly than anyone then realized. In 1954, the U.N. Visiting Commission had urged the British government to promise independence to Tanganyika within twenty or twenty-five years. At the United Nations two years later, Nyerere himself asked for independence within ten to

3

twelve years; and in 1959 he asked for it in five years. But neither he nor anyone else yet realized to what degree the colonial powers would accelerate the process of withdrawal; Tanganyikan independence, it turned out, came scarcely two years later—in December, 1961. In 1958 the Governor of Tanganyika paid a visit to the Belgian Congo. He later recalled, "Its governor-general, a pocket Napoleon, told me, 'We admire what you British are doing in Tanganyika, of course. But aren't you going about it too quickly?' Well! Eighteen months later . . ." Eighteen months later, the Belgians recklessly settled their accounts in Central Africa by granting the Congo an independence for which it was tragically unprepared.

Sir Edward Twining, a blustery idealist, was governor of Tanganyika from 1949 to 1958. He ruled from Government House with a strong hand—"like Robert Morley playing the sultan," a Tanganyikan once said. In his early years as governor he had deeply pleased the Hehe tribe of central Tanganyika by arranging, through a German museum, the return of the skull of a famous Hehe warrior, Chief Mkwawa, who had killed himself to avoid capture by the Germans in battle forty years before. It was both a magnanimous gesture and a shrewd one, but Twining, who took it upon himself to fetch the skull, apparently had some private doubt as to whether the museum had given him the right skull. When the Hehe asked him, "How can we be sure this is our chief's skull?" Twining replied, "Well, won't you recognize him?" An old man said, "*I* will. He had a great bump on the right side of his forehead." Twining told friends later, "My heart sank." The old man took the skull and studied it, turning it around and around in his hands for what seemed to Twining an eternity. At last he beamed and said, to Twining's relief, "*This* is our Mkwawa."

Twining never got on well with Nyerere, whom he dismissed as a racialist. "I've seen Twining so mad about Julius that he forgot he had gout," Father Walsh, who was a close friend of both men, has recalled. "In December 1954, I was with Twining at his lodge at Lushoto, his leg propped up on a chair. Oh, he was angry! He wouldn't listen to me at all. He said, 'Nyerere is not intelligent, he's just an emotionalist.' I said, 'All revolutions in the world have been inspired by men of emotion.' Twining was the last of the Kipling era, one of the greatest men I've met. But he was from the world of Kipling. They sang a Kipling hymn at his funeral—the one that ends, "Lest We Forget, Lest We Forget." He was the last of the

Photo: John Reader

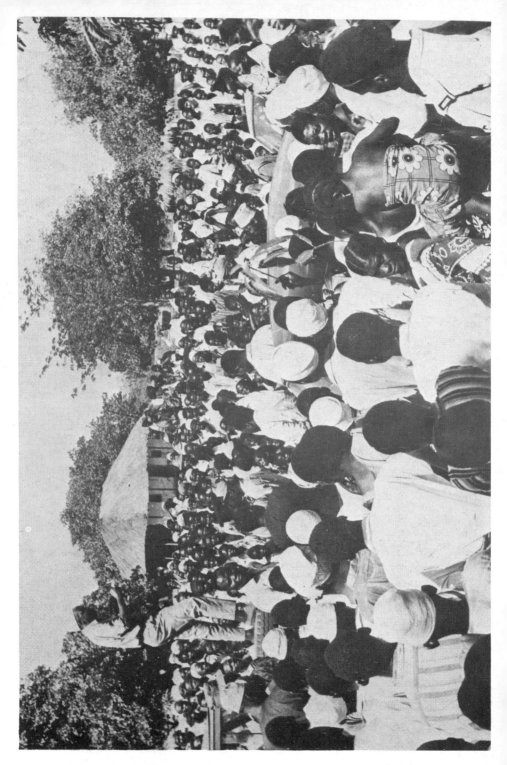

Photo: Tanzanian Information Service

empire builders, and Julius was the first of the radicals, and so they clashed. Both were honest, both were idealists. Twining said, 'He's trying to pull the chair out from underneath the British Empire!' He said, 'I'll destroy that man'—but of course he had gout, remember."

Another man who was close to both Twining and Nyerere was David Makwaia, of the Legislative Council. "It was difficult for me", Makwaia has since recalled. "One tended to be regarded as a stooge of the colonialists. But Twining once said to me, 'I've been trying to meet Julius Nyerere socially. He has kept promising he would turn up, and he never turns up.' Julius said, "He is quite right. If you are going up there today, I'll go,' and I took him to Government House that evening at six o'clock. Only one servant was present, and he quickly disappeared. Lady Twining was not there. I recall that both of them were reluctant to start the discussion. Then Twining, having poured himself a gin, said, 'Look, Julius, what do you want to drink? I'm having a gin, what about you?' Julius said, 'What about you, Chief?' I said, 'I suppose I can break the law in Government House and get away with it.' Julius said, 'Well, I'll have a small beer.'

"I said, 'Now, you wanted to talk. Why do you seem so shy?' Twining said, 'I feel the president of TANU and the Governor should discuss matters of state, because whatever I do will have some bearing on what Julius Nyerere wants to do.'" They began by discussing the terms "multi-racialism" and "non-racialism". "Then," Makwaia continued, "I said, 'You have said you are pre-paring Tanganyika for self-government or independence, and Nyerere is demanding there be a timetable. What is your objection to that?' Julius said, 'David is quite right. We would be very happy if the colonial government could state the number of years until independence.' Twining said, 'I'll tell you in confidence. I'd say fifteen or sixteen years from now, this country should attain inde-pendence. But you cannot expect me to say that in public.' Julius said, 'Why not? Such a goal is exactly what we want; and we would then work towards it.'"

Many years later, Twining—he was now Lord Twining—reflected on Tanganyikan politics from his apartment in Ashley Gardens in London. "The mandate was the foundation of our policy," he said. "It stated that we should bring Tanganyika to self-government and independence, but it set no time limit. We refused to have a time-table. The last visiting commission, in 1954, said it should be within twenty-five years. In 1958, I said I thought it would be within twelve or fourteen years. My policy was based on the accepted policy of the British government: non-racialism, with a gradual programme of turnover to African control; a plan of carefully graded objectives. Now, Nyerere's was a rabid African nationalism. Nothing in it about non-racialism: he wanted one-man–one-vote immediately! I told Nyerere, as long as they didn't break the law they could do as they wanted. But it got out of control; some TANU branches set up their own courts! Well, I thought Nyerere was a nice chap. Mild, moderate, intelligent. He would agree with me, and go off next day and address thirty thousand people and say the opposite. He is a very shrewd politician, an emotionalist, and that was the sort of stuff they wanted. But he is not greedy, not corrupt; I think he is a good man."

Long after the independence fight was won, Nyerere said of Twining: "He was one of the greater governors—to the extent that I can appreciate colonial governors. If I were to write a history of the colonial period, I would give an important place to Twining, and to Sir Donald Cameron; they were the most prominent.

"Twining came at the wrong time, and he stayed too long. But you must give him credit: he had ideas. But he had a fault. Who is the man referred to by the English poet Pope—'Should such a man, too fond to rule alone, bear, like the Turk, no brother near the throne'? Well, *he* was governor, and he didn't like anyone to tell *him*. He did good things. The British did little to develop this country, but to the extent that development took place, it was pushed by Cameron and Twining. The deep-water berths in the port are from Twining's time; the new Dar es Salaam airport is Twining; the tarmac road to Morogoro, the big school at Iringa, all Twining.

"Politically, he didn't like anyone near the throne. He saw some European settlers thinking of establishing here the kind of empire they had in Kenya, and he put a stop to that. There would be one voice, and it would be that of Government House! One voice and none other! I respect him. But we clashed as early as 1954. In his vague mind, I stood for racial dominance, and his party was 'multi-racial.' By 1955 he had come to realize he couldn't fight us alone, and he tried to revive the European voice—but it was too late."

In response to TANU's growing influence in the mid-nineteen-fifties, Twining, in December, 1955, organized the "multi-racial" United Tanganyika Party as an opposition to TANU. A year and a half later, he announced that the first elections in Tanganyika would take place in the first quarter of 1958. Each of ten constituencies was to elect three members of the Legislative Council—one African, one Asian, and one European—and each voter would vote for a candidate of each race. Since, under this system, only one-third of the Council members could be Africans, most of the TANU leadership thought the party should boycott the elections. At a party conference in Tabora in January 1958, Nyerere argued convincingly that TANU should participate, and his victory proved to be a crucial one for his country's future.

Nyerere's brother Joseph has recalled that, at the beginning, Nyerere was supported by only one member, the delegate from Tanga. "All the other delegates, more than a hundred, said no, we should boycott the elections. The debate had gone on for two days, and the last day I wasn't at the meeting. That day there were only two speakers—Bhoke Munanka and Julius. Well, I had the impression that the whole country was against our contesting the election. So when I came back and was told that we were going to participate, I said, 'But how can we, when there were only two who wanted it? How could they decide like that against the wishes of the people?' And I went to his place in the evening, and I said, 'You dictator!'

"Julius said, 'OK, I know you are fired up; now sit down and I'll tell you about it. If we don't participate this year, the UTP is going to win. All members will be returned unopposed. And TANU will be fighting from the outside. The only thing we could do is send a petition to the Colonial Office explaining our position; the Colonial Office would send a commission of inquiry; and the next election would be three or four years later; and by that time the UTP would be firmly established. We might get our independence by 1970 or 1975.

" 'But suppose we do contest it. Everybody says that TANU will elect only ten members, but that's not true. We also have Europeans and Asians who are friends of ours and will support us. We'll have thirty TANU-supported members. Then we'll fight from the inside *and* the outside. We'll demand a new constitution. In a few months we'll have self-government, and we'll be independent in 1961.' "

Joseph reflected on his brother's powers of persuasion. "Julius is not hurried in reaching a decision. We'll discuss something. Then he will say, 'OK, now let's go out for a beer, or take tea.' Then we'll come back and he will say, 'OK, tomorrow,' and you go on like that until he has convinced you."

On May 27, 1958, four months before the first phase of the elections, the TANU news-sheet *Sauti ya Tanu* (the name means "the voice of TANU") published an editorial by Nyerere cautioning party members to refrain from violence. "The reason why lunatics have been trying to provoke the people into violence," it said, "is the fact that they know we are virtually invincible if we remain a law-abiding organization . . . Fellow Africans, be on your guard. The enemy is losing the cold war because he has no argument against our case. Don't give him that chance. Don't be provoked into violence. Be as calm and good-humoured as you have always been." The editorial then singled out two district commissioners for criticism; it charged that one had put a chief on trial for "cooked-up reasons", and accused the other of trying to undermine TANU. However mild such comment may seem now, the colonial government saw fit at the time to file three counts of criminal libel against Nyerere on the basis of the editorial. The case dragged on for almost three months. In the end, Nyerere was found guilty, and was given a choice of paying a fine of £150 or serving six months in prison.

Many observers felt the authorities had behaved unwisely in pressing the case. Even Twining, in later years, blamed the incident on "an obstinate Irish attorney general" and added, "Under the British system, a governor can't interfere, any more than he can interfere with the chief justice." Whatever the truth of this statement, it was generally assumed in Tanganyika that Nyerere would seize the opportunity to become a "prison graduate" like most other African nationalist leaders. Indeed, Nyerere's friends like to recall how he wrestled with the decision. Resting at Lady Chesham's farm, he would say lightly, almost jokingly, "Shall I go to jail? Every other prime minister has gone to jail. But I *can't* go to jail—it's an election year."

The trial also coincided with another important event, the retirement of Twining and the arrival of a new governor, Sir Richard Turnbull. A tall, thin, erudite man, Turnbull had served as chief secretary in the Kenya government during the height of the Mau Mau Emergency. He took the oath of office on July 15, a week after Nyerere's libel trial had begun. To the surprise of virtually everyone in Tanganyika, Turnbull invited Nyerere to Government House for a talk on July 24, more than two weeks before the trial ended. "The British made a mess of the trial," Turnbull has said. "Tremendous feeling had been aroused. I had been through four years of the Emergency in Kenya, and I didn't want to go through that again. I couldn't wait for the judgment. I sent for him."

A friend recalls that Nyerere said at the time, "When I went to see Turnbull, I thought I should say something polite, so I said, 'I thank you for what you intend to do for Tanganyika.' But Turnbull put it aside. I took a deep breath and thought, 'Thank God, this man is shy. With him I can probably work.' "

Nyerere said in later years, "Turnbull could have fallen into Twining's footsteps and got into real trouble, because the political movement was now very militant. I was determined to go to jail. The showdown had come, and we were in the mood to fight. I expected that he would invite me to talk with him, but I thought he would wait until the trial was over. But he didn't wait. Well, I respect people even if they represent systems I am fighting. And also, we realized he had inherited difficulties not of his own making. I felt after our first discussion that it was absurd to precipitate crisis for the sake of crisis." He chose to pay the fine. As Turnbull has put it, "He did a very generous thing: he gave up the martyr's crown."

In the campaign that year, Nyerere ran for a seat in the Eastern Province against Chief Patrick Kunambi, an early TANU member who had fallen out with the party and decided to run as an independent. In one village, TANU supporters broke up a meeting of Kunambi's by throwing rocks. "I know Julius was very upset about this," Kunambi has said. "No, he didn't speak to me about it. He finds it difficult to talk about such things. He understood, I understood, that's all." In Dar es Salaam, Nyerere campaigned for the TANU candidate against a European named Tyrell, whose campaign slogan was: "You all know Tyrell." "We all know Tyrell," Nyerere said in his speeches, mimicking and animating the line until his audiences shook with laughter. "Who doesn't know Tyrell? Oh, we know Tyrell, all right." As Nyerere had predicted, TANU and TANU-sponsored candidates won all the seats they contested; Nyerere himself received 2,600 votes, as compared with 800 for Kunambi. The following March the Governor increased TANU's role in the government significantly by giving it five of the twelve ministerial posts. On that day in March 1959, Nyerere, with victory so clearly in sight, celebrated with his colleagues Amir Jamal, an Indian, and Derek Bryceson, an Englishman, by "jumping around the room, first on one foot and then the other," as Bryceson once described it, in a burst of joy.

Pounding away at his main theme, *uhuru na kazi*, freedom and work, Nyerere cried, "We cannot go around the world begging for money. We must work for the things we want. This is God's ordinance—not Nyerere's." Condemning the traditional practice of giving petty bribes to chiefs and elders, he declared, "The people can no longer afford to see justice purchased with gifts of goats and chickens."

When he attended a conference of independent African states at Addis Ababa in 1960, Nyerere delivered a study paper in which he said that the creation of an East African federation was so important that, if necessary, Tanganyika would be willing to have its independence delayed so that it could become independent with Kenya and Uganda simultaneously, and could federate with them immediately. An aide released the paper to the press by accident, and it quickly became apparent that Nyerere had not cleared the statement with his party leadership. "Every major TANU official in Dar called us to say that Nyerere couldn't have said such a thing," a former editor of the Tanganyika *Standard* has said. But Nyerere took responsibility for the idea, and later explained, "I felt we should become one country. The question was how? When? I argued that the best time to achieve federation would be at the time of independence—we could combine the freedom movement with the unity movement. Freedom was popular; unity could be popularized. You would be asking the states to achieve something, whereas after independence you would be asking them to surrender their sovereignty, and that's not easy. My point was: Don't wait until the day the flag goes up. So I said, 'We in Tanganyika will delay our independence until Kenya and Uganda get popularly elected governments.' But my friends [the British] didn't see it that way."

In the elections of August 1960, TANU candidates won seventy of the seventy-one seats in the new House, and Nyerere was called to form a government. "Success must not go to our heads," he told his followers. "We must not become bigheaded with ideas as big as Kilimanjaro, forgetting the past and future." In March of 1961, a constitutional conference attended by British officials and Tanganyikan leaders was held in Dar es Salaam to settle the details of a constitution for an independent Tanganyika. As a concession to the Colonial Secretary, Iain Macleod, Nyerere had agreed that when Tanganyika became independent—December 9th was the date they settled on—it should first become a monarchy, with a governor-general representing the Queen; only later did many of his colleagues realize that this meant waiting a full year before Tanganyika would become a republic within the Commonwealth. In May, Tanganyika achieved internal self-government—the last step before full independence—and Nyerere became Prime Minister.

A British journalist, John Collier, has recalled dropping by for a beer one day at Nyerere's six-room government bungalow in Dar es Salaam's Seaview district. "Yes, it's a beautiful view," Nyerere reflected, "but that car is in the way. Will you move it, John?" No, he had never learned to drive, Nyerere said wryly; why should he bother, when there were always so many people around who wanted to drive for him?

By this time, Nyerere's views on African affairs were being solicited regularly by the foreign press. According to a story still current in East Africa, a British reporter pleaded with Nyerere on one occasion that year to rephrase a point he was making in more colourfully African language. "Oh, I don't know," Nyerere is supposed to have replied. "You do it, you're good at that sort of thing." The reporter quoted Nyerere as saying that unless African leaders could find ways of meeting the aspirations of their people, "we shall fall, as surely as the tickbird follows the rhino," a line widely quoted thereafter. "Not bad," Nyerere told the reporter.

One of Nyerere's first acts as prime minister was to suspend the practice of supplying Tanganyikan labourers to South Africa's gold mines. The new policy cost Tanganyika £500,000 a year, but Nyerere regarded it as morally unavoidable. A few months earlier he had written: "In South Africa, the white man behaves like a man at a sleeping giant's throat. He dare not relent his grip for fear of the consequences. This fear drives him to suicidal madness and he tightens his grip until the giant wakes up feeling the pain." He was also beginning to speak of the non-alignment that would become a cornerstone of his foreign policy: "We shall not allow our friends to decide who our enemies shall be."

"Julius and TANU were very inexperienced in those days," Sir Richard Turnbull has said. "In Ruanda-Urundi, they supported the wrong people, the Watutsi, who had the quarrel with the Belgians, on the principle that the enemy of my enemy is my friend. In point of fact, the Watutsi were the immigrant aristocrats, the Hamitic overlords, the fifteen per cent in Rwanda, while the Bantu peasantry were the other eighty-five per cent.

"Two things I used to reflect on: One tends to underestimate the terrible poverty of Africa. One may say, 'Why don't the young men of Africa go back to the villages?' But how can they, when they

3*

don't have even two hundred pounds to buy fertilizer and essentials? The terrible drain of poverty.

"And secondly, the nature of the African family. There are no old-age benefits, the old and ailing have to be looked after. So when one acquires wealth, everybody shares it. As chief minister, Nyerere sometimes had as many as forty people staying there. Oscar Kambona once complained to me that his relatives took his clothes; he had acquired a new suit, and his father had taken it. Well, Julius found this terribly demanding, all these people wanting jobs, and Maria with forty people. All we could do to help was to paint his house frequently, and that meant pushing them all out. Of course, this happens everywhere in Africa; corruption is sometimes explained in these terms, the hordes of hangers-on who have to be taken care of. Julius never complained, but I know it was a burden to him."

The wives of the diplomats and civil servants gave "knife and fork" parties for the African wives so "they wouldn't be embarrassed using them," as a Briton later explained it. But the practice ceased abruptly after Rashidi Kawawa condemned it as "a blow to African customs". Turnbull has recalled that he used to teach Nyerere informally, sometimes using Herbert Morrison's *Essence of Parliament*. "When dealing with an African," Turnbull has said, "it's always better to quote a Labour man."

"We the people of Tanganyika," Nyerere had said in a Legislative Council speech two years earlier, "would like to light a candle and put it on top of Mount Kilimanjaro, which would shine beyond our borders giving hope where there was despair, love where there was hate, and dignity where there was only humiliation." On the night of December 9, 1961, a team of climbers planted such a torch on the summit of Africa's highest peak, while in Dar es Salaam, five hundred miles away, seventy-five thousand Tanganyikans and their guests, including the Duke of Edinburgh, gathered in the National Stadium to participate in the ritual of independence. At exactly midnight, the lights in the stadium went out. In the dark, the British flag was lowered and the green, black and gold colours of Tanganyika were raised. The lights went up to cheers and shouts of "UHURU!" And then, as Nyerere had been warning his countrymen since the early days of TANU, Tanganyika's real problems began. Towards the end of the first turbulent year of independence, Nyerere was asked what he felt was the most significant thing his country had accomplished. "We have learned this hard fact of life," he said, "that there are no short cuts to our aspirations."

VI

THE TWELVE MONTHS that began on December 9, 1961, when Tanganyika became independent, and ended on December 9, 1962, when it became a republic, have been characterized by Sir Richard Turnbull, who stayed on as governor-general, as "the year in the wilderness". It began with an unexpected series of deportations. The British manager of the Palm Beach Hotel in Dar es Salaam asked four Africans—one of whom, he later learned, was the mayor of Dar es Salaam—to leave the hotel bar. He was immediately served with a deportation order. At an inn in Korogwe, 130 miles north west of Dar es Salaam, three Britons got into an argument with a young African who turned out to be a parliamentary secretary. All three were deported. At Lindi, a coastal town near the Mozambican border, a Swiss citizen who had lived in Tanganyika for nine years was similarly expelled. According to the government, he had pinned an *Uhuru* badge to his dog's collar and "paraded the animal in front of the people . . . He was heard to say that his dog was just as good as the people who were celebrating independence." What alarmed the British press was not the fact that the Tanganyikan government had reacted angrily to racial incidents, but that it had expelled the individuals, usually on twenty-four hours' notice, without giving them a chance to answer the charges. "For once," said *The Economist*, Nyerere "showed an inept touch and did not ensure that justice was to be done". "It may be," said the *Guardian*, "that an African leader has to behave as a racist occasionally even though he is not one, and to talk like a politician even though he is a statesman. It may be that racism, like smallpox, is best prevented by vaccination." Even in Tanganyika, many observers seemed to believe Nyerere was simply allowing the party a bit of self-indulgence. "One principle outweighed all the rest; to avoid a quarrel with the party," Turnbull has said. "The law provided that [the deportees] had some recourse to the courts. This wasn't allowed them." But, he added, "there were the rich Indian merchants in their Mercedeses after independence, and there were the privileged Europeans, and the Africans were still in the same position, with nothing changed. What had they but national pride? The rash of deportations was very offensive to the national spirit, but it let off some steam."

Unhappily, the twenty-four-hour deportation became, in Tanganyika as elsewhere, a symbol not only of the African's rise to power but of the arrogant and even whimsical use of that power. (In Kenya a few years later, the government obliged one of its Cabinet ministers by expelling his American-born wife on a few hours' notice; the charge against her was "disaffection toward the Kenya nation.") But it was a practice for which Nyerere never apologized. "For many years we Africans have suffered humiliations in our own country," he said at the time. "We are not going to suffer them now." A few years later he added, "I think we were definitely right. You go through two stages in these colonial countries. One is when midnight comes; the clock strikes, and you are independent. Fine. But then begins a whole process of changing conditions and changing people. I had been talking to the people, telling them that the second process would not be easy. I'd been saying over and over, '*Uhuru na kazi*,' work, work, work, long before independence. Getting the people ready for the next stage: 'Don't expect miracles, don't expect a better house after midnight.'

"But," he continued, chopping his words in anger, "one thing *must change* after midnight: the attitudes of the colonial people, their way of treating the Africans as *nothing*. This must change after midnight. The colonized are now the rulers, and the man in the street must *see* this! If they have been spitting in his face, now it must stop! After midnight! This cannot take twenty years! We had to drive this lesson home."

Such incidents continued for more than a year as evidence of the abrasive relations between the new rulers and the old. In June, 1963, the Safari Hotel at Arusha was ordered closed without warning; its twenty-eight guests, mostly whites, were given an hour's notice to find other lodgings. The government's complaint, it turned out, was that the hotel had insulted Guinea's President Sékou Touré, who was in Tanganyika on a state visit. On the previous day, when Touré's party, led by Oscar Kambona, arrived at the hotel for lunch, nobody stood up as the distinguished visitor passed through the lounge; guests said they had had no idea whom the party consisted of. Peter Walwa, the regional commissioner and the ranking government official based in Arusha, complained that the hotel had neglected to display national flags or other decorations, and in addition had served "a poor meal". "When we came into the hotel, an attitude of mind showed up," explained Kambona, who had become Nyerere's Minister of External Affairs and Defence, "and we thought it was time we showed an example. One thing an African will never stand for is this lack of dignity accorded him as a human being. We are very sensitive to no appreciation of our dignity." Inevitably, the foreign press criticized the Tanganyikans for their hypersensitivity and arrogance; the local white community tended to blame Kambona and Walwa and to take refuge in the thought that Nyerere, had he been present, would have smoothed things over. The Safari Hotel's manager denied that any insult to the visiting dignitaries had been intended, and the hotel was allowed to re-open a few months later.

In a somewhat similar incident, sixty-nine members of the government and party applied for membership in the Dar es Salaam Club, a squat old relic of colonialism. The club refused to take them, but implied that the applicants might be accepted later if they were properly proposed and seconded. Of the club's nine hundred and eighty members at the time, only nine were Africans. By late 1963, the club had become the subject of angry parliamentary debate. "Here is a club which even President Nyerere cannot enter," shouted one M.P. "We don't know what's going on in this club, either. For the sake of our security, it's time the club was closed down." But Job Lusinde, the Home Affairs Minister, assured him that the government was watching the club's every movement: "Our security is such that even if a group of people meet in a hidden place for subversive activity, they will be found out. We wait until the iron is hot, and then we strike." Eventually the government decided to dissolve the club and take over its assets. Since the club had been started by Germans before the First World War, explained Lusinde, it was former enemy property and should have been confiscated long before. "This," declared a jubilant M.P., "is real African socialism." The club's veranda thereafter became a favourite meeting place of Tanganyikan politicians. As in the Safari Hotel case, Nyerere remained aloof from the controversy; a few years later, when the reorganized club fell into bankruptcy, he promised personally to see that its bills were paid.

Only six weeks after Tanganyikan independence, the London *Sunday Telegraph* carried a report that Julius Nyerere had resigned as prime minister. When shown a copy of the paper, according to the Tanganyika *Standard*, Nyerere "read the first few words, laughed loudly and said, 'Oh, boy.' " He laughed again after reading a reference to Oscar Kambona as "one of Nyerere's strongest opponents" and told the *Standard* reporter, "You can say I read it and laughed."

The next day, however, he announced that he had in fact resigned. "Today I relinquished my position as prime minister. Before doing this, I myself selected a new team of ministers, with Mr Rashidi Kawawa at its head." He had decided to devote himself to the rebuilding of the party, he explained, because he believed this was the best way to achieve "our new objective—the creation of a country in which the people take a full and active part in the fight against poverty, ignorance and disease." In addition to an able government, he said, the country needed a "strong political organization, active in every village, which acts like a two-way all-weather road along which the purposes, plans and problems of the government can travel to the people, at the same time as the ideas, desires and misunderstandings of the people can travel direct to the government. This is the job of the new TANU." He knew such a step was unusual, he said, but added, "We do not believe it is necessary for us to copy the institutions of other countries. We do believe we must work out our own pattern of democracy." He asked Tanganyika's friends abroad to "understand these changes and not to try and read into them a different significance than they have".

His request notwithstanding, Nyerere's resignation was widely interpreted as a strategic retreat. "It looks as if Mr Nyerere has met a too-common fate among African moderates," said the *New York Times* in an editorial on February 3, 1962. "The swiftness with which pressures from more radical and nationalistic elements rose against him and drove him out of office is disquieting." A better-informed judgment was offered by *The Economist*, which said in its January 27th issue: "If anyone had been asked to prescribe a nightmare formula that would do the most harm to the reputation of Tanganyika throughout the world, he could hardly have improved on the concoction brewed in Dar es Salaam this week." Even Jomo Kenyatta, Kenya's political leader, said he had heard "with great sorrow" of the resignation of his "dear friend". In Dar es Salaam, journalists interpreted the series of deportations as evidence of discontent within the party; they also noted the recent inclination of *Uhuru*, the party's Swahili-language weekly, to adopt a strident, racial tone; it had referred to the country's Indians as "snakes" and to the remaining British officials as "the prophets of colonialism". Indeed, the resignation became the first in a series of not-quite-explained incidents that were to become an odd hallmark of Tanganyikan politics.

If Nyerere had in fact had a serious quarrel with some members of the National Executive committee in the weeks following independence, he has never admitted it publicly. "I had known a month earlier that he might do it," Turnbull has recalled, "but I hoped that he was being unnecessarily pessimistic." There is no doubt, however, that Nyerere regarded the rebuilding of the party as the most urgent task facing the country; and that, when he told the National Executive committee of his plan, it took him some three days to win their consent. "We had deliberately tried to discuss nothing but *Uhuru,*" he has said. "But then the nation was asking, 'What next?' I couldn't sit here. I had to answer the vital questions."

The morning after his announcement, Nyerere called in Rashidi Kawawa, who was a minister without portfolio at the time, "And," Kawawa, has recalled, "he said, 'Look, Rashidi, you are the Prime Minister from right now. Take the chair.' I got the shock of my life! Yes, we had given him the green light [to resign] the previous evening. He argued with us for four hours that night; but he didn't tell us when he wanted to do it. This shocked everybody. He is always dramatic, you know."

"He was very agitated," Amir Jamal, another Cabinet colleague, has said. "He had already gone through the agony of the decision. He said, 'I'm asking Rashidi to become Prime Minister, and all you fellows are going to stay on.'"

When Nyerere told the Governor-General that he had finally decided to resign and that Kawawa would succeed him, Turnbull pointed out that Kawawa was scheduled to leave on a trip to Nigeria that very evening. "I said they'd better not let him get off. They hadn't thought of this." Turnbull was also disturbed about the effect the announcement would have overseas. "Julius was awfully bad at handling his public relations. I told him, 'Look, this will have to be very carefully explained to the world—in the towns here, in Britain, in the U.N., and in other African countries; you must tell each of them, and in a slightly different way. You must get your public relations chaps to work on it.' And I told him to tell the overseas staff by cable. But they didn't do any of this. The Tanganyikan High Commission in London wasn't told for a week. They didn't know if Julius was ill, or what."

Despite the lingering confusion, Nyerere never regretted his action. Several years later, long after he had returned to office as

President of the Republic, in December, 1962, he was asked if he thought he had been right to resign so suddenly after independence. "No question about it," he said. "If I made any mistake, it was that I came back." His listeners laughed, but he was deadly serious. "I was convinced my function was to lead the masses. If I regret anything, it is that it would be difficult now to go back to the masses. It changed the tone of the country. I will not say we are therefore different from other East African countries, but I think we are different from what we might otherwise have become. If this country has anything, it has a sense of purpose. I think my actions in 1962 helped give it that sense of purpose. I think it's the best thing I've done for this country."

Nor have his friends ever doubted that he made the right decision. "As a result of that resignation," Amir Jamal once said, "nobody will ever accuse him of hanging on to power for the sake of power. They know they're dealing with a very serious man."

Rashidi Kawawa was born in 1929 to a family of elephant hunters. "My father inherited this profession from his father, and he from his father," Kawawa has said, "and I learned it from my father." He belonged to the Ngoni tribe of Songea district, but grew up in several places in Tanganyika, including Kilwa and Nachingwea, because his father, a government game scout, was frequently transferred.

After his graduation from the Tabora School, where he heard Nyerere debate the merits of education over wealth, Kawawa became a clerk in the social welfare department in Dar es Salaam and, by accident, a film actor. The department had imported a film-producing unit from South Africa and had begun to make films of its own. "Well, I was a young man, you know, it was very exciting, so I decided to play a part in a film. I was given the leading role in a picture called *Bitter Cassava*. It was a story of a country boy who was attracted by town life and misled by it, and who decided to go back to his village. Another film was called *The Ship Is Sailing*. It was about a village girl who was misled by a town boy. She went to Mombasa and was abandoned by the boy. She decided to go back home and found that her fiancé had married somebody else. So she bewitched her old fiancé's wife, you see, and she was found out and taken to jail. That was her fate."

Later Kawawa worked in a camp where some of Kenya's Kikuyu tribesmen were being detained during the Mau Mau Emergency in Kenya. "At first the Kikuyu were very suspicious, they thought I was a spy. But then they discovered I could be very helpful. I organized them into committees, and took their complaints to the camp commander."

During his travels throughout the Territory, Kawawa helped to organize meetings of the Tanganyika African Government Service Association (TAGSA), in which his father had been active. As TAGSA's president, Kawawa helped raise money to send Nyerere to the U.N. in 1955. "But please," Kawawa cautioned Oscar Kambona, "when you receive the money, just give me a receipt, don't write 'Given to TANU', or I'll be in trouble." In October 1955 he became general secretary of the Tanganyika Federation of Labour, and the following year he resigned his civil service job and joined TANU. From then until independence, TANU and the TFL worked closely together. The brewery strike of 1958 was led by Nyerere himself. "If you drink beer, you drink the blood of your own people," Nyerere told his TANU audiences. "And it worked," Kawawa has said. "We paralyzed the beer bars everywhere, and within a month they had to give in to our wage demands."

From the day he took office as prime minister, Kawawa insisted that he was merely sitting in for Nyerere. "He is the Father of the Nation," said Kawawa, "and as president of TANU he is the most powerful and important man in Tanganyika. I am a member of the party, and I am always guided by it." After his election as President, Nyerere named Kawawa Vice-President, and Kawawa has since remained his closest political ally.

"JULIUS IS BACK WITH THE PEOPLE," reported a headline in the *Standard* soon after he resigned as prime minister. And indeed he was—travelling and speaking throughout the country. In the Lake Region, he complained to a group of villagers that too much money was being buried in the ground, and told of a man at Shinyanga who had shown him £500 in notes that had been partially eaten by ants. "We shall have a bank here," Nyerere declared. Still arguing for East African federation, he shouted, "If we want more places where we can have prime ministers, let us Balkanize Africa even more. Let every tribe go to the United Nations. You have no idea how many votes we would have from Tanganyika if that happened." In words strikingly like those of his Arusha Declaration five years later, he said, "Our emphasis must be on what we ourselves can do. We must produce more cotton, more coffee, more tobacco, and if, without too much government assistance, people can build a dam or a school or a road they must do it. This is what we can rely on—not outside assistance."

Under the government's self-help programme, villagers all over the country donated a day's work a week to a community project—a new road, a well, a school or clinic. According to one government announcement, the population built about £890,000 worth of projects during the first half of 1963, for which the government donated about £70,000 in materials. To understand the enthusiasm of many villages, a visitor had only to spend a day that year at a place such as Kibamba, fifteen miles west of Dar es Salaam, where two hundred villagers hoed and hacked at a new roadway to the rhythm of drums and castanets. One man, seemingly berserk with exuberance, raced back and forth through the crowd waving his pick-axe like a bayonet. There were, miraculously, no casualties. Prime Minister Kawawa, who had arrived to hoist a few ceremonial shovelsful of earth himself, seemed slightly put off by the pandemonium. "I think I have made you too joyful," he said. "We are all sweating," boasted the local TANU official, "from the Prime Minister down." Much of the early excitement faded when villagers waited in vain for the government to send a roof for a new community centre, or a teacher for a new school. If he could repeat the experience of the early months of independence, Nyerere said later, "I'd try to make better use of the people's enthusiasm—try to give more guidance about where a road should go, or whether a school should be built."

Six months after independence, the government abolished the jobs and salaries of the hereditary chiefs, whose powers and functions conflicted with those of government officials. "The reason the chiefs were not absorbed into the nationalist movement," a former chief has said, "was primarily due to their own short-sightedness. Most of them were too closely identified with the British authorities; and there were growing tensions between the old chiefs and the younger, educated ones. 'They are ambitious,' the old men would say, when the young ones favoured change. The colonial administrations found the chiefs useful in trying to carry out policy, and also as scapegoats if things went badly." For example, he recalled, the chiefs in Sukumaland—the region of Tanzania's largest tribe, the Sukuma—were pressured into supporting a plan for cattle de-stocking—reducing the number of cattle their people owned. "To the peasant, his cattle were his wealth. He couldn't care less if they were only skin and bone. Any effort to reduce his cattle simply meant the government was trying to make him poorer. Well, the old chiefs started accusing the younger chiefs. 'They want you to get poorer,' the old chiefs would tell their people. It was Machiavellian—a case of hunting with the hounds and running with the hares. Many of the younger chiefs decided to wait and see, and they got caught in the process. The nationalist movement was able to label them anti-people. As long as the chiefs had any power, they could be a headache to TANU. So it was expedient for the TANU government to get rid of them."

Another former chief has said, "There was feuding in Nigeria and Ghana between the chiefs and the democratically elected governments, and problems of double loyalties. To avoid these problems, TANU decided to abolish them altogether. TANU's aim was to streamline the government from the top down to the village level, and retaining the chiefs would have made a break in the direct line."

The only chief who survived as a powerful political figure was Abdullah Fundikira. A conservative and a traditionalist—who, in fact, had once said of himself, "I am tradition"—Fundikira became minister of justice and later was the first chairman of the Tanganyika Development Corporation. Because of his haughty manner and also because of his hereditary power, he was resented by many of the TANU leaders. Sir Richard Turnbull has recalled, "Fundikira was the doyen of the chiefs' corps; he was reserved and dignified, with a suggestion of the divine right of kings about him. I think he was contemptuous of some of the younger politicians, who were noisy and undignified. When an African is embarrassed, he often takes refuge in the guffaw. At Cabinet meetings, I would see them laughing their heads off at some insoluble economic problem, and would turn to see Fundikira looking at them."

Eighteen months after independence, Fundikira was arrested on charges of corruption; he was accused, as chairman of the National Agricultural Products Board, of having accepted £2,500 "to incite him to do something in relation to granting an agency for purchase of produce to certain merchants". Fundikira denied the charge, and was acquitted. In December 1963 he resigned from TANU, saying he disagreed with some of its basic policies. Two years later, he rejoined the party and subsequently became chairman of the East African Airways Corporation.

Soon after the Tanganyikan Parliament reconvened, in February,

1962, with former Prime Minister Nyerere seated among the back-benchers, the government announced that it favoured legislation to convert the system of land ownership from freehold to leasehold—an idea that Nyerere elaborated a few weeks later in an essay entitled "Ujamaa" ("Familyhood"), in which many of his other ideas about African Socialism were also explained. Nyerere wrote, "To us in Africa, land was always recognized as belonging to the community." Man's right to the land "was the right to use it; he had no other right to it, nor did it occur to him to try and claim one. . . . The foreigner introduced a completely different concept, the concept of land as a marketable commodity. According to this system, a person could claim a piece of land as his own private property whether he intended to use it or not. I could take a few square miles of land, call them 'mine', and then go off to the moon. . . . Such a system is not only foreign to us, it is completely wrong. . . . Unconditional or 'freehold' ownership of land which leads to speculation and parasitism must be abolished."

Shortly thereafter, the government announced the details of the new republican constitution that would go into effect on the first anniversary of independence. Under the new constitution, a President was to be elected by universal suffrage; the President would then appoint a Vice-President who in turn would preside over the National Assembly, or Parliament. Having an elected President, rather than a governor-general representing the Queen, said Kawawa, would "provide a new focus for loyalty" and would be "more capable of inspiring a sense of loyalty in the people." "The pattern of dictatorship emerges in Tanganyika," cried the London Daily Express, and there was widespread criticism that the strong powers handed to the Presidency could lead to authoritarianism. Reflecting his British tutelage, Nyerere told Parliament that "the ultimate safeguard of the people's freedom is the ethic of the nation." What was needed, he said, was a national ethic that enabled the government to say, "We cannot do this, this is un-Tanganyikan," and the people to say, "That we cannot tolerate, that is un-Tanganyikan." Without such an ethic, said Nyerere, "no constitution, how-ever framed, could insure that the people would not become victims of tyranny." As for political campaigning, he told the Assembly, "it is not a traditional African practice. It smacks of pride, vanity and sometimes stubbornness. A man standing before the public out-lining his good qualities—this is a shameful thing."

It was a foregone conclusion that Nyerere would become TANU's candidate for President. He combined electioneering with his TANU duties, stopping only at those villages that had undertaken self-help projects. In the November election he polled 98.1 per cent of the vote. Not long after that, an American visitor asked him if he had been surprised to receive so high a percentage of the vote. "Why?" he replied sharply. "I would not have been surprised to have received ninety-nine and nine-tenths per cent. We are a united people. I would not have been surprised for America to have had only one party in the beginning. You would have said, 'We've got to win the war and get this stupid King George out! The most important thing is unity! The issue is, should we be led by a monarch three thousand miles away?' We Tanganyikans want to govern ourselves. This is no issue. We laugh at the happenings in Kenya"—where, a year before independence, the two major parties were in conflict. "We say to the Kenyans, 'You have no sense of priorities—one hundred per cent unity is the answer.' My ideas of democracy are Western. I never questioned the two-party system until I was confronted with the problem in Tanganyika. Is it necessary for a democracy to have a two-party system? I said no. It's no good standing on Mount Kili-manjaro and shouting our disagreement."

For much of the preceding year, Nyerere had been pondering the meaning of a one-party system in a democracy. "What nonsense it is to have elections on this basis," he would tell his colleagues, "because people do not in fact have any choice. It's not democratic. So what do we do?" A friend has recalled, "He would scribble a draft, and play around with it, and this went on for several months."

Following the November 1962 elections, Nyerere announced that the National Executive committee had voted to ask the party's national conference to open party membership to non-Africans, and to grant "complete political amnesty" to all persons who had been expelled from TANU since 1954. "We were not racialist then, but we were realistic," he said of the former policy of excluding non-blacks from party membership. "We were the Africans of Tangan-yika fighting for our rights. Our aim was to be racial in composition and non-racial in policy." But as early as 1955, he said, the policy had become an embarrassment; that year the party had voted to accept any Tanganyikan who was half-African. In early 1963 Amir Jamal, an Asian, became TANU's first non-black member, and Derek Bryceson, a former Briton, became its second.

As for the other change, Nyerere explained, many members had been expelled in the past for failing to support TANU candidates, but the party realized that under a one-party system such practices made no sense. "We realize you can't have an election in Tanganyika between TANU and another organization, so it will have to be between members of TANU."

It was not until after the 1965 general elections, however, that Western criticism of Tanganyika's one-party system began to subside. Sir Richard Turnbull has said, "None of us realized at the time that the one-party state is the natural and proper way of governing a country like Tanganyika. How can there be two parties? Maybe in ten years, if they develop differing economic programmes. But the dominant thing is national pride and feeling, and raising the level of the people." The key point, as Nyerere wrote in January 1963 in a pamphlet called "Democracy and the Party System", was that parties such as TANU "were not formed to challenge any ruling group of our own people; they were formed to challenge the foreigners who ruled us. They were not, therefore, political parties, i.e., factions, but nationalist movements."

Would the country develop a two-party system at some later stage? "It does not necessarily follow," Nyerere said in 1964. "It could become a multi-party country, but I see no necessity for that. We are rejecting the idea that only a two-party system can be a democracy. The philosophical concept of freedom is not a matter of mechanics." He was also rejecting the notion of his Western friends who were "making allowances for us to go through an undemocratic period in the beginning." He added, "But look, brother, this is not right. We must not be undemocratic even in the beginning."

"I must confess," said a British resident of Dar es Salaam in late 1962, "I don't quite understand this security mania." "The ferocious desire for total unity," wrote the correspondent of The Times of London, "has led the government to introduce precautionary legislation out of all proportion to the mouse that squeaks defiance." And so it seemed. The opposition to TANU, insofar as it existed at all, consisted of a few dissident trade union officials and one or two tiny political parties. Nonetheless, the government in 1962 pushed through Parliament a labour law virtually banning strikes, and, under a certificate of urgency, a preventive detention law enabling the government to imprison without trial any person it deemed dangerous to the national security. "We feel that while this country is peaceful," Nyerere said, "its roots are not really all that deep." A few months later he explained further: "We know this law could be a convenient tool in the hands of an unscrupulous government. The point is, preventive powers are assumed by democratic governments at times they consider such powers necessary. Britain had such a regulation in wartime, India has one which she recently used. We hope we misjudged the danger. We don't want to use this drastic law. This is a huge country, with five hundred miles of coastline and borders with seven nations. And we have *eleven hundred men* in our army. Eleven hundred men! Our security is in the hands of the Almighty! I have no money for a large army or a large police force. But I can put this law on the statute books. It's a safeguard. And I think it has done some good."

The "Africanization" of the civil service was already under way. Since independence, several hundred British civil servants had left Tanganyika with their "golden handshakes" or "lumpers"—severance pay amounting to as much as £10,000 a man. By the end of 1963, roughly half the senior- and middle-grade posts were held by Africans, but there were many vacancies. Many of the Africans were insufficiently trained; many of the Europeans employed to fill upper-level and technical vacancies for which no trained Africans were available were newcomers on short-term contracts.

Since independence, the trade union leaders had pressed for accelerated Africanization. The head of the railway workers union, Christopher S. K. Tumbo, had threatened a strike; in Parliament he had called the white civil servants "mercenaries." In April 1962, perhaps to remove him from the domestic political scene, the government sent him to London as Tanganyika's new high commissioner. In August he resigned, however, dropping hints that he didn't really have to work for a living. Following his return to Tanganyika, Tumbo started his own political group, the People's Democratic party, but in late November he slipped across the border to Mombasa, Kenya, where he became a press agent for a cement factory.

The other opposition party was the African National Congress, whose leader, Zuberi Mtemvu, accused Nyerere in January 1962, of plotting to "introduce neo-colonialism" into newly independent African states—which meant that Mtemvu was discontented with Nyerere's moderate policies on racial matters. In May 1962 he announced a three-stage plan—"cool, warm and very hot"—to obtain a "purely African government" in Tanganyika within a year. For several months the government prevented the ANC from holding meetings, but lifted the ban in time for the November elections, in which Mtemvu was Nyerere's chief opponent. Mtemvu drew 21,276 votes to Nyerere's 1,127,978. A few days later Mtemvu asked to rejoin TANU. "The most significant result of the election," said a TANU statement, "is the refusal of our people to have anything to do with racialism."

The celebration of *Jamhuri* (Republic) in December 1962 was much like the ritual of independence a year earlier. At the National Assembly, an African sergeant-at-arms bellowed "Mistah Speakah!" and, carrying the mace, entered the chamber. He was followed by the bewigged Speaker, the chief justice and, finally, to the roll of a nineteen-gun salute, the Governor-General, who delivered his farewell address and prorogued Parliament. At a midnight ceremony another tattoo was played, fireworks were set off, and schoolchildren marched forward to slay the papier-mâché dragons of poverty, ignorance and disease. Nyerere, now President, moved into State House.

Most of the first year had been devoted to domestic problems; the emphasis of the second—in addition to a series of official visits to West Germany, the U.S., Canada, Algeria, Scandinavia, Guinea and Nigeria—was on African affairs. Nyerere ridiculed existing African boundaries as "ethnological and geographical nonsense"; "It is impossible to draw a line anywhere on the map of Africa which does not violate the history or future needs of the people." At the Afro-Asian Solidarity Conference, held in Moshi in February 1963, he said, "As we emerge successfully from the first 'scramble for Africa', so we are entering a new phase—the phase of the 'second scramble' . . . The events in the Congo have demonstrated that it is possible for a colonial power to leave by the front door, and the same or different external forces to come in by the back. . . ."At the founding session of the Organization for African Unity at Addis Ababa in May, 1963, he told the delegates, "The real, humiliating truth is that Africa is not free; and therefore it is Africa which should take the necessary collective measures to free Africa."

In June, Nyerere met in Nairobi with Prime Minister Jomo Kenyatta of Kenya and Prime Minister Milton Obote of Uganda, and the three announced that they had agreed to inaugurate an East African federation before the end of the year. "We cannot create a continental government overnight, but we can start in East Africa," Nyerere said. But the talks, designed to establish the basis of federation, broke down at the ministerial level, and in December 1963,

Nyerere called the failure to achieve federation the major disappointment of the year.

Some observers speculated that the June 1963 announcement of federation had been a cynical attempt to induce the British government to advance the date of Kenya's independence; Kenyatta, in fact, once implied as much. "If it was a pressure technique, it was quite unnecessary," a former British diplomat has said. "Britain was as anxious for Kenya's independence as the East Africans were." The Tanganyikans have insisted, however, that this was not the purpose of the negotiations, and that at least several of the Kenya delegates—notably the late Tom Mboya—were as determined to achieve federation as the Tanganyikans were.

Both Kenya and Zanzibar became independent in December 1963.

"If you don't believe in human equality, quit the party," Nyerere had said the previous July. "Those who do not believe in the principle of human brotherhood had better burn their membership cards." Africanization—the policy of giving job priority to black Tanganyikans—was a kind of discrimination, he said, but was "justifiable" to redress past inequities. But on January 8, 1964, in a critically important move, Nyerere announced that the government's two-year-old policy of Africanization was being ended. Thereafter, he said, Tanganyikan citizens of all races would be equally eligible for government jobs. "It would be wrong for us to continue to distinguish between Tanganyikan citizens on any grounds other than those of character and ability to do specific tasks. We cannot allow the growth of first- and second-class citizenship. This action is not taken for the sake of people with brown or white skins, but for Tanganyika."

The announcement was harshly denounced by trade union leaders in Tanganyika, and was tragically misunderstood by the men of the Tanganyika Rifles. It was a prelude to the most serious crisis of Nyerere's life.

In the meantime, four days later, revolution broke out on Zanzibar, twenty-four miles away.

VII

JULIUS NYERERE'S FRIENDS recall that he had long worried about the closeness of Zanzibar to the Tanganyikan mainland. "If I could tow that island out into the middle of the Indian Ocean," he had said a few years earlier, "I'd do it." At a dinner party in Dar es Salaam a year or two before independence, he had remarked that he thought one of Tanganyika's biggest problems in later years would be Zanzibar. "No, I'm not joking," he said at the time. "An alien monarchy, with the sons dabbling in politics. It's very vulnerable to outside influences. I fear it will be a big headache for us."

If Nyerere's friends were sceptical of this prediction, it was partly because Zanzibar Town in those years seemed like nothing so much as a magnificent old theatre set, a relic whose grand but evil history had passed it by. Besides, the British Protectorate of Zanzibar was tiny, compared to the neighbouring territories of the East African mainland, consisting as it did of two principal islands, Zanzibar and Pemba, with a total population of 319,000 and an area of only 1,020 square miles. Zanzibar Island, the larger of the two, is fifty-three miles long and twenty-four miles wide at its broadest point.

But Zanzibar had always seemed more menacing to the mainlanders than its dimensions warranted. In an earlier time, the island's Arabs used to say, "When the pipes are played on Zanzibar, all Africa east of the Lakes must dance." It was a proud boast and an accurate one, for Zanzibar was the base from which the Arab slavers and traders set off by dhow for Bagamoyo on the mainland coast, and on by caravan toward the Great Lakes of Central Africa. Zanzibar was the centre and the symbol of the Arab tyranny in East Africa, the marketplace and shipping point for the mainland's exports—its rhino horns, ivory and human beings. It was also the point from which the great explorers, Burton, Speke, Livingstone, Stanley, set off on their expeditions to the interior.

The Arabs and Persians visited it from ancient times, the Portuguese took it in 1503, and the Arabs of Oman seized it in the seventeenth century. In 1832 the ruler of Oman, Seyyid Said bin Sultan, moved his capital to Zanzibar, bringing with him the cloves that were to become the island's major export crop. He also brought the sultanate's red flag that survived as the flag of Zanzibar until January 12, 1964. Towards the end of the nineteenth century the Germans explored and annexed some sixty thousand miles of what had been regarded as the sultan's mainland territories. Faced with the prospect of having an aggressive European power as a neighbour across the channel, the Sultan of Zanzibar willingly submitted to the protection of the British Crown in 1890.

During the seventy-three years that Zanzibar remained a British protectorate, its territories included a ten-mile-wide strip of land that ran for fifty-two miles along the Kenya coast and included the port of Mombasa. This land was administered by Kenya but remained a part of the sultan's dominions, and the Zanzibar government received £11,000 a year in rent for it.

Zanzibar's decline coincided with the gradual abolition of slavery. In 1872 the slave trade was banned within the sultan's dominions, but the island remained dependent on slave labour to work the Arab-owned clove plantations. In 1897 all slaves who "cared to apply" were freed. By 1963, the year of independence, there were few visible traces of the heritage of slavery except for the Anglican cathedral that stands on the site of the slave market as a memorial to the victims of slavery. By that time Zanzibar had become a tranquil but marvellously vivid place, pungent with the aroma of cloves and other spices, a land of coral beaches and lustrous palms and the decaying remnants of lost reigns. Old Arab guides took visitors to see the Beit-el-Ajaib, the ornate "House of Wonders"; to the residence where David Livingstone spent several weeks preparing for his last expedition; to the Jubilee Gardens beside the ocean wall. A world asleep, or so it seemed; a place where British civil servants, in tropical shorts, worked until midday and spent the long afternoons at sailing and other sports, and evenings at the English Club. But even then there were a few forebodings. There had been, for example, the riots at the time of the 1961 elections in which seventy persons were killed. Of these, sixty-four were Arabs.

For a visitor, it was no easy task to distinguish between the Arabs and the Africans on Zanzibar. Of the island's population of 319,000, 650 were "Europeans"—mostly British, with an occasional German, Italian or Greek; 20,000 were "Asians"—Indians, Pakistanis and Goans; 50,000 were classified as Arabs; and the rest as black Africans. Some called themselves Shirazis, claiming to be descended from Persians who visited the region in ancient times. Of the Arabs, a few were more or less pure-blooded and looked, in fact, like creatures out of *The Arabian Nights*. Most, however, were as black as the Africans. As a British resident explained at the time, "The way the local people sort it out, those who belong to the Arab Association, or *used* to, are classified as Arabs."

There were three political parties in Zanzibar. The oldest was the Zanzibar Nationalist party (ZNP), which had been founded in 1956 from the ranks of the Arab Association. Much of its membership was African but its leadership was purely Arab, and practically every Arab in the island belonged to it. The party was loyal to the Sultan and flew his red flag as its own. The party's leader, Ali Muhsin, was a former civil servant and an educated man. He was also something of an Arab sentimentalist, and was rumoured to advocate the establishment of a loose Moslem union with Somalia, Sudan and Egypt. He rejected any notion of association with East Africa, and his declaration that "Zanzibar shall not become a district of Tanganyika" had a strong appeal to many Zanzibaris, particularly the Arabs. The ZNP's hierarchy contained most of the educated men of Zanzibar; primarily for this reason, the British clearly favoured the party over its rivals.

Also within the ZNP was a clever young leftist named Abdulrahman Mohamed Babu, who returned to Zanzibar in 1957 after spending five years in London. He became the general secretary of the party and the organizer of its youth wing. He made trips to China and the Soviet Union, and he became the editor of a small newspaper, *Zanews*, that was sponsored by the New China News Agency. The 1961 rioting frightened the ZNP's leaders, and caused them to send several groups of Babu's youth wing members to Cuba for military training so that, in the event of further trouble, they would be able to defend themselves.

In 1962 Babu was jailed for fifteen months on a criminal-libel conviction growing out of an item he had published in *Zanews*. Shortly after his release the following year, he had a quarrel with Ali Muhsin over how many parliamentary seats the ZNP would allot to Babu's youth wing leadership in the elections that year. Accordingly Babu resigned, taking his youth wing with him, and established the *Umma* ("Masses") party. By this time a number of youth wing members had returned from Cuba, and signs reading ZANZIBAR SÍ, YANQUI NO were beginning to appear mysteriously on such places as the walls of the American consulate. The improbable blend of Communist political agitation with the traditionally soporific spell of Zanzibar led one Western diplomat to observe, "It's as if part of Fantasyland had slipped its moorings. The leftist front here amounts to only a handful of people."

The British authorities sought in 1963 to curtail Babu's political activities overseas by withdrawing his passport. But the resourceful Babu paddled to the mainland by canoe, talked the Tanganyikans into giving him an emergency passport, and showed up in London to attend the Lancaster House conference at which the Zanzibari constitutional details were settled. Then he paid a visit to Peking and arrived home shortly after independence.

The second major political organization in Zanzibar was the Afro-Shirazi party (ASP), which was founded in 1957. It was the island's black African nationalist party, and it had links with mainland parties such as TANU. Its president was Abeid Karume, a big, burly, un-educated former dock worker and boatmen's union official whose forebears had come from Nyasaland. Another leader, and an enemy of Karume's, was Othman Shariff, a Makerere College graduate and a veterinarian. A third was Kassim Hanga, who had shared a London flat with Oscar Kambona for a while in 1958, and later studied in Moscow. He returned to Zanzibar in 1961 and became the party's deputy secretary. The party suffered grievously from a lack of edu-cated leadership. One British Labour party member, after meeting the hulking, unprepossessing Hanga in 1958, concluded, "If this is a leader of the ASP, the ASP is not the party we should support."

Yet it was clearly the most popular party in Zanzibar. In the June 1961 elections, the ASP received 49.9 per cent of the vote, the ZNP 35 per cent. But each won ten seats in the Legislative Council. The remaining three seats were taken by the Zanzibar and Pemba People's party, which received 13.7 per cent of the vote. The ZPPP had broken away from the ASP four years earlier after a personality clash between Karume and the head of the ZPPP, Mohamed Shamte. It was Shamte himself who broke the tie in 1961. The wily old Shamte cast his vote in the Legislative Council for the ZNP, thereby permitting the party to form a government. Shamte demanded and received a handsome reward for his co-operation: he became chief minister.

The Afro-Shirazis were angry at the election outcome; they felt victory had been snatched from them by the Arabs and their Sultan with the connivance of the British. As a constitutional monarch, the Sultan was supposed to be above politics; but his young son Jam-shid, who was best known for his love of sports cars and speedboat racing, had openly favoured the ZNP. "At the moment," a British diplomat commented in July 1963, "the Sultan is not serving a very useful purpose, and if he were, he might not remain."

Less than a month later, the Sultan, Seyyid Sir Abdulla bin Khalifa, died suddenly, and his son Jamshid succeeded him. Jamshid's sultanate lasted barely six months.

The Afro-Shirazis, as well as their allies in the mainland governments, had been urging the British authorities to reshape the constituencies to ensure that the party with the largest popular vote would lead Zanzibar to independence. The constituencies were in fact redrawn, and the Afro-Shirazis assumed that they would be the beneficiaries. "I'm certain," said Othman Shariff, "that we can get seventeen seats." But the July 1963 elections, held under the watchful eyes of several hundred British marines, produced a repetition of the 1961 stalemate. The Afro-Shirazis polled 54 per cent of the popular vote but took only thirteen seats. Together the ZNP and the ZPPP won eighteen seats, and Mohamed Shamte became prime minister. At the Lancaster House conference in September, the British tried to persuade Shamte to form a national government of all three parties; but Shamte refused.

The independence celebration on the night of December 9, 1963, was attended by dignitaries from seventy countries, including the Duke of Edinburgh and the Aga Khan, but none of the East African heads of state chose to attend. "We appreciate that *Uhuru* does not mean distribution of loot," said Shamte. "There is no loot to distribute." To many Africans in Zanzibar the occasion was called *Uhuru wa Waarabu*—Arab independence day.

The government of Prime Minister Shamte was jittery from the beginning. It seized the passports of several opposition leaders, and is said to have handed out weapons to many Manga Arabs, who were fiercely loyal to the Sultan. It also speeded up the process of "Zanzibarization" of the police force, whose ranks had previously been filled largely with mainland Africans, including a number of Makonde tribesmen from southern Tanganyika and northern Mozambique. These discharged policemen remained on the island, unemployed and embittered.

Then, in early January, the government banned the Umma party and appeared to be on the verge of arresting Babu, but Babu escaped to Dar es Salaam. "I had been charged that week with possession of a weapon," he explained later. "It was a very old gun that my child had found in a garden. I had made a speech two weeks before, and they said I had attacked the Throne [of the Sultan]. I heard they intended to put the two matters together and make a charge of treason. They intended to arrest me on Thursday at four in the morning. But a policeman I knew tipped me off, so I went to Dar es Salaam to get a lawyer. I didn't want to be arrested over there and not have a lawyer to fight it." Babu's three-year-old daughter had been killed by an automobile a few days earlier; there were rumours that the police had hoped to arrest Babu after the child's funeral, but he failed to appear.

The Afro-Shirazi leaders, who had worked closely with Babu since his resignation from the Nationalist party the previous July, were convinced that the government would arrest them as soon as it was finished with the Umma leadership. An ugly fight had broken out within the Afro-Shirazi leadership, meanwhile, between Othman Shariff and Abeid Karume. Shariff attacked Karume as "an utter failure" and demanded that he resign as party leader. There were also rumours that Shariff was negotiating with Prime Minister Shamte, who happened to be his brother-in-law, and might try to form a new coalition party.

"We had all speculated about how long it would take for trouble to arise," a former British civil servant on Zanzibar has said. "I guessed it would come in the second quarter of 1964. The ministers had decided they would not recognize Umma, and the ASP youth element had said, 'Right, we're next for the block.'

"Immediately before this, the ministers had been very touchy. Some thought the Makonde tribesmen, with their bows and arrows, were plotting. It scared the daylights out of the locals. Then the ministers thought bombs were being landed to the north. I thought we were chasing wildcat rumours. Or it could have been a smoke screen—to get part of the force out of town. We had long pressed the ministers to make an agreement with the British for defence. In the event of trouble, the East African mainland countries would obviously have been the best source of help; but the Zanzibar government couldn't get that support. We told them, 'You must mend your fences.' "

Sultan Jamshid said, much later, "On Saturday [January 11] a friend told me, 'There will be trouble tonight or tomorrow.' I had planned to go hunting for wild pig. I called a minister and told him. You know, people in the outlying districts were the ones who had been in danger in June 1961, when seventy people were killed. He assured me everything was all right."

Babu, who by that time was in Dar es Salaam, has said, "On Friday I heard over here in Dar es Salaam from someone—a member of the Afro-Shirazis—that something would happen very soon. Well, you know, you always heard those stories. But I thought this might be true."

"This was the whole point," Julius Nyerere remarked later. "The ASP was a popular movement. [In earlier years] I kept telling the British to do what I was convinced they would do in Kenya and Tanganyika." It was clear, he said, that they would yield to African majority rule on the mainland. "But I kept saying I was afraid about Zanzibar. That in their *very British way*, they would feel they were fulfilling their function if they handed Zanzibar over to the Sultan. I said, 'Yes, of course we are prepared to deal with a ZNP government—but the Zanzibar people will not accept it.'

"I did say to the Americans, 'Look, you tell the British: they must do in Zanzibar what I know they will do in the rest of East Africa. They must not cook up things in Zanzibar!' [Iain] Macleod was the one British leader who understood what I was talking about. I thought, good. In no time, he was out as colonial secretary, and we went back to [Duncan] Sandys.

"In May 1963, Sandys was right here in this office. I said, 'Of *course* we'll co-operate with whatever government they have, but we don't believe the Nationalists can be elected if you don't cook things up.' He said"—mimicking Sandy's smooth, patronizing tone —" 'Mr Nyerere, why don't you like the Sultan?' He said, 'Our lawyers have told us, we didn't have a sound legal claim on the coastal strip of Kenya. The Sultan was extremely decent with us. He asked only that the Kenya government look after his citizens there.' I said, 'Fine, Mr Sandys. If you had no legitimate right to stand on the Kenya coast, you have no legitimate rights on Zanzibar either. Why don't you pension him?'

"*This was the eleventh hour!*"

It started late Saturday night, January 11, 1964, on the last weekend before the beginning of Ramadan, the Moslem month of fasting in commemoration of the first revelation of the Koran. The narrow streets were crowded with townspeople, and the Afro-Shirazis were holding a dance at the Raha Leo community centre. Despite the festive air, many Zanzibaris were apprehensive; one African was told by a friend, "Go home early and sleep very soundly tonight." Late in the evening, the field police on duty at the Mtoni mobile

Nyerere with Zambia's President Kenneth Kaunda.

force armoury were ordered to the town, four miles away, to stop some rioting, The order could have been based on a genuine report, but it was more likely a ruse to get the policemen out of camp.

Sometime after midnight, bands of men attacked and overwhelmed the guards at the Ziwani police armoury, on the outskirts of town, and then at the Mtoni camp, seizing hundreds of machine guns and automatic rifles. Both Ziwani and Mtoni had fallen by five o'clock. By six, the only real resistance was coming from the Malindi police station near the harbour in Zanzibar Town. "I didn't sleep that night." Sultan Jamshid said later. "At about one-thirty I heard shots. Around nine they called me and said that all was lost, and that I should go to the boat in ten minutes." Under the protection of the Malindi station, Jamshid and his party escaped on the steamer *Salana* and were later transferred to the Sultan's yacht, the *Seyyid Khalifa*, in the Zanzibar Channel.

An hour or two earlier, Prime Minister Shamte had asked the British High Commission to send troops to Zanzibar to put down the uprising. It was, as a British diplomat later described it, "a rather hysterical request." He added, "Of course, there was no defence agreement between Zanzibar and Britain. HMG was under no obligation at all. No, Britain never had any intention of responding to the request of a government that no longer existed." Nor does there appear to have been any chance that Shamte could have gained the support of any East African country, since this would have involved the use of African troops to put an Arab government back into power over an African state. Shamte also sent a small plane to Pemba Island to bring back weapons, but the road to the airport was blocked before the plane returned. At 2.10 on Sunday afternoon, radio operators along the East African coast heard the Zanzibar tower operator say, "This is getting serious. A truckload of thirty men has just driven up. An armed party is down below. I'm going down to meet them now." The Dar es Salaam operator replied, "Best of luck." The government of Zanzibar had fallen on the country's thirty-fourth day of independence.

Nobody knew exactly who the rebels were. By Sunday afternoon one embassy in Zanzibar was calling it an Afro-Shirazi take-over; another reported that "the Afro-Shirazis are providing the bodies, and Umma the brainpower." On Sunday evening, a man who identified himself on Radio Zanzibar as "the field marshal" announced in Swahili that the Afro-Shirazi party and the three-month-old Umma

4

party would form a new government. He said that Zanzibar had been declared a republic, and that the President would be Sheikh Abeid Karume, the Afro-Shirazi leader. Curiously enough, he also called on Karume to "come back and take your job".

The next day the field marshal introduced himself to his radio audience as John Okello, a name previously unknown in Zanzibari politics. He announced that the Sultan had been banished for life and that his palace and property had been confiscated. "His foot may never touch our soil again." Amid reports of widespread fighting in the *shambas*, the field marshal asked the Tanganyikan government to send a planeload of medical supplies, and called for nurses to return to their hospitals.

In Mombasa, Kenya, an American destroyer, the USS *Manley*, which was in East Africa on a good-will visit, was dispatched to Zanzibar to pick up the employees of a US satellite tracking station, and on Tuesday morning the *Manley* reached Dar es Salaam with ninety-nine evacuees, including fifty-three Americans. Two Dutch students on the *Manley* said they were convinced that a rebel leader who wore a green cap and claimed to be a "Persian" was in fact Cuban. Some thought they heard him speaking Spanish. Throughout the week, a number of persons arrived in Tanganyika with similar reports, giving rise to the early headlines that Zanzibar had become, overnight, the "Cuba of East Africa". Even a visiting American diplomat claimed to have talked to a "definite Spanish-speaking type". But who was in charge? Karume had been away from the island at least once since the shooting began; Babu had been in Dar es Salaam during the entire period; and nobody had ever heard of Okello.

Every night the field marshal delivered chilling radio addresses. "I shall take severe measures," he declared. "Eighty-eight times more severe. There will be no divorce. Anyone who gets a divorce will be given sixty-five strokes. The Sultan was a devil. Imperialists and capitalists are devils. Do you reject these devils?" Another night he shouted, "It is I, the field marshal, who speaks. You will see how we hang people and burn them like chickens. Others will be cut into pieces and spread on the streets. Others will be thrown into the sea, and others will be tied to trees and shot. Anyone who tries to be a hypocrite will be punished by fifty years. Anyone looting even a bar of soap will be liable to eight years. I can make one hundred grenades an hour." To an Arab named Harusi he vowed, "Kill yourself and your sons or we will do it for you."

Photo: Adarsh Nayar

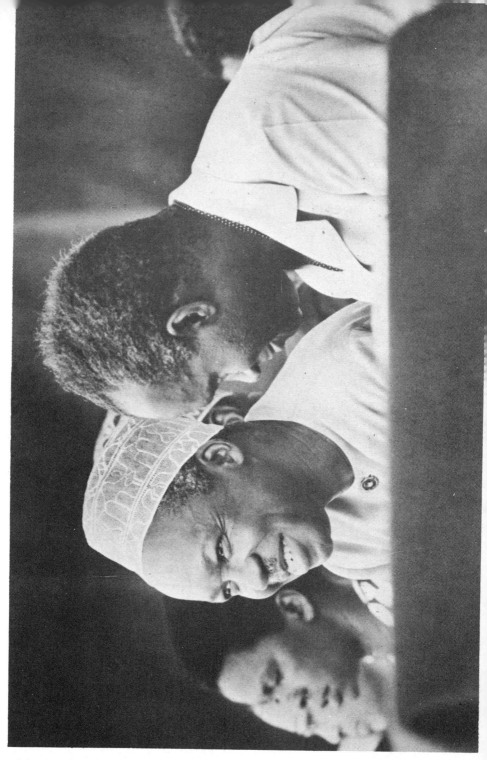

Photo: John Reader

On Monday, Karume had appealed to his countrymen for peace. On Tuesday, Okello said four former ministers would be hanged. On Wednesday, Karume contradicted him: there would be no hangings and no reprisals. On Thursday, Karume flew to Dar es Salaam with Babu and Hanga to urge Nyerere to recognize his regime and provide some mainland policemen to help restore order. Okello, apparently unaware of Karume's trip, said he had made Karume President and that Karume had played no part in the revolt. That night he declared himself President, with Karume as his deputy. Later he denied that he had made such a statement.

By this time, East Africa was full of contradictory rumours about John Okello. He was said to have received military training in Cuba; he was reputed to be a former Zanzibar policeman. Everyone agreed that he spoke Swahili with a mainland accent and that his apocalyptic words had the strange quality of an Old Testament prophet gone mad.

On Thursday afternoon, on the fifth day of the revolution, Okello arrived at his headquarters, the yellow-stucco Raha Leo, the radio station and community centre where the Afro-Shirazis had held their dance on the previous Saturday night. In front, hundreds of Africans milled around, scraps of yellow or green cloth pinned to their shoulders presumably to indicate their participation in the revolution. Many swung rifles carelessly. At the front door, two women waved guns and knives at visitors. Next door was a hastily improvised camp where scores of frightened pure-blood Arabs were being held. When the field marshal appeared in his black uniform, the crowd cheered, shook his hands and shouted, "*Jamhuri, Jamhuri!*" —Republic, Republic!

Upstairs, a few steps from the radio studio where he spoke several times a day, Okello welcomed his visitors and, with the help of a translator, spoke at some length about himself, seemingly with relish. Like his radio oratory, his words had a dreamlike quality; but unlike the broadcasts, they were simple and without rancour except when he spoke of the Arabs. He was twenty-seven, he said, a Lango tribesman from Uganda who had moved to Kenya and had served for three years in the Mau Mau, rising quickly to the rank of brigadier because "I had the power of interpreting dreams". He said he had moved from Kenya to Pemba Island five years earlier, had become a house painter and had taken an interest in Afro-Shirazi politics. He had planned the revolution by himself, he said, training small groups of people in rural areas by using pieces of wood as practice guns. "I started the revolution," he said, "because I heard that the Arabs were slaughtering the poor Africans." The first attack, he said, was made with pangas, knives and bows and arrows. He had named the new cabinet on Sunday night without consulting Karume and Babu, he claimed, and he implied that he didn't care much for Babu. He hadn't even told Karume about the revolution beforehand, Okello said, lest Karume try to stop it.

He rambled on about other matters. His new government would be "entirely democratic and won't lean to any bloke". Or did he mean bloc? His visitors laughed, and he smiled shyly too. Whom did he most admire among living men? Churchill and Khrushchev. He had never visited Cuba or anywhere else overseas, he insisted: "I never had enough money to go to Nyasaland." It was a not unreasonable statement, since many Zanzibaris of African origin had come from Nyasaland (now Malawi).

It was a strange interview, but his visitors came away with two impressions. In the first place, Okello seemed clearly to have the support of the little army of unprofessionals who lingered around the Raha Leo. The trained and uniformed young men outside the Zanzibar Hotel, to whom Okello's name meant little or nothing, were a different breed; these were Babu's Umma members, with their beards, berets and occasional words of Spanish, who had joined the revolution sometime on Sunday morning. Secondly, Okello seemed to believe what he was saying. The story about his participation in the Mau Mau was bizarre, especially for a Ugandan and a man who was a member of neither the Kikuyu nor a closely related tribe. But who could say? Could an interpreter of dreams have insinuated his way into the Mau Mau?

The situation on Thursday had been somewhat complicated by the illegal arrival of seven Western journalists— four Americans, two Britons and a Canadian—by dhow from Bagamoyo. It was also the day that Karume, Babu and Kassim Hanga had flown to Dar es Salaam to plead with Nyerere for recognition and to ask for his help. Evidently they succeeded, because the first of three hundred Tanganyikan field policemen began to arrive a day or two later. The young American chargé d'affaires, Frederick Picard, had spent much of the afternoon discussing the case of the journalists, who had been placed under house arrest at the Zanzibar Hotel, with the amiable Othman Shariff, who had been appointed minister of education in the new government—to his great surprise, in view of his recent open fight with Karume over the Afro-Shirazi leadership. In the early evening, Picard, Shariff and several of the journalists sat drinking beer in a corner of the Zanzibar Hotel lobby.

Suddenly the bulky Karume strode angrily into the room, followed by half a dozen of his revolutionary colleagues. Standing over Picard, he bellowed in his broken English, "Why are you causing us trouble? Why are you interfering in our affairs? Why? Why? You Americans, why did you evacuate your people without telling us? Why do you not recognize us?" Picard protested gently that he had informed the Zanzibaris of the withdrawal of US citizens, but Karume railed on. Abdul Aziz Twala, one of his younger aides, snapped, "We have wasted enough time. We do not need the Americans." Then Karume shouted at Picard, "You have called our ministers and interfered in our affairs. Get out of here in twenty-four hours—no, twelve hours." Picard, running after him, asked, "You mean you want me to take my staff and leave?" Karume replied, "Go to your house and do not leave it." Karume stalked out, and Picard was led away by revolutionary soldiers.

The precise reason for Karume's anger at that moment was never explained. It was true that Picard had had close ties with the deposed government and was also friendly with Othman Shariff, Karume's enemy. It was also believed that, in the evacuation of the Americans earlier in the week, Picard—presumably for humanitarian reasons—had withdrawn one or two Zanzibaris who were friendly with the old regime and who had been employed by the American embassy. Karume was undoubtedly upset about Okello's latest broadcasts, and was presumably annoyed by the arrival of the seven Western journalists. As Babu later explained, with a hint of amusement, "The reporters coming by dhow without proper papers— how could they do that? Suppose we did that in America? Would they have tolerated our landing in America that way? And it could have been very dangerous. The Sultan was still in those waters, and we thought there was a danger that he might go to Pemba and set up a government there, and we were trying to push him out of those waters. So, to have a load of foreigners arrive suddenly by dhow, of course they were accused of being spies, of course it was dangerous."

The next day Picard was declared *persona non grata* in Zanzibar and was flown to Dar es Salaam. The journalists and a number of British residents were evacuated the same night to Mombasa, Kenya, on the British survey ship HMS *Owen*. In Washington, five days after the revolution, a State Department spokesman concluded, "We just don't know what's going on. The situation is impossible to grasp." He was sceptical about reports of Cubans on the island, however, and noted that Hanga was supposed to be Soviet-trained, Babu Chinese-trained and Okello a Cuban-trained freedom fighter. "If these reports are true," he said, "no wonder nothing from Zanzibar makes sense."

The revolution appears to have come without warning to the mainland governments. Nyerere had expected trouble in the future but apparently knew nothing of the conspiracy that succeeded. He told one visitor a day or two later that he had called in Babu on Sunday, the day of the coup, and Babu said he didn't know what was happening, either. Oscar Kambona said in later years, "The revolution itself was a complete surprise to us; I think also to most Zanzibaris."

Despite the confusion on Zanzibar, the Kenya government recognized the revolutionary regime on Monday afternoon, scarcely thirty-six hours after the fighting began. Kambona had flown to Nairobi and Kampala on Sunday; he telephoned Nyerere from Nairobi to advise him that Kenya and Uganda were granting recognition immediately, and urged Nyerere to do the same. Nyerere said no. He couldn't be sure that Abeid Karume and the Afro-Shirazis were in control, he said, and he didn't like the violence. Friends have said that Okello's radio broadcasts worried the Tanganyikans and further contributed to the delay. Kambona also told Nyerere that Kenya had decided to refuse permission for the Sultan to land his yacht at Mombasa; Kambona said he assumed Tanganyika would also deny him entry. Again Nyerere disagreed. As it turned out, he allowed Jamshid and his party to land in Dar es Salaam late in the week and to remain until preparations had been made for them to fly to London.

On his way back to Dar es Salaam early on Sunday afternoon, Kambona is said to have telephoned the Zanzibar airport tower, which had not yet been taken by the revolutionaries. "You bastard," said the tower operator. "We asked you for help six hours ago. Where are your troops?"

Reconstructing the events of the Zanzibar revolution with certainty is not yet possible because most of the principal characters still have important reasons for obscuring part of what happened. All the Afro-Shirazi leaders claim to have played a part in planning the revolution. The official Zanzibari version, in fact, is that the coup was a project of the Afro-Shirazi party under the guidance of Abeid Karume; this version takes little notice of Okello because his presence became an embarrassment and because he was not a member of the party leadership. John Okello's account, on the other hand, as narrated in the "autobiography" he published in Nairobi in 1967 with the assistance of the East African Publishing House, is that Okello conceived of the revolution on his own, trained a small army in secret, gained the support of some Afro-Shirazi youth league members in the final week of preparation, and led the attack himself.

The confusion is compounded by the fact that two or more coups may have been in the planning stage in January 1964. Many observers in East Africa believe that the Afro-Shirazis, probably with the support of the Umma party and perhaps with unofficial Tanganyikan backing, were preparing to launch a coup a few weeks later.

The best judgment that can be made at present is that the revolution of January 12 was planned by a group of persons who called themselves the "Committee of Thirteen". The group, which was formed a few weeks before the revolution, included several members of the Afro-Shirazi youth league; among them were Seif Bakari, the head of the youth league; Said Bavuwai and Said Washoto; all later became members of the Revolutionary Council. The committee probably also included Yusef Hemidi, who became the Zanzibar army commander soon after the revolution. It did not include Abeid Karume and probably did not include Kassim Hanga; in fact, it may not have included any of the members of the revolutionary cabinet that John Okello announced on the evening of January 12. Nor did it include Edington Kissasi, the senior African superintendent of police, whom the revolutionaries awakened on the night of the attack and promoted to police commissioner.

The committee assembled a band of several hundred fighting men, and trained them in small groups hidden in the bush and among the palms. They had no weapons except their pangas, sticks, and bows and arrows. In recruiting members, the leaders relied heavily on Africans of Kenyan and Tanganyikan origin, many of whom had been discharged from the police force by the Shamte government. Among the mainlanders was John Okello, a Ugandan who had lived on Pemba and had in fact served there as a local branch chairman of the Afro-Shirazi party. For at least four or five months, and probably longer, Okello had been living on Zanzibar Island, where he worked as a house painter and stone cutter. He also ran a small coral quarry on the east coast of the island. He was not well known.

There are at least three versions of how John Okello came to prominence in the revolution. The first is that a few days before the revolution, the leaders of the committee recruited Okello because they wanted somebody who could blow up the ammunition storage area at Mtoni in case the attack should fail; among his many past jobs, Okello was said to have worked with explosives in a Kenya mine. A few hours before the fighting began, somebody attempted to ease the tension among the group by asking, "What rank would you like after our victory?" Okello, taking the question in earnest, is supposed to have replied, "Field marshal," and everyone laughed. For a man who later claimed to have lived and fought with the Kenya Mau Mau, it was a logical enough answer, since the Mau Mau organization was full of forest fighters who called themselves field marshals.

The second version—Okello's own—is that he had been training a handful of freedom fighters ever since the previous July and that in September he got in touch with Seif Bakari, the head of the Afro-Shirazi youth league, and joined forces with him. On the night of the attack, Okello wrote, the men cut the barbed-wire fence and entered the Ziwani compound, and then all but thirty or forty fell back afraid. It was then that the fanatical Okello, believing himself called by God, rushed forward, seizing the rifle of a sentry and killed him with its bayonet, thereby giving the rebels "the first modern weapon in our revolution".

The more or less official explanation is that Okello was picked by the coup leaders as a scarecrow; they hoped that his mainland accent, not to mention his terrifying rhetoric, would frighten the island's Arabs into surrendering because it would make them think that Kenya and Tanganyika were behind the revolution. One European who was in Zanzibar at the time has said, "They *did* make use of Okello to frighten Arabs, I think. The Arabs thought him a super-human devil. They're superstitious people, and he scared them more than aeroplanes could have done. After twenty-four hours, I don't think they thought of resistance. But I'm sceptical; I can't imagine anybody in the Afro-Shirazi leadership thinking up such a scheme. Babu could have, but he wasn't there." Babu, who never claimed to have been part of the coup at the beginning, has said, "Okello was taken in, a short time before the revolution, because of his accent. To enhance the prestige of the revolution. As soon as he got hold of the mike"—a sputter of laughter—"he couldn't leave it."

Karume himself, minimizing Okello's role, has said, "He was here for labour. Radio was free. Anyone going to radio to announce any-thing he wants. During revolution, we had no field marshal here." Then he turned to his Afro-Shirazi colleagues and roared with conspiratorial laughter.

It is impossible to prove or disprove Okello's record as a battlefield hero. But it is difficult to believe that Okello's position of power following the revolution was based solely on his radio performances. Sometime just before or after January 12, the Committee of Thirteen was enlarged to fourteen to include Okello. When the Zanzibar *Gazette* of January 25 published the names of the thirty members of the Revolutionary Council, it listed first the members of the govern-ment and then the members of the Committee of Fourteen, starting with Field Marshal John Okello.

There is ample evidence that the rebels were poorly trained and organized. After seizing the armouries, they fell to looting. They allowed the Sultan to escape, failed to capture the airport until about twelve hours after the fighting started, and never bothered to take the Cable and Wireless office at all. They had no direct help from out-siders, either from the mainland or overseas; the "Cubans" were the young men of Babu's Umma party who joined the attack sometime on Sunday morning. A Briton who observed some of the early fight-ing was convinced that the rebels had no rifles or other modern weapons until they captured the police arsenals. "When we went into the town two days later," he has said, "the only weapons I saw at roadblocks were the .303 rifles from the armouries—bolt-action, ten rounds before reloading. Okello, I think, had a Sten gun, and had had pictures taken of himself with it. And there were a few auto-matic pistols. All these came from the arsenals. It was at least two weeks later before weapons of Communist origin began to appear."

For several days after the Sultan's escape, the revolutionaries feared that he would land at Pemba and try to organize a resistance, or at least tarry there while he attempted to get military support from Britain or the mainland. But Jamshid, a placid young man with seemingly little taste for leading armies, has said that such a plan was never considered: "We didn't know our friends in Pemba were in control."

Several of Abeid Karume's political enemies have claimed that the Afro-Shirazi leader was unaware of the coup beforehand, and that he fled from the island sometime on Saturday night, either because he didn't know who was leading the rebels or because he didn't want to be on Zanzibar if the attempt failed. This, however, is not true. Two

British residents—John Cameron, an architect, and his wife—started out early on Sunday morning on a fishing trip, unaware of what had happened during the night. They were stopped by the rebels near the Mtoni armoury, north of the town, and were driven to the Raha Leo, which was already being used as the revolutionary headquarters. There they met Abeid Karume, who was wearing slacks and a sports shirt. He seemed surprised to see them. "I've given strict orders that no Europeans be arrested, " he told them. "I'll arrange transport back to your house."

A few hours after this, Karume did in fact slip away to the mainland in a small boat. His reason for leaving at that point, when the fighting was almost over, is not at all clear. Could he have failed to realize that the revolution had already succeeded, or was he alarmed by Okello's sudden power? Karume himself has said, "I went to Tanganyika to explain to Julius Nyerere how the revolution took place." But could he not have telephoned? The phones were working that morning, as were the telegraph lines. Again he has explained, "Julius Nyerere delayed to recognize our government and the Sultan was requesting Tanganyikan assistance." But the Tanganyikans had not yet had a chance even to discuss the recognition question. Instead Karume left in a boat—a dug-out canoe, some say—and spent most of the day on a rough sea, reaching Dar es Salaam exhausted in the early evening.

Kassim Hanga, whose post in the new government was first announced as prime minister but was quickly changed to vice-president, insisted in later years that the Tanganyikans had known about the revolution beforehand. He himself had flown to Dar es Salaam a day or two earlier, he said, to forewarn his old friend Oscar Kambona. He also claimed that the revolution had almost taken place twice previously—in late December and on January 7—but that on neither occasion had the time been right. He further asserted that he and another Afro-Shirazi, Abdul Twala, had spent two months in Tanganyika in late 1963 being trained in the use of firearms by a Tanganyikan policeman. No other sources ever confirmed any of these details. If they were valid at all, they might have referred to an Afro-Shirazi coup that was to have taken place sometime later in 1964.

In any case, Hanga also left Zanzibar for the mainland on Sunday. Like Karume, he sailed alone in a small boat. His purpose, Hanga said later, was to get more rifles.

That night in Dar es Salaam, Karume met with Nyerere, who felt

Karume's stabilizing influence was needed on the island and urged him to go home immediately. On Zanzibar, Okello meanwhile was announcing the names of the new cabinet, and was calling on Karume to return. Oddly enough, none of the Zanzibar officials in Dar es Salaam that evening could remember Okello's name. Okello referred to himself that night as "the field marshal" and "Field Marshal *Huyu*"—a Swahili word meaning "this man" or "X"—and didn't announce his real name until the following day.

Unable to fly back to Zanzibar because the airport was closed, Karume and Hanga enlisted the aid of a European named Misha Fainzilber, who was engaged in the fishing business and had been friendly with the Afro-Shirazis in Zanzibar in previous years. So at two o'clock on Monday morning, twenty-four hours after the revolution began, the group left from Silver Sands, a small resort north of Dar es Salaam, in Fainzilber's glass-bottom boat. The crossing took them six and a half hours because the engine broke down en route. When they finally arrived at Kizimkazi on Zanzibar in the early morning, the whole village came down to the shore to welcome them. The new leaders of Zanzibar requisitioned the schoolteacher's car and drove straight to the Ruha Leo, where they were greeted by Field Marshal Okello and sat down with him to a big meal. Then Karume and his cabinet retired to another room to hold a meeting.

Nobody will ever know how many Zanzibaris died during the week of the revolution and in the unsettled period that followed. "Okello said nine thousand, nine hundred and ninety-nine, didn't he?" asked a European who formerly lived on Zanzibar. "And Karume said about twelve hundred? My guess is somewhere in between. Maybe six thousand, mostly in the outlying districts."

In the public mind, the symbol of the bloodshed was John Okello. A week or two later, a Briton who had known Okello as a house painter on Zanzibar had a dream in which Okello was painting the Briton's new boat, not with a paint spray but with a machine gun.

Ten days after the revolution, the Anglican bishop of Zanzibar, the Right Reverend Niall Russell, was finally able to return to Zanzibar Island from Pemba, where he had been marooned by the fighting. On the boat with him was Field Marshal Okello, who had been making a triumphal visit to his former home. "He was very respectful," the bishop later recalled. "He asked me to read Matthew Twenty-three to him—about the scribes and the Pharisees. He said to me, 'I don't mean all those things about burning people in oil, you know.' I said I thought it was time to quieten things down, and he said, 'Nobody tells me these things.' I invited him to come to church, and he did come once; he sat very quietly. He was very convinced he had been sent by God."

VIII

JULIUS NYERERE'S ANNOUNCEMENT in early January 1964 that he was ending his government's two-year-old policy of Africanization, and that citizens of all races would henceforth be equally eligible for government jobs, produced a chorus of angry protests from trade union leaders. The railway union promised to resist the policy change "at all costs", and the head of the local-government union accused Nyerere of taking the country "back to the colonial days". He added, "If Tanganyika is to gain respect outside by neglecting its indigenous citizens, then we don't want that kind of respect."

Nyerere was preoccupied with the Zanzibar revolution during the week of January 12. On Sunday night he saw Karume at State House and urged him to return home immediately. On Tuesday he flew to Nairobi to see Prime Minister Kenyatta. On Wednesday the Sultan of Zanzibar landed in Dar es Salaam to await transport to London, and left four days later. On Thursday Nyerere saw Karume in Dar es Salaam for the second time that week. Apparently he promised help to Karume in restoring order and bolstering the new regime, because, by the following weekend, some three hundred Tanganyikan field policemen were being flown to Zanzibar for temporary duty. Although nobody realized it at the time, their absence upset the existing power balance between the army and field police in the Dar es Salaam area.

The weekend of January 18–19 was calm enough for Nyerere to devote some time to ceremonial duties. He unveiled a plaque after officially opening a new swimming pool at the Missions to Seamen in Dar es Salaam, and he gave a cheque for £3,000 to the Algerian ambassador for the victims of recent Algerian floods. On Sunday night he had a chat with Field Marshal John Okello, who had come over to Dar es Salaam for a brief rest, and urged him to work in good faith with President Karume.

A few hours later, at 1.50 a.m. on Monday, January 20, the British commander of the Tanganyika Rifles, Brigadier Patrick Sholto Douglas, was awakened at his home near Colito Barracks, some ten miles north of Dar es Salaam, by the sound of bugles and sirens.

Dashing into the street in his pyjamas, he saw a dozen of his officers rushing down the hill to the camp. At the foot of the hill, he later learned, they were arrested by enlisted men armed with rifles and Sten guns, and were locked up in the guardroom. Half of his army—the eight-hundred-man First Battalion—had mutinied.

Collecting his wife and six-year-old daughter, Douglas ran out the back door of his house and through the bush for a mile and a half, borrowed a car from a friend and drove into Dar es Salaam. The city was quiet. Leaving his wife and daughter with the Australian high commissioner, Douglas drove on to the home of an army staff officer in the suburb of Oyster Bay, just north of the capital. There he tried desperately to reach Nyerere and Vice-President Kawawa by telephone, but couldn't get through. Then he called Oscar Kambona, the External Affairs and Defence Minister, and asked that three DC-3s be sent to Tabora, four hundred miles away, to bring back elements of the Second Battalion, which, so far as he knew, was still loyal to the government. Kambona agreed. Moments later, Douglas learned that the mutineers had already blocked the road to the Dar es Salaam airport, thereby separating the pilots from the planes.

Fearing that the post office had also been seized and that the mutineers could trace his telephone calls, Douglas ran from house to house in Oyster Bay. As he dashed into one house, a group of soldiers roared past in a Land-Rover, shooting wildly at the front door. Douglas quickly exchanged his uniform for a check shirt and khaki trousers, ducked out of the back door, jumped hedges and walls, ran straight through the house of the German ambassador, and finally reached the residence of the British high commissioner, where he remained in hiding for five days.

Nyerere narrowly escaped. Douglas had telephoned the police inspector general, who walked to Rashidi Kawawa's house on the State House grounds and awakened him, and the two ran on to State House together. "We had a lot of trouble persuading the President to leave," Kawawa has recalled. "He wanted to stay and argue with them. He wanted to ask them, 'What is the problem?'" (Nyerere's colleagues have pointed out that he once went straight into the middle of an Indian riot at Douali and talked the rioters into going home. His friends were appalled; one said to him later, "My God, Julius, if one stone had touched you, there wouldn't have been an Asian left alive the next day." "I know!" he said. "But I didn't think of it at the time.")

"The argument," another friend of Nyerere's has said, "was over preventing him from going out to talk to the mutineers. His wife was on her knees to him. His security men helped Bhoke Munanka [a State House aide] get him into the basement, with Maria pleading. And one of his security men then walked slowly down the State House drive to stall the mutineers. 'It's not the President you want, it's your minister," he told them. 'Why don't you go and see Mr Kambona?' " While this argument was taking place, Nyerere and his wife and Kawawa were leaving the State House grounds by another entrance.

The President's younger brother Joseph was awakened by a neighbour, who warned him, "Don't go to town. There has been an army revolt." Joseph drove to State House, where soldiers stopped him and said, "You can't go in there; State House has been taken over." Joseph told them. "OK, you can take over State House, but you can't take over my mother," and drove through the gate. Inside he found his mother unharmed. As he started to leave, one of the soldiers recognized him as the President's brother and as the man who had recommended that soldiers should be asked to work in the fields. "That's the fellow," said one, "who says we should go to Kilombero"—the huge sugar estate. So they arrested him and took him to Colito Barracks.

For most of the next two days, Nyerere remained in hiding somewhere in Dar es Salaam. Where he stayed during that brief period has never been disclosed, and has remained one of the more tantalizing minor mysteries of the country's political history. There have been endless rumours: that he took refuge in a mission, a church or an embassy, in a hut on the beach or a ship in the harbour, or that he went as far as Arusha or even Nairobi. "No, it was not a ship," Rashidi Kawawa has said. "I don't think it is appropriate for me to tell you where; we went to a place where we felt safe and could get information from time to time. Then later, when everything was all right, we came back." Nyerere was criticized for failing to keep in closer touch with his people, and he himself admitted later, "I think I made a big mistake." If such an admission implies that he would behave differently in the event of another mutiny or coup, the lesson he learned was probably a fallacious one; his quick disappearance that January morning may have been responsible for the preservation of his government and perhaps even his life.

The first day. The mutiny was led by a small group of soldiers, mostly non-commissioned officers, whose primary aim was to get rid of the British officers. The Europeans didn't understand their grievances, they said; one soldier testified later that he joined the group—which called itself the Army Night Freedom Fighters—because an officer had recently ordered the "slaughter" of some chickens the men were keeping; the hen-house, he complained, wasn't clean enough. The soldiers also demanded an increase in basic pay from 105 shillings a month to 260 shillings; even a houseboy was paid 150, they said. At a meeting late on Sunday night, the conspirators decided to proceed with their plan immediately. "Today," said a soldier named Pius Francis, "we shall give back Mr Kambona's teachers."

Having seized Colito Barracks by shortly after 2 a.m., the mutineers—no more than forty men at first—broke up into several groups and drove into Dar es Salaam. One group, led by Sergeant Francis Hingo Ilogi, forced its way past the guards at State House and tried to find the President. Failing in this effort, Hingo's men drove to Oscar Kambona's house and brought him back to State House. There, in the gatehouse, Hingo told Kambona, "We have locked up our officers. We do not blame you ministers, because you are civilians. You do not know a soldier's difficulties. If you will come with us to hear the men's complaints, the officers will be released." Kambona agreed to go with them to Colito. As a precaution, however, he drove behind the army Land-Rover in the police commissioner's car.

At Colito, Hingo told Kambona the soldiers wanted the army Africanized immediately—and completely. Kambona replied that such a plan was already being considered, but that he had to settle certain problems in the Defence Ministry first. He asked them to choose some representatives to discuss the soldiers' grievances in Dar es Salaam. Several men shouted, "Shoot him!" and "Beat him up!" and Hingo insisted, "No. We want everything today."

Seeing that the mutineers were determined to remove the British officers immediately, Kambona asked them who they thought should be the new commander of the Tanganyika Rifles. "I remembered from the Congo," Kambona has said, "that the worst thing is to have an army without officers." Somebody shouted "Nyirenda"—Alex Nyirenda, the young, Sandhurst-trained officer who had planted the *Uhuru* flag on the summit of Mount Kilimanjaro on December 9, 1961. The suggestion was quickly shouted down; "Nyirenda is a European," said one man, referring to Nyirenda's polished manner.

Then another young African officer, Second Lieutenant Elisha Kavana, was nominated, and was accepted by all. "When they urged Kavana to take over," Kambona has said, "I told him he must do it. They forced Douglas' brigadier's cap onto Kavana's head. I was surprised at how bitter they were."

Kambona then refused to sign an agreement on the new appointments until he had had a chance to consult the President, so he and Hingo's group drove back to State House for a second time. Soldiers lined the State House drive, but none had entered the building itself. Some wanted to go in with Kambona, but Hingo restrained them. Nyerere had left State House at least two hours earlier; but Kambona, after remaining inside for a few minutes talking with the President's aide-de-camp and also the President's mother, emerged to tell the mutineers that Nyerere had agreed to their demands. "Liar!" someone shouted. "The President is not inside." But the group seemed satisfied and returned once more to Colito Barracks, with Kambona again following in the police commissioner's car.

This time, following a meeting in the education centre, Kambona agreed to the removal of the British officers and arranged for their immediate transport to Nairobi. At one point, some said later, he reassured the frightened British wives that their husbands were safe and that he personally would look after them. Before noon Kambona succeeded in getting all or most of the mutineers back to their barracks. Later he called some of the soldiers back to Dar es Salaam to restore order after looting and rioting broke out. In Magomeni township in Dar es Salaam, an Arab shot two soldiers and two African civilians, one of whom had been looting the Arab's shop. Angry soldiers fired mortars at the Arab's house, then killed him and his six-year-old daughter as they ran from the flames. Five other members of the family were burned to death inside. According to the official count, seventeen soldiers and civilians were killed in the rioting.

Earlier in the day, Kambona had asked the Kenya government for assistance in putting down the mutiny, but the request was soon withdrawn by Job Lusinde, the Home Affairs Minister. In a broadcast to the nation, Kambona announced, "This is your Minister of External Affairs and Defence. The government is still there. . . . There has been some misunderstanding between the Africans and the British officers in the Tanganyika Rifles. At my intervention, the soldiers have now returned to Colito Barracks." Curiously, he failed to mention Nyerere at all, perhaps because he simply didn't know where Nyerere had gone. A subsequent statement to the press by George Rockey, Nyerere's British press secretary, that "*Mwalimu* is safe, well and in command", was thus not altogether reassuring. Throughout East Africa there were rumours that Kambona was in the process of seizing power; even later, some of Kambona's enemies asserted that he had been working with the mutineers but had become alarmed by the depth of their anger and by the fact that Nyerere had escaped, and had pulled back. The best argument against this thesis is that, if he had had the soldiers' support, there was very little to have prevented him from staging a coup that day if he had chosen to do so. Kambona interpreted such rumours as further evidence that he was disliked and misunderstood by many Europeans. "The British looked to Mr Nyerere as the moderate leader," he has said. "They felt my image had been boosted by the events that day, and they were angry."

Kambona soon realized that the crisis was not yet over. "At first," he has recalled, "the soldiers seemed very happy that the British officers had been removed. They cheered me." At the funeral of the two soldiers who were killed by the Arab, however, Kambona noticed that Hingo Ilogi was acting strangely. "He wouldn't talk to me or even look me in the eye. I suspected further trouble, and put on security men to track him."

The second day. The government learned that the Second Battalion of the Tanganyika Rifles had mutinied at Tabora shortly after receiving news of the mutiny of the First Battalion at Colito Barracks. In the midst of the Tabora rebellion, a cable arrived from Oscar Kambona announcing that he was naming a new battalion commander, Mirisho S. H. Sarakikya, a mountain climber and runner who, while attending Sandhurst, had set an academy record by running the mile in four minutes and eighteen seconds. Sarakikya, who was under arrest at that moment, along with other officers, asked the mutineers' permission to read the cable, and told them to read it aloud. Then he ordered them to stand at attention, unfix their bayonets and unload; and they obeyed him. That night he arranged for the evacuation of ten British officers and non-coms.

Sometime on Tuesday morning, presumably at the place where he had gone into hiding. Nyerere tape-recorded a short speech that was broadcast in the evening. In three minutes of tense Swahili, Nyerere urged his countrymen to remain calm. "Yesterday was a most dis-

graceful day," he said. "Some people went around spreading
rumours and claimed that I was no longer here, and that there was
no government. Such rumours make a little trouble seem much
bigger than it really is." Didactically he added that rumour-monger-
ing was "a sign of not being grown-up, a grown man is calm," and
closed with a bitter comment: "My hope is that we shall never see
such a disgraceful day repeated in Tanganyika."

"But where *is* he?" many Tanganyikans asked after hearing
Nyerere's terse message, and some wondered if he had been taken
prisoner by unknown enemies. As a precautionary measure, the
British government prepared to send two thousand additional troops
to East Africa. The frigate *Rhyl* was already standing by off Dar es
Salaam, and the carrier *Centaur* sailed from Aden with six hundred
marine commandos aboard. Almost unnoticed in the excitement,
Sultan Jamshid of Zanzibar reached London by plane from Dar es
Salaam.

The third day. Suddenly Nyerere reappeared on Wednesday
morning. Riding with his wife and Job Lusinde, he toured every
section of Dar es Salaam from Magomeni, where some of the worst
rioting had occurred, to Kiungani, where an Indian shopkeeper
greeted him warmly: "*Karibou, Baba.*" At TANU headquarters a
crowd sang the party song, "Tanu yajenga nchi" ("Let TANU
Build the Country"). At every stop Nyerere said, "What happened
is a disgrace, but it is over, and there's nothing to be afraid of."
People peered uncertainly from their houses; some waved timidly.
Once, after six people scurried away at the first sight of his procession, Nyerere walked after them saying, "Why did you run away?
There's no reason to be afraid."

The fourth day. Nyerere held a press conference at State House at
which he spoke about the effects of the mutiny and took the blame
for failing to keep the public better informed. "It would be foolish
to pretend that these events are unimportant," he said, "or that they
have not damaged Tanganyika's reputation overseas." In reply to
questions, he said that the soldiers' demands for higher pay were
being discussed, and that he did not expect to call in British troops:
"We can handle our own situation." Then he was asked if he intended to punish any of the soldiers in the revolt. He smiled thinly,
paused for a full five seconds, and replied, "Thank you very much,
gentlemen," closing the conference. The awkward pause underscored the predicament he faced at that moment; his government
had accepted a lawless solution, had capitulated to a mutinous army

and was powerless to punish it. The soldiers had simply returned to
their barracks. "There is nothing the government can do," a Western
diplomat said that day, "to prevent them from seizing Dar es Salaam
again tonight if they want to."

That evening at Karimjee Hall, Nyerere received a five-minute
ovation before delivering a lecture sponsored by the Dag Hammarskjöld Memorial Foundation and entitled "The Courage of Recon-
ciliation". "It dealt with law based on enforceable power," as one of
his aides said later, "and it was given at a time when he had no enforceable powers himself."

During those days, one of his friends has said, Nyerere "was
pretending that the problem would heal itself; he expected the
soldiers to be as shocked by the seventeen deaths as he was." On
Thursday he issued a directive to the men of the First Battalion to
put on their dress uniforms. "I wanted to see if they would respond
to an order," he said later. They refused.

The fifth day. Negotiations between the government and the army
over the mutineers' demands were breaking down, and the soldiers
were becoming rebellious again. On the previous Monday, the
mutineers had lacked a political leader and even a political motive.
Now there were reports that trade union leaders had been meeting
with the soldiers at Colito Barracks, and that the unions were planning a general strike for the weekend in alliance with the mutineers.
There were also reports of a plot at the town of Morogoro, headquarters of the plantation workers' union. According to one story
that circulated later in Dar es Salaam, a woman sitting in an out-
house in a Morogoro garden had heard two men conspiring against
the government, and had called the police.

The Tanganyika army mutiny had sparked off similar but less
serious rebellions in the armies of both Uganda and Kenya. At the
first sign of trouble, Uganda's Prime Minister Obote and Kenya's
Prime Minister Kenyatta requested British military assistance.
Nyerere was extremely reluctant to take similar action. It has long
been said that he was not convinced of the existence of a conspiracy
against the government until someone showed him a list of the proposed Cabinet that the plotters had prepared; but Nyerere has
specifically denied this. "The thing that finally convinced him,"
Kambona once said , "was that one of his friends was approached by
the conspirators and asked to be the new Vice-President."

Sometime on Friday afternoon, in any case, Nyerere apparently
became convinced that his government was in danger. At 5.30,

accordingly, he called the British Acting High Commissioner, F. Stephen Miles, to State House and requested military assistance. The request was immediately transmitted to London. Kambona then went to the high commissioner's house, where Brigadier Sholto Douglas had been in hiding all week, and asked for his help. That night Douglas and another officer took a launch from an isolated beach to the *Centaur*, which had arrived from Aden and was lying offshore. By the time Douglas boarded the carrier at 2 a.m. on Saturday, he learned that the British government had approved the Tanganyikan request.

The sixth day. At 6.20 a.m., six helicopters lifted sixty British marine commandos from the *Centaur* to the playing field just south of Colito Barracks. At 6.30 the carrier and the destroyer *Cambrian*, which had also been standing by offshore, began firing attack airbursts to frighten the Tanganyikan soldiers. From a distance of fifty yards, Douglas told the soldiers over a loudspeaker that he had resumed command, and ordered them to come out of the barracks with their arms in the air and to sit down in the road. He was giving them ten minutes to reply, he said, and began a countdown in Swahili. Then the marines fired at the guardroom with a rocket launcher, tearing away part of the roof and breaking windows. Immediately the soldiers began to surrender; one hundred and fifty appeared within ten minutes, and another hundred and fifty in the next hour. "By seven-thirty it was all over," Douglas said later, "although we spent the morning rounding up stray men who had fled into the bush." Three Tanganyikan soldiers had been killed and five wounded; there were no British casualties. No incident has illustrated more dramatically the vulnerability of the young African states; the Tanganyikan mutiny had been started by no more than forty men and was put down by sixty British marines.

British troops in Uganda and Kenya had acted simultaneously that morning. In Uganda they drove before dawn from the Entebbe airport to Jinja Barracks, where they overpowered the guards and took the mutineers captive. At Lanet Camp in Kenya, where troops of the Eleventh Battalion of the Kenya Rifles had seized arms on Friday night, the British Royal Horse Artillery arrived at dawn, captured the armoury and disarmed the soldiers. From Saturday morning, British troops were protecting three East African governments from their own armies.

Early that morning, a frightened Tanganyikan soldier had appeared at the Dar es Salaam office of the East African External

Telecommunications Company. He wanted to send the following message, he said, to the Secretary General of the United Nations, U Thant: TANGANYIKA RIFLES CAPTURED BY UNKNOWN TROOPS HELP QUICKLY SEND U.N. TROOPS. The message was to be dispatched at the "priority" rate and was signed "Lieutenant Colonel Ilogi, Commanding Officer." Testifying at the trial of the mutineers four months later, Michael Wright of the cable company said the man had appeared "very distressed". Wright was unable to identify him positively as Sergeant Francis Hingo Ilogi.

Many observers overseas thought it curious that mutinies had broken out in three East African armies at almost the same time, and only a week after the revolution on Zanzibar; but no evidence of an inter-army conspiracy was ever found. All three armies had previously been components of the King's African Rifles, and their men had certain grievances in common. Tanganyikan officials tended to blame their British officers for having failed to keep the government better informed. "I think the mutiny could have been avoided," Rashidi Kawawa once said, "if only the army commander could have told us the truth, which he did not. There was no proper system for telling us the thinking of our own army." For their part, many of the British officers felt Kambona had mismanaged the army and failed to understand military discipline; on one occasion he had talked to the enlisted men, in the absence of their senior officers, and invited them to air their grievances. Most diplomats in Dar es Salaam believed Kambona had behaved well during the week of the mutiny, however, although the rumours about his deviousness continued; when one London newspaper referred to him as "Moscow's man in East Africa", Kambona sued for libel and won.

On Saturday afternoon Nyerere denounced the ring-leaders who had tried to "intimidate our nation at the point of a gun", and explained to his people why he had been forced to call in the British to punish an army that had "tasted the poison of disloyalty and disobedience". A friend of Nyerere's, recalling how he had once remarked, "The British have been through the furnace, we have never been through it," asked him after the mutiny, "Is this the furnace?" "Yes," Nyerere said, "a little of it." He had always been fond of saying that, in the long struggle for independence, not a single life had been lost; in the week of the mutiny, at least seventeen were killed. "The whole week," said Nyerere, "has been one of most grievous shame for our nation. It will take months and even years to erase from the mind of the world what it has heard about these events this week."

In the days that followed, Nyerere disbanded the First Battalion and dismissed hundreds of soldiers from the Second. Suspecting others of involvement in the conspiracy, he also discharged about ten per cent of his 5,000 policemen; ordered the questioning of more than 400 persons, some of whom were trade unionists who had been in touch with the mutineers at Colito Barracks; and arrested 550 people under the Preventive Detention Act, most of whom were quickly released. He disbanded the Tanganyika Federation of Labour and in its place established the National Union of Tanganyika Workers, with his Labour Minister as general secretary. He appointed a new army commander, Captain Sarakikya—the man whom Kambona had chosen to head the Second Battalion during the crisis—and promoted him to brigadier. He increased the soldiers' wages to almost exactly what the mutineers had asked: from 105 shillings to 240 shillings a month. He sent a telegram of thanks to the British government, and then called an emergency meeting of African foreign and defence ministers to discuss "the grave danger to the whole continent" posed by army revolts. The meeting, in effect, absolved him of blame for calling in the British troops, and endorsed his plan for borrowing soldiers from other African states until his own new army had been trained. In early April the British troops were withdrawn, and were replaced by the Nigerian Third Battalion under Lieutenant-Colonel James Pam, who was to die two years later in a coup in his own country. Sergeant Hingo Ilogi was sent to prison for fifteen years for his part in the army mutiny; thirteen other soldiers received five- and ten-year sentences.

One day in February that year, Nyerere spoke about the damage caused by the mutiny. "This is a very proud country," he said. "Our country feels let down very much. It's a double shame—shame at being let down by our own men, and shame at having to call in the British. It's clear as anything to me—the British should be here as short a time as possible."

The mutiny had caused Nyerere to ponder what kind of army his country should have. "The King's African Rifles never taught the men to become soldiers of Kenya, Tanganyika and Uganda. They were just battalions with British officers. So what did we do when we took over? We changed the uniforms a bit, we commissioned a few Africans, but at the top they were still solidly British. There were no African field-grade officers. We had inherited an impossible situation. You could never consider it an army of the people. When I suggested, 'Here are these able-bodied men, why can't they help in building bridges?', the officers answered"—he affected a clipped British accent— " 'These are soldiers!' I said that in wartime, British soldiers built bridges. They replied, 'Wartime is different.'

"An army, I think, must accept the political ethic of a country. Our army didn't know what our political ethic was. The British allow political dissent within their army, but that's part of their ethic. I had some of the British officers to dinner here, and one of them talked politics to me. He said he was voting socialist against the Tories. Well, that's fine. But can you imagine a KADU colonel"— KADU being Kenya's opposition party at the time—"in the Kenya army? If we had an opposition here, the damned fellows would be overthrowing the government the next morning. Here the opposition would be subversive. *On that day* [during the week of the mutiny] *they were talking with the army*. Where is the future opposition leader I can call in, as Lord Home can talk to Wilson? Whom I can call in and say, 'Look, brother, here is the security situation as I know it'? There is no such thing here.

"*I* don't need to be convinced of the need for an opposition. The West should talk to the opposition, not to me. It should tell them, 'If you want to be the opposition, don't be subversive, don't be disloyal.'

"One of the soldiers said during the mutiny, 'How can we overthrow the damned government? It's too popular.' Can you imagine that?" He repeated the question, obviously pleased with it. "What we need is the kind of criticism that pushes a good government. I got a letter recently implying that I hadn't kept a promise I made in 1958. This is the kind of opposition you like."

His goal, he said, was "an army that understands the problem of building a nation, not an army isolated from the people." Some of his friends had protested that he should not build a political army, he said. "But to me a political army is simply one that accepts the political ethic of its country."

In retrospect, the mutiny seems to have marked the zenith of British-Tanganyikan relations in the post-colonial period. When asked why he believed the British rescue of the Tanganyikan government had failed to create better relations on a sustained basis, Sir Richard Turnbull replied, "No independent country likes to see its army put down by sixty young men. Of course we had the equipment.

But it was a great humiliation for Julius and Tanganyika. Nobody likes having a good turn of that sort done to them. People don't like to be helped in that way."

Looking back on the mutiny four years later, Julius Nyerere said with growing confidence, "The recovery is complete—and early. The mutiny was a strike of the army people, and it went out of control. It shocked the country. But every cloud has a silver lining, as the British say. It enabled us to build an army almost from scratch. Many institutions we have inherited, but the army is something we built ourselves."

IX

President Nyerere wishes it clarified that the word Tanzania should be pronounced Tan-za-ni-a, with the emphasis on the penultimate syllable, as is the practice with the Swahili language.

State House announcement, *November 1964.*

IN THE UNEASY WEEKS following the Zanzibar revolution, the three hundred Tanganyikan field policemen remained on the island. Their stated purpose was to help the Zanzibaris restore order and guard against an Arab counter-coup, but the more important effect of their presence was to bolster the regime of Abeid Karume against other revolutionary elements. The new President announced a fortnight after the revolution that Zanzibar had become a one-party state; the one legal party was, of course, the Afro-Shirazi, so Abdulrahman Babu went on the air immediately to say that his Umma party was joining the ASP.

Almost from the beginning, the new government began the seizure and distribution of large quantities of Arab plantation holdings to African peasants. It also nationalized the island's "racial" clubs while Duncan Sandys, the British Commonwealth and Colonial Secretary, was having tea in one of them, the English Club. "No," he replied later, in response to a reporter's question, "nothing would surprise me on Zanzibar." In another symbolic and highly popular action at about the same time, Karume burned the island's few remaining rickshaws at a ceremonial bonfire, promising £100 in compensation to each rickshaw owner. He had long advocated an end to the degrading practice in which men worked as animals, he said, but the previous government had laughed at him.

During this unsettled period, while hundreds of revolutionaries carried weapons carelessly in the streets and killings continued intermittently in the remote districts, the British community of five hundred dwindled to less than fifty. At least seven hundred Arabs and five hundred Indians fled the island. Dhows that were authorized to carry thirty passengers were loaded with as many as one hundred and fifty. One such dhow went down off the coast of northern Kenya; only the captain survived.

On February 20, Field Marshal John Okello flew to Nairobi, where, at a press conference, he denounced foreign "devils" and said he was willing to start revolutions in southern Africa wherever the colonialists were still in power. Then he went off to Uganda to see his family. When he reappeared in Dar es Salaam a few days later, he denied to journalists that he was Field Marshal Okello; his name was Gideon Baker, he said. He was lingering in Dar es Salaam waiting for Abeid Karume, Okello later explained in his autobiography, but Karume failed to arrive. After four or five days Okello heard a rumour that he was unwelcome in Zanzibar, so he flew to the island to find out what was happening. At the Zanzibar airport he was greeted by Karume and the rest of the Revolutionary Council—armed, as usual. Karume bundled Okello into a Tanganyikan government plane, saying Nyerere had something to tell them, and the two flew back to Dar es Salaam. The following morning, when Okello was taken to State House, Nyerere said to him, "There have been some misunderstandings. Does the government belong to you or Karume?" Okello answered with oracular ambiguity, and the next day Karume returned to Zanzibar alone. When he finally managed to see Nyerere a week later, Okello wrote, Nyerere told him that Karume wanted him "to go to my home in Uganda and rest for six months, after which time the question of my returning to Zanzibar would be reconsidered".

Okello complained that he had no money and had even left his suitcase at the Zanzibar airport the week before; and what about his three months' army pay? Oscar Kambona brought him the suitcase the next day, but nothing else. "The Sultan had been well received in Britain," Okello wrote sorrowfully, "and my own brothers had expelled me. I caused the Sultan to lose his regime, yet my fate was much worse than his."

Okello wrote how he then wandered, penniless, from Nairobi to Uganda. He failed to mention, however, how he happened to come into possession of a new Peugeot sedan, which he wrecked completely on March 14 while driving to Uganda. On April 7 Okello wrote a letter to Karume and received a cable from the principal immigration officer in reply: YOU ARE INFORMED THAT YOU ARE AN UNWANTED PERSON IN ZANZIBAR.

The speed with which the new Zanzibar government welcomed

technicians and aid from China, East Germany and the Soviet Union dismayed many East Africans who had supported the overthrow of the Arab regime. Having recognized the Karume government as quickly as possible after the revolution, the Soviet Union sent a freighter loaded with trucks, mortars, anti-tank and anti-aircraft guns as well as small arms. In late February, Babu announced that Zanzibar had accepted £185,000 in aid from China. "That's only the beginning," he said. Colonial names were replaced by Communist ones; within a few weeks a stadium had been renamed for Mao Tse-tung and a school for Fidel Castro, and Chinese doctors had begun to practice the art of acupuncture at the V. I. Lenin Hospital.

The Zanzibaris were doubly angry with the West. They resented the early press reports that Zanzibar had become the "Cuba of East Africa", and they were particularly annoyed that Britain, the United States and many other Western countries had withheld recognition. The West German government sent a Foreign Ministry official to Zanzibar in early February; he returned to Bonn convinced that the Zanzibaris had agreed to establish relations with West Germany and not East Germany. Shortly after that, however, the Zanzibaris admitted an East German chargé d'affaires to the island, and Hassan Moyo, Zanzibar's Acting External Affairs Minister, dismissed a West German protest as "presumptuous".

The sole remaining American diplomat on the island, Donald Petterson, drove around the town with two Tanganyikan policemen as guards. His main chore was looking after the NASA tracking station, as well as the homes and property of the station's evacuated American employees. Every day at 9 a.m. and 3 p.m. he talked over an open telephone line with the US embassy in Dar es Salaam.

On February 19, President Karume impatiently ordered the British high commissioner and the acting American chargé d'affaires to leave Zanzibar within twenty-four hours because their countries had not recognized his regime. Recognition followed immediately, and the order was rescinded. The United States named Frank Carlucci, a young diplomat who had served in the Congo, as its new chargé. For a while Karume seemed mollified, but in early April he asked the United States to remove its satellite tracking station permanently "in the interests of the security and defence of Zanzibar". He was incensed over a statement made in New York by William Attwood, the American ambassador to Kenya, that China and East Germany were attempting to turn Zanzibar into a "kind of non-African state". The statement was valid, but its timing was unfortunate. On the same day that Karume ordered the tracking station removed, he accepted the credentials of the new Chinese ambassador, Meng Ying, saying that Zanzibar looked to China "not as a friend but as a real brother".

The question has been debated endlessly in East Africa in the years since 1964; but the prevailing view is that, although the Communist powers were not involved directly in the planning of the Zanzibar revolution, they attempted immediately thereafter—and with considerable success—to exploit it to their own ends. It is generally agreed, furthermore, that the Western countries made a serious mistake by failing to recognize the Karume regime for six weeks after the revolution, while China, the Soviet Union, East Germany, Czechoslovakia and Cuba deluged the Zanzibaris with blessings and support. It is by no means certain, however, that early Western recognition would have affected Zanzibar's subsequent foreign policy significantly. Abeid Karume was an uneducated man whose problems and nightmares ranged from a wild field marshal to the danger of an Arab counter-coup. Inevitably he relied on the guidance of the young, educated Marxists who had joined his regime, and they quickly moulded its policies. Israel, for example, should have become the new government's first and closest friend, because the Israelis had been one of the largest contributors to the Afro-Shirazi party in the years before independence. But when, after the revolution, the Israelis tried to establish relations with the Karume government, they encountered an inexplicable amount of resistance.

Julius Nyerere was deeply angered that the West failed to understand what had happened on Zanzibar. He was particularly furious that the British, having turned the island nation over to an Arab minority government, should seem to be unable to grasp why the African majority had seized power. Later he would dismiss as irrelevant such questions as whether the Afro-Shirazi party was the sole instigator of the coup, or what role John Okello played in the planning; the point was that a black majority, twice denied the right to govern by an electoral process inherited from the colonial power, had taken it by revolutionary means.

"What happened was what the whole world should have known," he said two years later. "But the West declared a Communist take-over! Absurd! We had been talking about this [danger of revolution] for years. These fellows with bows and arrows and pangas took over. But the Western countries said, 'It's Communist!'

"Well, the Communists jumped in. The Zanzibaris had no experience in government. They were ordinary people. Ordinary people! And the Western powers *pulled out!* The Americans were the first to pull out. Why? It was the Nationalist party that asked them to remove their tracking station. The Afro-Shirazis never had. "These people had had no experience. Go out and look at them! They had no external support whatever, and they had fear that the British might put the Sultan back. And the Russians, the Chinese and the East Germans were recognizing them. As they say, 'When you are sinking, you try to cling even to a reed.' What did they know or care about the Cold War? They thought, these were good people who were helping them, and bad people who were not. That's all they knew."

But, considering the leftist influences within the new government, would it not have adopted anti-Western policies in any case? "There were left-wing socialists, yes," Nyerere said, "but they were a minority in a minority"—Umma was a minority in the ZNP—"and a splinter from a minority. They would have urged left-wing policies, but it would not have become a Cold War matter. What identified them with the East was the refusal of the Western countries to accept Zanzibar."

On April 22, Nyerere flew to Zanzibar for the first time since the revolution to pay what his aides described as a one-hour "courtesy visit" on Karume. The following day it was announced at State House in Dar es Salaam that Nyerere and Karume had in fact signed "articles of Union", and that the Republic of Tanganyika and the People's Republic of Zanzibar had agreed to unite.

The news came as such a surprise that nobody knew quite how to interpret it. "Observers regard Union in one of two ways," said an editorial in the *East African Standard* of Nairobi, "either as strengthening Zanzibar's revolutionary regime against extreme elements and containing them offshore, or as an entry of extreme influence to the mainland." Even a few of the supposed participants seemed to have been caught off balance. Zanzibar's External Affairs Minister, Babu, was returning from a trip to Indonesia when the announcement was made; he said in Pakistan, on his way home, that he had no comment. The following day, after arriving in Nairobi, he said he had known about the plan all along and had approved it. At the People's Palace in Zanzibar, Abeid Karume told his followers on the day after the announcement that Union would not make it necessary for Zanzibar to change its friends, and Julius Nyerere insisted in an address to his National Assembly that the move was inspired by the desire for African unity and had nothing to do with Cold War politics: "There is no other reason. Unity in our continent does not have to come via Moscow or Washington."

Under the interim constitution of the new country, which was to be called the United Republic of Tanganyika and Zanzibar, Nyerere was designated President, Karume First Vice-President and Rashidi Kawawa Second Vice-President. Karume was also named "President" of Zanzibar, although this title was later changed to "head of government". After naming a new Cabinet of twenty-two members, Nyerere held a press conference at which his answers were almost as choppy and defensive as the ones he had given during the week of the army mutiny three months earlier. Where would the new capital be? "Dar es Salaam." Would the Zanzibari forces be disbanded? "They will become part of one army." Would political prisoners be released? "They don't cease to be political prisoners because of the Union." Would confiscated property be returned to former owners? "Why?"

Inevitably, to Nyerere's anger and political embarrassment, the Union was widely interpreted as a triumph for the West. There has been endless speculation about the events that led to the merger, but Nyerere has always insisted that the simplest explanation was the accurate one. According to Nyerere, TANU and the Afro-Shirazi party had always worked closely together and had talked about unity; and one day in March that year, when Karume visited him in Dar es Salaam, Nyerere had said to him, "Look, I have made it clear to Prime Minister Kenyatta and to Prime Minister Obote that when they are ready for East African federation, we are ready. I am now saying to you, 'When you are ready for federation, we are ready.' "

"And," Nyerere continued, "he said, 'What do you mean, when we are ready? We are ready now!'

"This was in March. Union would have been in March. But in March we were holding a series of talks with the other East African countries, and there was just a possibility that we might have federation. So Zanzibar and Tanganyika waited." But on that day in March, Nyerere said, Karume had told him, " 'Call the press—tell them we are ready now.' " And Nyerere had said to him, " 'It must take time.'

"I think genuinely," Nyerere continued, "these are simple, honest leaders of the people. They mean what they say, these true leaders of the people. We had all been saying we wanted to unite, and here was one leader saying, 'We've always said we wanted it when we gained our independence, and now we have it, so let's go ahead.' "

Shortly after his conversation with Karume, and at least six weeks before the announcement of Union, Nyerere called in Roland Brown, his attorney general, and told him, "I want you to do some secret work for me." The Zanzibaris were interested in a union with Tanganyika, said Nyerere, and asked Brown to consider what kind of arrangement could be worked out.

Despite the early agreement between Nyerere and Karume, there is evidence of considerable vacillation on the part of the Zanzibaris. Kassim Hanga is said to have favoured the merger, while Babu opposed it, and Karume wavered. Babu's opposition was based, at least in part, on his precarious political position in Zanzibar. A half-caste himself, he held the personal allegiance of only a small number of Zanzibaris; but because of his intelligence and skill, he had made himself invaluable to the Karume government. He knew that TANU and the Afro-Shirazi party were closely aligned, and had no way of knowing what his role would be in a united government. According to one participant, Babu even brought in a lawyer from the mainland to strengthen his argument that, under a Union government, Zanzibar would be swallowed by Tanganyika. He is said to have left for Indonesia believing he had convinced Karume to hold off, at least for the time being.

Nyerere faced an ugly dilemma. As Oscar Kambona once described it to an American journalist, "Our first concern was the growing Communist presence and, second, the danger of the Cold War coming in. The Cold War was in the Congo already—it would have been a straight line across Africa. And there was another problem: he had to show he had his own reasons. The problem was how to isolate Zanzibar from the Eastern countries, yet not be used by the West for its own purposes." Nyerere has never defined the problem in exactly these terms, and might well take exception to Kambona's comment. There is no doubt, however, that his primary motive was to prevent Zanzibar—and Tanganyika—from being drawn into a Big Power confrontation. A friend has recalled that Nyerere said once in high fury, " 'China on the island, and the Americans saying I'm fighting Communism, and it's Vietnam in Africa—and I damned well won't have that.' "

He was deeply worried about the military build-up on the island

and the continuing violence, but he was in no position to intervene even if he had wanted to; his own army had been largely disbanded, and he was relying on the Nigerians for his own security. He was also concerned about the safety of the three hundred Tanganyikan policemen who were still on duty in Zanzibar. Some observers in Dar es Salaam have said that Nyerere was ready to remove the policemen, if there were to be no Union, because he didn't want their lives endangered in the event of renewed fighting; and that this prospect, which might well have changed the military balance on the island, is what convinced Karume that he should unite with Tanganyika immediately.

Karume's vacillation is said to have continued until the last moment. He even threatened to stay away from the Dar es Salaam ceremony at which the instruments of Union were to be exchanged, perhaps in anger because the TANU newspaper *The Nationalist* had published the Union announcement prematurely.

For a long time, Nyerere had sharply resented the way in which the British and American press characterized him as "moderate" and "pro-Western". In the post-Union period, when the Western press congratulated him for fighting Communism by seizing the island, Nyerere reacted with rage. Not only did he feel that such tributes had the effect of misinterpreting and perverting his motives; they could also have damaged, if not destroyed, the Union itself by embarrassing the Zanzibaris. It can be argued, of course, that the Zanzibaris were too simple and too preoccupied with their problems to pay much attention to what the overseas press was saying; but it is almost axiomatic in modern African affairs that the exploitable, sooner or later, is exploited by somebody. Nyerere was particularly vulnerable to such charges that year, moreover, because he had called on the British for military assistance. In Cairo at the African heads of state conference in July, Ghana's President Kwame Nkrumah declared that he could not understand why the training of African freedom fighters had been entrusted to an "imperialist agent"—an obvious reference to Tanganyika, where most guerilla training camps were located. Nyerere angrily replied that, when his country had gone through the "humiliation" of asking help from the former colonial power, "the ambassador of a brotherly African state celebrates and rejoices, and I am forced to request that he be removed". The Tanganyikan government had in fact asked the Ghanaian ambassador to leave for such reasons. Nyerere continued, "I am becoming increasingly convinced that we are divided between those who genuinely want continental government and patiently work for its development, and those who simply use the phrase 'Union government' for the purpose of propaganda. Some people are willing to use their great talent to wreck any chance of unity on our continent, as long as some stupid historian can record that they wanted unity at a time when nobody else did."

In June, *The Economist* had declared, in an article entitled "The Perils of Nyerere", that the President had "managed half the work of a python". It continued: "He swallowed Zanzibar all right but he did not crush its fighting force first. The live animal is a long time digesting, and its kicks are being felt hurtfully, and possibly even fatally, deep inside Tanganyika's body politic." Such criticism—an accurate reflection of serious continuing problems within the Union —led to a series of stinging articles in *The Nationalist* against Britain and the United States. One particularly virulent editorial asserted that "the British put their finger on the trigger to incite the [January] mutiny in order to give them sufficient reason to come back." Britain, it added, "wants to manipulate President Nyerere as if he were a marionette." Soon after that, the National Assembly in Dar es Salaam passed a resolution "deprecating the hostility of the British and American press toward the United Republic". The government, said Rashidi Kawawa, "sadly supported" the resolution.

When asked, two years later, if the anti-Western propaganda campaign had not in fact been a brilliant smoke screen for obscuring whatever pressure Nyerere was trying to apply to Zanzibar that year, a mainland official replied, "It was not a smoke screen. Call it brilliant, if you like, but not a smoke screen. It was an act of insulation."

In August the government invited suggestions for a new name for the United Republic "which gives a sense of unitedness and should be easy to pronounce. The prize for the accepted proposal will be ten pounds." Two months later, Nyerere announced the winning title: United Republic of Tanzania. The contest attracted 1,534 entries from more than forty countries. The favourite names suggested, besides Tanzania, were Tanzan and Tangibar. Five days passed before the government, amid general uncertainty, made its brief further announcement: the correct pronunciation was Tan-za-*ni*-a.

The mainland Tanzanians were distressed to find that Zanzibar changed very little following its union with Tanganyika. Abeid Karume, driving around the island in a black Austin Princess, was still referred to as "the President"; the United Republic was practically never mentioned. Special visas were still required for travellers from Dar es Salaam, as they had been since the revolution, and there were a few incidents in which Tanganyikan government officials were refused entry to the island. The Zanzibaris continued to conduct their revolution in their own curious way. In June they nationalized the Zanzibar Electricity Board, as Liberation Army troops surrounded the offices and power station. Yet, as it happened, the Board was already a quasi-governmental organization controlled by a board of six men who, since January, had been appointed by Karume.

All that year, the Union was rumoured endlessly to be on the verge of collapse. At one point Nyerere was said to have asked the Nigerians to send in a detachment of troops that would serve as a counter-force to the Zanzibar Liberation Army; but Nyerere has insisted that no such request was ever made. The three hundred Tanganyikan policemen, however, were re-equipped with sub-machine guns.

The problem was complicated by the Zanzibaris' foreign friends, who were reluctant to sacrifice the diplomatic position they had achieved there. The Tanzanian government requested that all embassies on the island be reduced to consular status from June 30, but the East Germans failed to remove their embassy for almost a year. The Chinese continued to send military aid directly to Zanzibar, but they announced that they were extending a £10-million interest-free loan to mainland Tanzania, as well as a £5-million loan to Zanzibar.

Early in 1972, eight years after the Union, Zanzibar was only partly integrated with Tanganyika. Under the revised interim constitution of 1965, the Union government controlled foreign affairs, defence, citizenship, external trade, customs, harbours, civil aviation, posts and telegraphs. The police force was unified but the two branches of the army, now known as the Tanzanian People's Defence Force, were not. The Revolutionary Council still ruled by decree; there was no independent judiciary or legislature in Zanzibar, and visitors from the mainland still went through immigration formalities at the Zanzibar airport. TANU and the Afro-Shirazi party had not yet merged. The Zanzibaris voted in the Union's presidential elections of 1965 and 1970, in which Nyerere was re-elected unopposed, but there had been no parliamentary or local elections on the island since the revolution. When interviewed in 1968 by the Tanzania *Standard*, Karume said he didn't expect free elections on Zanzibar for fifty years. "Elections are a tool of the imperialists to sabotage the people," he said, referring yet again to the pre-independence elections in which the Afro-Shirazis won the popular vote but failed to win a parliamentary majority. In July 1970, Nyerere was obliged to use the same sort of reasoning in explaining to his Parliament why the Zanzibaris would not be taking part in parliamentary elections that year; the islanders were still afraid that attempts might be made to subvert the revolutionary regime, he said, and return the masses to minority control. But he said he hoped that talks on a new and permanent constitution would be held during the life of the new Parliament, which will sit until 1975.

From the beginning Nyerere has handled the Zanzibaris with the utmost permissiveness. "The Zanzibaris are a proud people," he said in 1965. "No one has ever intended that they should become simply the Republic's eighteenth region." On the contrary, the Zanzibaris have been considerably better represented in the Union government than they deserved. Zanzibar's population is 350,000, out of the United Republic's 13,000,000; Zanzibar is smaller, in fact, than any of the mainland's seventeen regions. Yet from 1967, for example, seven of Nyerere's 22 Cabinet members were Zanzibaris, as were 40 of the 183 members of the Tanzanian Parliament. Unlike his colleagues from the mainland, no Zanzibari had been elected to Parliament; he held his seat by virtue of his membership in the Revolutionary Council or his post in the Zanzibar government. Nyerere has worked consistently to convince the Zanzibaris that they were benefiting from the Union. His reasoning, presumably, has been that no matter how slow and painful it might be to achieve complete integration, it was better to have the Zanzibaris in the Union than outside it.

Such influence as Nyerere has had among the islanders has been based largely on his considerable powers of persuasion. When Karume's old enemy Othman Shariff came home in 1965 after serving as Tanzania's ambassador to Washington, the Zanzibar government charged him with "pre-revolutionary crimes" and locked him up. Nyerere is believed to have arranged for his release to the mainland, where Othman was given a job as a government veterinarian in Mbeya; there he remained for four years before becoming involved in further intrigue. In 1968 the Dar es Salaam government was reported to be discussing retirement terms with the members of the Zanzibar Revolutionary Council—an almost certain prerequisite to free elections and reform—but apparently no agreement was reached, and since that time the Council has remained in power.

In countless matters, the Zanzibaris have continued to go their own lawless way, to the consternation of the mainland authorities. "Zanzibar is our cross," one Tanzanian official has been heard to grumble from time to time. In 1966 the Zanzibaris published a law making it illegal for parents to withhold consent for their daughters' marriage. Karume had advocated such laws as a way of overcoming racial differences, but the Arabs and Indians recognized it instantly, and rightly, as an attempt to make their daughters more easily available to powerful African politicians. The Anglican bishop, the Right Reverend Niall Russell, spoke out against the new law, and was promptly expelled from the island.

The controversy was revived in 1970. After four young Persian girls refused to marry the sixty-five-year-old Karume, he ordered the arrest of ten of their male relatives for "hindering the implementation of mixed marriages". He swore he would deport the men, then that he would expel all of the hundred-odd members of the Persian Ithnasheri sect to which the girls and their relatives belonged. And then, after a quiet talk with Nyerere, Karome dropped the charges. A few months later, four Persian girls—apparently different ones— were forced to marry members of the Revolutionary Council, with a fifth member of the council performing the ceremony. Eleven of their male relatives were ordered jailed and flogged by a "people's court" judge who accused them of "sowing the seeds of racism". Mainland women's groups protested angrily, and the *East African Standard* of Nairobi denounced the case as "an appalling throwback to the time of slavery".

One young mainland official tried to explain the situation to a foreign friend: "You must understand it in terms of Zanzibar. Look, Zanzibar was a place of slavery, a symbol of slavery in all Africa. In all that time, if a rich Arab liked an African girl, he took her, that's all. And marriages were arranged by parents, always. But only within each community.

"Now, since the revolution, freedom to the Zanzibaris means the reverse. When an African says to an Arab—or an Indian—'I like your daughter,' the Arab says, 'Oh, no.' The African says, 'Why not?' The Arab says, 'Well, let's ask her.' The African says, 'What do you mean? It never worked that way before. Why won't she marry me? I'm not a criminal.' "

The mainlander concluded, "You can say to them, 'This is ridiculous, this isn't what freedom means.' But they don't see it that way."

The incident strained relations between Dar es Salaam and the island, and greatly embarrassed Nyerere. His friends were also upset about the damage it caused his moral position in arguing about such African problems as the continuation of the trade embargo on Rhodesia and the British government's plan to resume arms sales to South Africa. "How can we talk about human rights," said one, "when this is going on?"

In August 1969, the Zanzibar authorities accused fourteen men of plotting to overthrow the Karume government. Among these fourteen were Kassim Hanga, Othman Shariff and two others who were arrested on the mainland and turned over to the Zanzibar government by Tanzanian authorities. Weeks passed. Finally, in November, Karume announced that, following a secret trial, four of the alleged plotters had been executed, nine remained in prison and one had been acquitted. In a gesture that was both slovenly and cruel, he failed to specify which four had been executed. Three years later, the deaths of Hanga and Shariff had not yet been confirmed, but, as a European who knew both men put it, "I haven't talked to anybody who believes they are alive."

Karume's announcement meant that Nyerere had unwittingly condemned as many as four men to death without a proper trial by surrendering them to the Zanzibar authorities. When asked why he had agreed to let them go, he said later, "For cross-examination. I wanted to be satisfied that there was a case. How could I say to Karume, 'Since you think you have a case, you come to the mainland to talk to them'?" Nyerere's decision was made at a time when petty plotting was harassing the government in Dar es Salaam as well as Zanzibar, and he apparently believed the plotting was all part of the same conspiracy, as it may well have been. His decision to surrender Hanga and Shariff was a serious mistake nonetheless.

Unwilling and perhaps unable to settle such Zanzibar problems by force, Nyerere seems to have developed a fatalistic attitude about the Union's ultimate chances of success. "I believe in African unity," he said in late 1969. "But the damned boundaries are not sacred. They were created by the imperialists. The people of Africa are more sacred than those boundaries. I have two bits of a union. Even if the Zanzibaris were not rejected by Tanganyika, if they simply felt the

Union was of no use to them, and broke away, and this was the genuine feeling of the Zanzibaris, I could not possibly kill Zanzibaris. If they came in freely, they can leave freely. We did not conquer Zanzibar. And if they remain, this must be of their own free choice.

"This is the only basis on which to build a nation. An empire you keep down by enlarging the army. A nation you keep together by strengthening the internal will to unity."

In the years since he was declared an unwanted person in Zanzibar, John Okello has been imprisoned again and again, mostly on immigration charges. In October 1964 he spent ten days in jail in Mwanza, Tanzania, before being deported to Kenya and taken to the Uganda border. Later that year he wandered back to Kenya and was jailed for eighteen months for entering the country illegally. Shortly after his release he returned to Uganda, where, for undisclosed reasons, he was held in preventive detention from July 1967 until September 1968.

In February 1969 he was jailed once more for entering Kenya illegally. The magistrate at Kakamega found Okello guilty of spreading "prohibited publications", and sentenced him to three years in prison. Okello's reputation as a person of magical powers and an exporter of revolutions had preceded him, and the village magistrate was taking no chances. On appeal to the Kisumu High Court, Okello's sentence was reduced to one year. On February 16, 1970, he was released and was flown to Uganda by police aircraft.

In February 1964, a month after the revolution, Sultan Jamshid moved from London to Southsea, near Portsmouth, with his wife, children, and twenty-five other relatives and aides. Two years later, he was visited in his three-storey brick house in Victoria Grove by an American journalist. He seemed surprisingly contented, a shy and amiable young man who was making the best of his new life. A Renault sports car stood in front of his door. He watched television, he said, went sometimes to the pictures, and visited his mother down the street. That summer, he said, he had made a three-month trip to Saudi Arabia and Aden to "see my people", the ones who had fled Zanzibar. He expressed in hardly more than a whisper the ancient hatred of the Arab islanders for the black mainlanders: "They call it revolution, but we say invasion." He had received many reports of life in Zanzibar. "It is not a real union," he said. "The Communists are in control." Recently, he said, he had been visited by some

Africans from Kenya who told him that, on a trip to Zanzibar, they had been followed by security men. "I like them to be honest with me," he said. But that was not exactly true. Like political exiles in every age—"I know," the playwright Aeschylus wrote, "how men in exile feed on dreams"—he doted on scraps of hopeful news from home.

Abeid Karume survived for more than eight years as the phlegmatic but oppressive dictator of Zanzibar. In his last years, thanks to a sharp rise in the price of cloves, he managed to accumulate £30 million in foreign exchange reserves which, to Nyerere's embarrassment, he carefully kept out of the hands of the Tanzanian government. He was as erratic and unpredictable as ever; he suspended a malaria-control programme on the grounds that Africans were "malaria-proof," and he "abolished" the island's prisons and released hundreds of inmates.

One evening in April 1972, as Karume was playing cards with his cronies in the white-walled, Arab-style headquarters of the Afro-Shirazi Party, four gunmen burst into the room and shot him four or five times, apparently killing him instantly. One of the assassins was shot dead on the spot by Karume's bodyguard; two were killed later in a battle with security forces; and the fourth, according to Radio Zanzibar, committed suicide. Three of the assassins were said to have been former Umma Party supporters. But one, a young army lieutenant named Humud Mohammed Humud, had a personal motive as well; when Karume threw open the prison gates, Humud had learned that his father, who himself had been a convicted assassin, had been tortured and executed while serving an open-ended sentence.

X

SOON AFTER TANGANYIKA'S UNION with Zanzibar, Nyerere began to feel the pressure of Western powers that he bring an end to the prevailing chaos on the island and reduce the size of the Chinese and East German presence there. He bridled against such advice, partly because he resented the persistent interest in his country's internal affairs, and partly because he was in no position to enforce his will upon the Zanzibaris. In August 1964, when he let it be known that he was going to accept seven Chinese instructors and four interpreters for his army for six months, a Western diplomat asked him if he realized the risk he was taking. "The maximum risk is that the army will revolt," Nyerere snapped. "My army revolted in January. It was not trained by the Chinese." Expanding on the theme at a press conference, he demanded, "Are the Zanzibaris supposed to sit down like a pack of damn fools and do nothing? They accepted military aid from Russia and China. They had no choice." As for his own army, he said, he had asked several non-aligned countries for instructors and they had turned him down. "What am I supposed to do? The Chinese offer is the nearest thing to what I wanted. What is this Chinese problem?

"This simple request is a little attempt to show that we are non-aligned. But when it comes to actual facts, this country is completely Western, in government, in business, in schools, in everything. The influence of this country is Western. The fact that I, as President, have to explain why I am accepting Chinese aid is itself a big humiliation. This is my explanation and my protest." There were other examples of what the Tanzanians regarded as overbearing pressure, and they continued to react sharply if not always publicly. A few months later, when they were casting around for Western assistance in building a rail line to Zambia, a Western ambassador told Nyerere, "I think you'll find that the railroad to Zambia passes through Zanzibar." The remark sounded to Nyerere like a scarcely veiled threat that he could expect no Western help for the railroad as long as the Communists exerted so much influence on the island.

The first diplomatic dilemma posed by the Union was the problem of what to do about relations with the two Germanys. Since

5*

independence, Tanganyika had had extremely cordial relations with West Germany and was counting on Bonn to make a sizeable contribution to the new five-year plan that was to be announced in May. In fact, Tanganyika, which constituted most of what had once been German East Africa, had enjoyed a sort of foster child's relationship with the West Germans. On the other hand, East Germany had rushed into Zanzibar after the revolution and established an embassy, its first in Africa. To protect their diplomatic foothold, the East Germans began to build the Zanzibaris a radio transmitter and sent a freighter laden with clothing and other goods; they also promised to rebuild an entire township in the Ngambo district of Zanzibar Town. Karume assured the East Germans that the islanders would allow nothing to spoil their newly found friendship.

Faced with such a curious problem, the Tanzanians expected the West Germans to approve of the Union and to agree to some sort of compromise, such as the presence of an East German consulate in Zanzibar. The United Republic would refrain from recognizing East Germany, the Tanzanians promised, and the net result would be that East Germany would lose its only embassy in Africa. Instead the Bonn government of Chancellor Ludwig Erhard insisted adamantly that such an arrangement would violate the terms of West Germany's Hallstein Doctrine, under which Bonn refused to have diplomatic relations with any nation except the Soviet Union that had relations with East Germany. The matter remained in stalemate until February 1965, when the Tanzanian government announced its decision: while withholding formal recognition, the United Republic would permit the East Germans to open a consulate general in Dar es Salaam in compensation for the closing of their embassy in Zanzibar.

The West German government retaliated with astonishing swiftness. It cancelled a military aid programme to Tanzania, which had included £4 million in capital aid to be used for the purchase of military aircraft, and withdrew its air and naval training teams virtually overnight. Bonn also announced that the West German Cabinet would, at its next meeting, consider "further moves to put pressure on Tanzania". The West German response represented precisely the sort of clumsy diplomatic bullying of a weak nation by a powerful one that Nyerere most deeply resents. He asked the West Germans to cancel all remaining aid immediately, including £3 million in technical aid that had also been promised. "A hungry dog will accept food in any way you give it to him," he said, "even if you throw it at him. It is different with a human being. You have to be careful with the way you give food to a hungry man. He has his dignity to preserve." He later remarked that some people had "expected the union of Tanganyika and Zanzibar to solve the problem of German reunification, but it did not."

During this troubled period, when the mainland Tanzanians were trying to bring peace and order to Zanzibar and were contending with a wider range of diplomatic problems than they had ever faced before, three incidents occurred that severely damaged Tanzania's relations with the United States. In November 1964, Oscar Kambona returned unexpectedly to Dar es Salaam from a vacation in Arusha, in the northern highlands, and called a press conference to announce that the government had "concrete evidence" that "certain Western powers", specifically the United States in league with Portugal, were preparing to attack Tanzania. Seemingly enjoying his role as the Tanzanian Paul Revere, Kambona cabled the Organization for African Unity at Addis Ababa: HAVE HONOUR TO INFORM YOU THAT THE UNITED REPUBLIC HAS GATHERED SUFFICIENT DOCUMENTARY AND FACTUAL EVIDENCE TO REVEAL THE EXISTENCE OF A PLOT BY CERTAIN WESTERN POWERS TO OVERTHROW THE TANZANIAN GOVERNMENT AND SUBVERT THE NATIONALIST AND LIBERATION MOVEMENTS. Two days later he told a crowd of seven thousand angry Tanzanians at Moshi, "We liked the Americans because they knew how sweet freedom is, and because they pressed the British to give us our freedom. Why are they now trying to undermine our government?"

While anti-Americanism raged across Tanzania, the United States embassy in Dar es Salaam waited for almost a week to see the "documentary evidence", which, as it turned out, consisted of three photostats. All three, written in careless French, were reputed to be Western diplomatic messages. One document referred to "special arrangements to overthrow the government of Mr Julius Nyerere to one still being studied by the Department of State". Another said that the United States sought to obtain "assurances from Great Britain that she will not intervene". The third, reputedly addressed to an ambassador, asked for £9,000 for recruiting South Africans for a "putsch". An American diplomat said at the time, "It will be no problem demonstrating that the documents are forgeries. The real question is whether the evidence presented will be accepted."

Nyerere had been spending the week at Lake Manyara in northern Tanzania. He was said to have received the documents from his old friend Andrew Tibandebage, who was Tanzania's ambassador to the Congo, and to have given them to Kambona saying, "Deal with this." When Nyerere returned to Dar es Salaam a few days later, Westerners hoped he would make a statement that the documents were false. Instead, at an afternoon rally of about twenty thousand people at the Jangwani playing fields, Nyerere gave a long, emotional speech about world power problems in which he referred again and again to the possibility of a mistake. "It may not be true in this case," he said. If the documents were not genuine, "I would be the first to thank God." The Americans had denied the documents' authenticity, he said, and would be given a chance to prove their claim.

Western diplomats were disappointed that Nyerere had not been more explicit, but tended to place most of the blame on Kambona, who had blandly told them that such public disclosure of unproved allegations represented "the African way of dealing with problems". Some even believed Kambona had used the incident to damage the position of the United States in Tanzania and to embarrass Nyerere in his relations with the Western countries.

Both Kambona and Nyerere insisted in later years, however, that Kambona was not responsible. "I was only the announcer," Kambona has said. "He called me from Lake Manyara, and asked me to make them public. Whether they were true or not, we thought this was the best defence against them." Nyerere has essentially agreed. "It's unfair to blame Oscar for that," he has said. "If I hadn't wanted that announced, I wouldn't have given it to him." Yes, of course, Nyerere said, he himself might have used different words or different methods, but basically the responsibility was his.

The documents case was still fresh in the minds of Tanzanians when, later that November the second incident occurred: Belgian paratroopers borne by United States Air Force planes dropped on Stanleyville, in the Congo, to save the lives of a thousand whites who were being held hostage by the Congolese rebels. The airdrop took place while negotiations for the hostages' release were being held in Nairobi between William Attwood, the American ambassador to Kenya, and Thomas Kanza, the "foreign minister" of the rebel movement that had captured much of the eastern Congo. Of all the statements of protest from African heads of state, none was angrier than Nyerere's: "In an action reminiscent of Pearl Harbour, foreign troops were flown into the Congo at the very moment that negotiations were taking place to secure the safety of all." Oscar Kambona added that the airdrop was "the meanest, most unwarranted and provocative interference by the Western world in the affairs and peace of the African continent."

Westerners in general were astonished at the extent of the African reaction against an operation that may well have saved several hundred hostages' lives, and were irritated that the African leaders said little or nothing about the rebels' murder of fifty hostages, including Dr Paul Carlson, an American missionary.

The key to the reaction against the airlift lies in the Africans' consciousness of their vulnerability. Nyerere had distrusted Moise Tshombe ever since Tshombe led the Katanga secession and at one point had actually suggested to Nyerere the possibility of merging Katanga with Tanganyika. In the years of Congolese fighting, Tshombe had become a symbol of the African who used white support and white mercenaries to kill his brothers and destroy his own country: the black man who hires whites to murder blacks. In Tanganyika during those years, there was no uglier epithet than to call a man a "Tshombe". Nyerere regarded Tshombe's return to Leopoldville as Premier in 1964 as a betrayal of Africa. "There are three dead men who, if they should come to life today, would ask, '*What* is happening?' They are President Kennedy, Dag Hammarskjöld and Patrice Lumumba." He also believed apparently that the paratroop landing in Stanleyville was aimed not just at rescuing hostages but at ending the Congo rebellion and thus helping the Tshombe regime. It is true that Nyerere and other Africans overreacted to the news of the airdrop; it is also true, however, that, in failing to exert greater pressure against Tshombe's accession to power in Leopoldville, the Western powers failed to understand the depth of the African leaders' hatred of him. When asked why Nyerere had reacted so violently to what was, after all, a humanitarian mission to save lives, a European friend of Nyerere's replied, " 'You'll do all that for a thousand white skins!' That's what the Africans would say. 'And you don't do anything at all about the millions of Africans in South Africa and Rhodesia.' That's the African reaction. Nyerere is not a racialist, but he's a fanatical African."

Nyerere himself tried to explain it to an American visitor in 1966. "One of the best things that could happen to Africa would be for the United States to understand her. This should not be difficult. The

United States fought its own revolution in 1776, defining in language that can never be bettered why an otherwise peaceful, sensible people would take up arms and fight. Of the countries born of revolution, the greatest is the United States. Today you have an ethic based on freedom. You judge society by that ethic. You find Alabama intolerable because of your own ethic. I find it very natural that during World War II, Roosevelt should have said to Churchill, 'How can we fight for freedom elsewhere in the world, and yet you stop the Indians from governing themselves?' One accepts that an American would ask, 'How can we justify preserving an empire while we are fighting for freedom elsewhere?' But then something went wrong.

"I think the United States is schizophrenic in this matter. It says, 'You must back up the United States in the anti-Communist struggle.' In some corner of its mind, it accepts that Africans have a right to independence. You relegate Africa's case to some corner; it does not matter very much. If there is a conflict, you back up your allies and not freedom.

"All right. The Congo becomes independent; trouble takes place; there is danger of the Congo getting dismembered. No Communists were involved. What started it off was the mutiny, so the natural effort was to stop the disintegration. On the whole, I think, Kennedy avoided letting it become a Cold War issue; he wanted to work through the UN to help Lumumba and the central government.

"All right, then there was a puppet regime, with Cyrille Adoula as Premier. But we didn't quarrel. But eventually the Katanga man was back and Adoula was kicked out! I know the United States is not as old in this game as the Europeans, but still: their man was pushed out. I don't believe the United States was responsible for bringing Tshombe back—but there he was! The very fellows who had been fighting the UN force bring back this fellow—and the United States embraces him!

"All right, the United States—a very honourable man—says, 'We joined in the [Stanleyville] operation to rescue the missionaries,' and then the United States is extremely surprised at our reaction! When Africa almost unanimously condemned this! Now I ask, 'Why is the United States surprised? Why this failure to understand?' Killing had been going on in the Congo; why did this particular threat of killing disturb them? Mercenaries had been recruited who *enjoyed the killing of Africans*—why doesn't this worry the United States?

"Out of its own ethic, the United States should have been our ally in all this: in stopping the mercenaries, these haters of the human race, who enjoyed killing. Why pick *this*? And then turn it around and say that we want the missionaries to be exterminated, to be eaten up!

"I've said before, in trying to explain this, try to imagine a Jew who recruits ex-Nazis to go to Israel and assist him in his power struggle. How would the Jews take it? Then suppose he has a powerful ally. And if the Jews react against this man, would his ally be surprised when the Jews react that way?

"The best thing that can happen for us in Africa would be for the United States, this power with a good ethic, to understand us. Our continent is a continent we don't control, and we feel strongly about this."

The third incident impairing relations between the United States and Tanzania was the most serious. In January 1965 Nyerere called in the American ambassador, William Leonhart, and told him he believed that two of Leonhart's men were engaged in subversive activities, and were therefore being expelled within twenty-four hours. The two were Robert Gordon, who had been counsellor of the embassy in Dar es Salaam for about six months, and Frank Carlucci, the chargé d'affaires in Zanzibar, who had seemed to be performing admirably under difficult circumstances. Nyerere is said to have assured Leonhart, moreover, that he understood that neither the ambassador nor his embassy was involved in these activities.

The implication seemed to be that the two men were Central Intelligence Agency employees who were plotting to overthrow the regime in Zanzibar—a plot which the State Department didn't know about but which, when completed, it would approve of. At a subsequent meeting with American diplomats, a member of Nyerere's staff asked, "What about the ammunition they were getting?" The embassy concluded that the source of the accusation lay in the twice-daily telephone conversations that Gordon and Carlucci conducted between Dar es Salaam and Zanzibar. It was also assumed that the conversations had been tape-recorded regularly by intelligence services on one or both sides of the Zanzibar Channel.

The United States government retaliated by expelling the counsellor of the two-man Tanzanian embassy in Washington, and by calling Leonhart home for consultations. Tanzania, in consequence, recalled its ambassador, Othman Shariff, and relations remained strained for many months. The Tanzanians were surprised and angered at Washington's action and pointed out that Nyerere—in a curious gesture perhaps intended to help the United States save face—had written to President Johnson that the dispute was between Tanzania and "two American individuals . . . who happened to be servants of the American government". Nyerere refused to produce evidence to support the charge against the diplomats and replied: "We are a small country, but we are as much a sovereign state as the United States. . . . We do not bully, and we do not like being bullied."

What had actually happened, apparently, was a minor classic of American bureaucracy in action. Carlucci, who had been anxious to give First Vice-President Karume a favourable impression of the United States, had told the ambassador a few days earlier that he would like to have President Johnson send a message of greetings to Karume on January 12, the first anniversary of the Zanzibar revolution. But which day was Tanzania's national day? Was it Independence Day, December 9; or Saba Saba, July 7; or Revolution Day, January 12; or Union Day, April 26? Leonhart reasoned that the proper national day was December 9, and that the message of greetings should be sent from President to President, Lyndon Johnson to Julius Nyerere. Carlucci persisted: Then how about a message from Vice-President Humphrey to Vice-President Karume? Again Leonhart said no. But he later added that if he was wrong, and other nations sent congratulations, the United States would have another chance on the "second twelfth". This meant February 12, which was being celebrated that year as the anniversary of the revolution because January 12 fell during Ramadan. He also said he didn't think anybody "higher than Williams" (Assistant Secretary of State for African Affairs G. Mennen Williams) should sign the message.

A day or two later, Carlucci complained to Gordon on the telephone that he wasn't satisfied with what Leonhart had told him. Gordon replied, "Why don't you go direct? The boss doesn't want any part of it"—meaning: Ask Washington yourself if you want to, but the ambassador doesn't want to get involved. In inveterate bureaucratese, one of the men even used the phrase "Operation Second Twelfth" and the words "enough ammunition"—meaning the information necessary for making a case to Washington.

Not surprisingly, the Tanzanian intelligence agents who listened to the conversation failed to comprehend the American jargon. Or

perhaps it was the Zanzibari intelligence agents who misunderstood.
Or perhaps someone heard the conversation and understood full
well its potential for exploitation. In any case, the incident occurred
at a time when the level of hysteria was very high. The government
was worried about the situation on Zanzibar and about Western
reaction to what was happening there. It was also preoccupied
with security precautions after the events of the preceding year;
visitors noticed copies of *The Invisible Government*, a book about
the workings of the CIA, in the offices of several Tanzanian
ministers.

Nyerere's friends and colleagues gained the impression that
Nyerere genuinely believed the diplomats were plotting, or at least
believed it plausible that American agents might be resorting to such
methods to overthrow the regime on Zanzibar. "But whether the
President understood or not is irrelevant," one Tanzanian has said.
"The Zanzibaris did not understand."

In subsequent years, the Vietnam war became an important source
of friction. "The United States must recover from the delirium of
power," Nyerere told a party conference in 1967, although he
characteristically matched his criticism of US policy with a tribute
to Americans who opposed the war. Not all Tanzanians were so
gracious. For several years the TANU-sponsored daily newspaper,
The Nationalist, had maintained a stridently anti-American line that
probably caused more damage to their relations with the United
States than the Tanzanians realized. One casualty of the ill feeling
was the Peace Corps. In 1961 Tanganyika had been the first African
country to ask for volunteers, and by 1966 the number of Peace
Corpsmen in Tanzania had reached five hundred and eight. But the
Corps was criticized steadily by *The Nationalist*; Nyerere himself
said in 1967 that the idealism of the Corps had waned and that the
organization had been infiltrated by "people whose motives are no
good." In late 1969 the last volunteer went home.

In the early years of its independence, Tanganyika probably inspired and impressed more young visitors from America and
Western Europe than any other African country. A Ugandan political
scientist, Ali Mazrui, published an article in the East African magazine *Transition* in 1967 in which he described a contagious social
phenomenon he called "Tanzaphilia." He defined it as "the romantic
spell which Tanzania casts on so many of those who have been
closely associated with her," adding: "Many of the most prosaic

Western pragmatists have been known to acquire that dreamy look under the spell of Tanzania." Particularly susceptible, he wrote, were Western liberals who saw in Tanzania—largely because of Nyerere's personality and ideas—a place where they could achieve the political goals on which they had failed at home. Tanzania still has a cult of overseas admirers, but the group's size has been reduced by the ill feeling and misunderstanding of the last several years.

Americans who live in Tanzania find the antagonism and suspicion difficult to accept. But, as one Tanzanian commented in late 1967, "We are intimidated by the power of the United States—the idea that the United States could move in on us any time it wanted to, and there would be nothing we could do. There was Stanleyville, and there is Vietnam. There is also Tanzania's growing relationship with China, and the realization that the powerful United States doesn't like this and might do something about it. But most of all it is a continuation of 1964 [the army mutiny and subsequent events], when we felt so helpless."

Relations between the United States and Tanzania have gradually improved since 1965, but have never returned to their pre-1964 warmth. High officials of both the Johnson and Nixon Administrations have tended to visit only those African countries where their reception was most likely to be friendly, and they rarely stop in Tanzania any more. Nyerere paid a state visit to Canada in 1969 but was not invited to make a stop-over in Washington. He visited the United Nations in October 1970 but did not meet Richard Nixon.

Nyerere's most serious dispute with the West occurred in December, 1965. At that time, he broke off diplomatic relations with Britain after the British government failed to take effective action to end the unilateral declaration of independence by the white-minority government in Rhodesia. The dispute had really begun at a Commonwealth Prime Ministers' Conference held in London in June of that year. At the meeting, Nyerere dissociated Tanzania from the portions of the final communiqué that dealt with Rhodesia and with Vietnam. "We tried for a long time," Nyerere said, "to get an assurance from the British government that whatever negotiations they were carrying out were aimed at the achievement of independence in Rhodesia on the basis of majority rule. We were unable to receive this assurance." He also took exception to Harold Wilson's proposal that the Commonwealth send a peace mission on Vietnam to Washington, Saigon, Moscow, Hanoi, and Peking. "I am merely suggesting," Nyerere said, "that the Commonwealth as such should not appear to be backing Mr Wilson or the United States on this issue. . . . For all I know, China might say it would receive the mission. But I am saying that it is not for us to take action which, going by past performance, appears to be one-sided, and is putting China in the dock." Wilson managed to isolate Nyerere completely; no other member supported his position on either issue.

Nyerere told a friend at the time of the debate, "It's terrible. It makes me seem arrogant. As I started speaking, I knew people in the conference would say, 'Nyerere is taking the position because he wants to establish himself as a radical leader—or because of commitments to China.' I could almost *hear* them thinking this."

As early as September 1965, Nyerere threatened to withdraw from the Commonwealth if Britain should negotiate independence with the Rhodesian government headed by Prime Minister Ian Smith. Like many other African leaders, he feared that an independent Rhodesia would inevitably align itself with South Africa and the Portuguese territories of Angola and Mozambique; and he felt that Rhodesia's whites, who numbered less than a quarter of a million, should not be allowed to perpetuate their hold over the colony's four million black Africans. At the OAU heads of state conference at Accra in October, in what turned out to be the twilight of Kwame Nkrumah's power, the organization passed a unanimous resolution in which its members urged Britain to suspend Rhodesia's constitution, using force if necessary, and threatened to break off diplomatic relations with Britain if the British allowed the Rhodesian minority regime to declare independence.

The Rhodesian declaration came on November 11. At first Nyerere counselled caution; Britain, he said, should be given a chance to solve the problem in its own way. On December 3rd, the Foreign and Defence Ministers of the OAU nations met in Addis Ababa and voted that member nations would break off diplomatic relations with Britain on December 15th unless the British crushed the Rhodesian rebellion by that date. Friends have said that Nyerere thought the ultimatum was stupid but concluded, "If we don't do it, nobody will ever take Africa's word again, and, worse, *we* won't believe in our word either."

Surely knowing that nothing would happen to settle the Rhodesian crisis within ten days, Nyerere began immediately to prepare his people for the break in relations on December 15. "My decision could mean hardship," he told a rally at TANU headquarters. "Are you ready to accept it?" Besides the loss of existing British aid, it meant the cancellation of a £7.5-million loan agreement that was ready to be signed. He also began to reassure British citizens in Tanzania, and warned his people that violence against British residents would not be tolerated. "No British subject need have any fear for his personal safety either from the institutions of the government or from the people of the United Republic." When a group of students set fire to the British high commissioner's car, Nyerere ordered them to go back and apologize.

In the days before the December 15 deadline, support lagged among other OAU members, and Nyerere noted that the decision at Accra had been unanimous. "But now," he said, "some African leaders have gone back to their capitals and started to look at their bank balances. This is ridiculous!" When the British complained that the rebellion could not possibly be settled before the deadline imposed by the resolution, Nyerere replied, on December 12th, that what was needed was "clear evidence of Britain's intention to take strong action". The African demand, he pointed out, was for independence "on the basis of majority rule". On December 14, Nyerere delivered his "Honour of Africa" address to the National Assembly, explaining why Tanzania would stick to its OAU commitment. The speech was delivered in English because there wasn't time to translate it into polished Swahili. At midnight, Tanzania broke relations with Britain. Eight other African countries followed suit: Guinea, Ghana, Mali, Egypt, Mauritania, Congo Brazzaville, Sudan and Algeria. Twenty-six did not.

Oscar Kambona and Labour Minister Michael Kamaliza led demonstrations in Dar es Salaam in support of the decision. Publicly Nyerere said, "If Mr Wilson has some ambition to be the British Prime Minister who broke the Commonwealth, I can regret it, but I cannot stop him from fulfilling his ambition." And what if Britain should take measures following the deadline? "I will be very pleased if I prove tomorrow to be the greatest fool that Africa has produced." Privately he was dejected by the lack of support and also by the break itself. "They were my friends," he said of the British. Tanzania and Britain did not resume diplomatic relations until almost thirty-one months had passed.

Almost simultaneous with the diplomatic break was the beginning of co-operation between Tanzania and Britain in airlifting emergency supplies of oil to Zambia, the former British territory of Northern Rhodesia, which had gained its independence in 1964. The British government had imposed an embargo on oil shipped by its nationals to Rhodesia; the Salisbury regime responded by cutting off the flow of Zambia's oil, which had traditionally passed through Rhodesia from the Mozambican port of Beira. Later the airlift was replaced by a road haulage operation between Dar es Salaam and Zambia, and eventually by a 1,000-mile pipeline.

Nyerere agreed in December 1965 to let the Royal Air Force use Tanzanian airfields temporarily, but asked that the British switch to civilian planes as soon as they could. Shortly after that, the British navy sent a frigate laden with oil drums from Aden to Dar es Salaam without securing the permission of the Tanzanian government. Nyerere then asked that no warships be brought to Dar es Salaam. The bluff skipper of the frigate made the correct gesture: he invited the President for lunch. Later, when he was asked by the local press if he had expected the President to accept, he replied, "Why not? Breaking diplomatic relations is no excuse for being rude." Nyerere, who has often shown a great fondness for British character and eccentricity, is said to have laughed heartily at the story.

The diplomatic community in Dar es Salaam tended to respect Nyerere's decision to break relations but viewed it as excessively rigid. "When he has made up his mind," said one Western diplomat, "he sticks to it. It made no sense to break with Britain. It tended to defeat the very thing he was trying to bring about."

Nyerere, however, apparently never regretted the decision. "No," he said a few months later, "we couldn't have lived with ourselves otherwise. We went to Accra, we heads of state. I was there. I could have dissociated myself, I could have said, 'This is absurd.' But I thought it was reasonable, and the matter serious. A few months later, there was a follow-up. I sent my Second Vice-President. They considered what steps might be taken, and they settled on the matter of diplomatic relations. This was something all were capable of. We can't march armies to Rhodesia—we don't *have* the blessed armies. But we could make a strong expression of Africa's feelings on the question of racialism. Fine!

"In private relationships, there are some people we know whose yes means yes and whose no means no. It must be the same here: so that the world can look on this yes as meaning something. Or else they will say, 'Those Africans, you can't rely on them, you never know if their yes means yes.'

"Would it help Tanzania to establish a reputation for undependability? Can young nations afford to be cynical about morals? For old nations, morals become an instrument of power. Can young nations afford this? No!"

XI

In September 1965, a few months before the break with Britain, mainland Tanzania had held its first general elections since 1962. Until that time, most Members of Parliament had assumed that they would be renominated by the party and thus would be assured of re-election. Instead, the party adopted a new system, under which the National Executive committee selected two candidates for almost every constituency; only six incumbent Members, including Second Vice-President Rashidi Kawawa and five other Cabinet members, were unopposed. Nyerere was also unopposed. His popularity was such that the party was not prepared to nominate anyone to oppose him; in all likelihood, no one would have chosen to run against him anyway. Such discontent as existed in Tanzania was rarely expressed except in private.

On Zanzibar there were no parliamentary elections; it was still too soon after the revolution, the government explained. But the Zanzibaris, like the mainlanders, had a chance to vote for or against the President. In answer to a question during the campaign, Nyerere told a group of voters on Zanzibar that it would be dangerous for him to be appointed President for life. "If that happened, you would be right back where you were under the Sultan," he said. "I could even call myself Sultan Nyerere."

He devoted much of his campaign to an explanation of the use of the ballot. "Those who do not wish me to be President for the next five years," he would say, "have simply to put a tick in the space on the ballot paper underneath where it says *hapana* [no]. But if you feel I should continue as President, I hope you will go to the polls and vote for me by putting your tick on the ballot under the word *ndiyo*."

At the beginning of the campaign, the TANU Central Committee selected two symbols, the *jembe* (hoe) and *nyumba* (house), and assigned one to each candidate. The committee assumed that the symbols were of roughly equal value, but political scientists and students who were analysing the campaign discovered that the symbols themselves quickly became an issue in many constituencies, and that the candidate whose symbol was the *jembe* had a distinct advantage over his opponent.

A British political scientist, Belle Harris, wrote of the campaign in a local magazine, *Mbioni*: "Again and again this kind of phrase occurs in the students' reports: 'All wealth comes from the *jembe*'; 'How many of you have a *jembe* at home?' answered by a roar of '*Ndiyo*'; 'Should we as a nation sleep or wake up and dig?' One Junior Minister carried a hoe around during the campaign. . . . Only in one or two constituencies was the symbol of the house used as effectively. For example, in Mbeya the local-born candidate emphasized the common bond of 'our houses are here'. He won."

Another factor in the campaign was the candidate's ability to show that he had not lost the popular touch. Miss Harris wrote: "The students reported that where a candidate adopted the Western 'educative' manner of explaining and justifying government policy, he was considered to be speaking 'above the heads of the people'."

The scene on election day was much like that of other African countries: as long lines formed at polling places beneath flame trees and baobabs, each voter's thumb was daubed in red indelible ink to prevent him from casting any more ballots that day.

Considering Nyerere's continuing popularity, the size of his victory was hardly surprising. In 1962, in a two-man contest, he had drawn ninety-eight and one-tenth per cent of the vote; in 1965, when he ran unopposed, he received nearly ninety-seven per cent. The surprise came in the number of incumbent Members of Parliament who were defeated. In Rufiji, the proud Bibi Titi Mohamed, the Junior Minister for Community Development and the president of the national women's organization, was badly beaten. Another casualty was Paul Bomani, the Minister of Finance and one of Nyerere's ablest colleagues. Bomani's friends pointed out that the voters blamed him for introducing the new five per cent development levy on salaries three weeks before; but it was also true that the Bomani family was widely resented in Mwanza for its wealth and specifically for the power it wielded within the large cotton co-operative, the Victoria Federation of Co-operative Unions.

All told, two ministers and six junior ministers were defeated, in addition to three other junior ministers who had failed to secure the party's nomination for re-election. Nine backbench MPs were also defeated, and another 37 either did not seek re-election or were not renominated. Of the 107 constituency members of the new Parliament, 86 were freshmen. Among the winners were Derek Bryceson, the Minister of Health and the only European in Nyerere's Cabinet, and Amir Jamal, the only Asian; both were re-elected over African opponents, Bryceson by a majority of almost five to one.

In choosing candidates to fill the ten "nominated" seats in Parliament, Nyerere took the position that these appointive posts should not be used to save the careers of politicians who had been repudiated at the polls—a decision that angered Bibi Titi Mohamed, among others. Then, making an exception to his own rule, Nyerere named Paul Bomani to a nominated seat and appointed him Minister of State in the Directorate of Development and Planning; Bomani, he explained, was too valuable a man to lose. Jamal replaced Bomani as Minister of Finance.

A few months later, Nyerere was asked whether he felt the elections had proved the validity of the country's one-party system. "I think it has vindicated what we have been saying," he said. "By definition, democrats are free people. And the machinery of elections must not be confused with the essentials of democracy. I don't blame Westerners for being sceptical. The only democracies they have known have been multi-party systems, and the only one-party systems they have seen have been non-democratic. But: a multiplicity of parties does not guarantee democracy."

He added, "I can't say we have proved it yet. You don't establish a system with one election. But we have shown we can have *one* free election under our system. My hope now is that we can create the necessary conditions that our experiment can live. And it may lead Westerners to say, 'Well . . . perhaps . . .' "

In a television interview later that year, he pursued the point. "To some extent there are safeguards," he said. "But I have sufficient power under the constitution to be a dictator. And frankly, I don't believe yet that we can claim the system is safeguarded. The safeguard is not one election, it is a tradition; the true safeguard of democracy is a tradition of democracy."

Nyerere has occasionally referred to Dar es Salaam as "Rumourville". This might seem to a casual visitor to be a very odd thing to say about that sleepy little harbour town, fragrant with the smells and spices of the East African coast, whose name in Arabic means "haven of peace".

It is true, however, that a sort of free-floating paranoia sometimes seems to hang suspended in Dar es Salaam's heavy air. Some observers have gone so far as to explain the suspicion and distrust of foreigners as a Tanzanian character trait, a legacy from the age of slavery. In any case, many foreigners seem to have learned to make allowances. A Briton who had lived in Dar es Salaam and served the Tanzanian government for many years once commented wistfully to a visiting American, "You know, we have to allow them to distrust us."

A European psychiatrist who formerly lived in Tanzania attributed the symptoms to a malady that he called "uhuruitis" and described as follows: "Depression, fatigue, almost a return to tribal fears; a considerable increase in anxiety at all levels; a certain amount of secondary guilt that comes from having rejected a father. Another element is the break-up of family ties; the drift from the villages to the towns." The constant bubble of rumour, he felt, was a manifestation of the tension.

Nyerere sometimes complains to friends, "I'm fed up with all this suspicion", and conducts periodic campaigns against it. Once he actually identified a dozen local people who were accused of spreading false rumours and warned them to stop it. At a mass rally on Union Day in 1966, he mentioned some of the prevailing gossip—of dissension within his Cabinet, and of the imminent break-up of the Union. "Three times we had rumours of three different coups," he said. Then he turned and addressed Brigadier Sarakikya, the young army commander, "By the way, Brigadier, what happened to that coup we were supposed to have this morning?"

Discussing the problem one day in 1966, Nyerere said, "Well, I think there are two sources of these rumours. One we can control: the internal source of rumour—mere gossip, born of ignorance or misunderstanding; local mischief. Dar is not big enough to be free of this, and yet not small enough for people to know everybody else and what is happening.

"But there is another source as well, I think. After the army mutiny, I was having a discussion with a foreign diplomat. I was explaining what was happening: 'You know, the town was full of rumours on that Friday.' And he made a remark—I'm a naïve fellow, so to me it was quite significant—he said, 'Have you ever considered establishing your own rumour factory?' Well, I have the feeling there are deliberate rumour factories."

Lady Chesham, who has remained in the Tanzanian Parliament as a national member, remarked tartly in 1966, "There are too many [foreign] wives here who haven't anything to do but write home and tell their friends about how brave they are to be here." She once recalled how, following a private meeting that Nyerere had held with Members of Parliament, a local British journalist had asked her, "Is

it true he told you of an attempted coup and named the conspirators?" Lady Chesham replied, "God no! Would he have confided
to one hundred and fifty people who had conspired against him?
Use your brains, man!" She later added, "The blinking idiot. He's
always backing me into corners at sundowners." At the meeting,
Nyerere had spoken of Tanzania's role in the world power struggle.
"But this has nothing to do with you," he said. "Your politics is the
development of Tanzania. You must be on your guard against influences from outside. Pay attention to rumours and, if they are
serious, you should report them."

Part of the suspicion, of course, is soundly based. The experience
of slavery was followed by a long period of colonialism, during
which the Tanganyikans saw Kenya become the centre of industry
for East Africa and the recipient of a disproportionate share of the
colonial power's investment and concern. After independence came
the trauma of the army mutiny and the revolution on Zanzibar and
the endless series of military coups and civil wars throughout Africa.
The Tanzanians also realized that they were taking a measured risk
by providing hospitality for at least a dozen refugee organizations
or "liberation movements" from South Africa, South-west Africa,
Rhodesia and Mozambique; there is even a group from the French-
owned Comoro Islands.

Some of the organizations are little more than store-front offices
that serve as gathering places for young men who have fled north to
Tanzania and are looking for jobs or scholarships. A few are genuine
guerilla movements, the most active being the Frente de Libertação
de Moçambique (the Mozambican Liberation Front, or FRELIMO),
which for about six years has been conducting a spasmodic military
campaign in northern Mozambique and has virtually controlled two
provinces during much of that period. In early 1969 FRELIMO's
leader, the American-educated Dr Eduardo Mondlane, was killed
near Dar es Salaam when he tried to open a package that had the
appearance of having been sent from somewhere in Europe. Early
reports had it that the book-size bomb package had borne an East
German or a Soviet postmark; subsequent rumours added West
Germany, France and even Japan. In any case, Tanzanian authorities concluded that the package had been slipped directly into the
local postal system or even into FRELIMO's post-office box. The
case remains officially unsolved; speculation has centred on everybody from the Portuguese, who obviously benefited from a weaken-
ing of the guerilla movement, to Mondlane's enemies within the

refugee community. Whatever the truth may be, the assassination underscored the vulnerability of African leadership to espionage. It reminded the Tanzanians that it would be to the great advantage of South Africa and Portugal if all of independent Africa, and particularly Tanzania and Zambia, were led by governments of a different character than those of Julius Nyerere and Kenneth Kaunda: governments such as that of Hastings Kamuzu Banda of Malawi that would be willing to live with, trade with, and accept gratuities from the white regimes of southern Africa.

"Africa is in a mess," Nyerere said on his return from an OAU summit conference in 1966. "There is a devil somewhere in Africa. I am a good superstitious African, and I believe in devils." At the conference, the delegates had refused, if only temporarily, to renew the budget of the OAU Liberation Committee; the committee provides funds for the various guerilla movements, most of which are based in Dar es Salaam. "I think the African countries will have to make up their minds," Nyerere said, "whether they will give priority to Africa or to their associations with foreign rulers."

Such outbursts against other African governments are notable for their rarity. For the most part, Tanzania's disagreements with its neighbours are treated with as much discretion as disputes within the councils of TANU or those between the mainland government and the Zanzibaris. Nothing angers the Tanzanians more than for a foreigner to use Dar es Salaam as a platform from which to denounce another African state or its leader.

The creation of an East African federation composed of Tanzania, Kenya and Uganda has never again seemed as imminent as it did in 1963. In 1967, however, the three countries converted the East African Common Services Organization—an inheritance from the colonial period—into the East African Community, whose headquarters were established at Arusha.

The Community, a common market and administrative union, operates a wide range of services for the three countries. It collects income taxes, customs and excise duties; it operates four independent corporations that run East Africa's airline, railways, harbours, and post and telecommunications. Its branches include an appellate judicial system and a development bank. After intensive bargaining, the three countries agreed to a plan that would give Tanzania and Uganda some assistance in catching up with Kenya's more advanced state of development.

Until early 1971, relations between Tanzania and its Community partners wavered between the cordial and the correct. The most serious threat to the Community's continued existence has been caused by the overthrow of the Ugandan President, Milton Obote, in January 1971, and by Tanzania's subsequent dispute with Uganda's new military ruler, General Idi Amin Dada. Nyerere continued to recognize Obote as Uganda's President, and offered him refuge in Tanzania. When Amin declared, in mid-1972, that he would expel some 50,000 Ugandan Asians who had retained their British citizenship since Uganda's independence, Nyerere attacked Amin's action as racialism. In September 1972, a band of Ugandan rebels loyal to Obote invaded Uganda from Tanzania, and for a few days it appeared that open warfare might break out between the two countries. The events in Uganda have accelerated Tanzania's tendency to look southward towards Zambia, with whose government Tanzania is probably friendlier today than with any other.

Tanzania's relations with the Congo improved immediately after the removal of Moise Tshombe as premier in 1965. Presumably because he despised Tshombe so intensely, Nyerere was prepared to work more closely with the new President, Joseph Mobutu, even though Mobutu was a military man who had seized power. When the Mobutu government conducted a public hanging of four former Cabinet ministers in 1966, Nyerere said simply, "I can tell you this: it would not have happened here."

One of the Tanzanians' noisiest quarrels with another African country has been with Malawi, the former Nyasaland. In fact, one measure of the present bitterness is the fact that the Tanzanians stubbornly refer to the lake that separates the two countries by its colonial name, Lake Nyasa, whereas the Malawians have long since changed it to Lake Malawi. At the heart of the dispute is Dr Banda, the President of Malawi. Dr Banda has had a rather odd career. He left his country at the age of thirteen, studied in South Africa, the United States and Britain, and practised medicine in London and later in Ghana. In 1958, after an absence of almost forty years, he was called back to Nyasaland to lead the country's independence movement. His colleagues were a group of young men who referred to Dr Banda as "our father"; he in turn called them "my boys".

In 1964 Nyasaland attained independence and Dr Banda's boys became his ministers. Within a few weeks, however, several of them were running for their lives following a dispute with Dr Banda. Four or five of the former ministers settled in Dar es Salaam; among them was Kanyama Chiume, who had been Oscar Kambona's great friend and fellow teacher at Dodoma years before.

Dr Banda subsequently accused the Tanzanian government of supporting the rebel ministers, and it may well be that the Malawians received some assistance for a while from one or more Tanzanian leaders, perhaps Kambona. For their part, the Tanzanians have grown increasingly uneasy as Dr Banda co-operated with the Portuguese and established diplomatic relations with South Africa; they fear that Banda might some day allow the South Africans to use Malawi as a base from which to attack Tanzania and Zambia.

A minor irritant, in addition, has been a dispute about the owner-ship of Lake Malawi and its shoreline. In his characteristically grandiose style, Banda was once quoted as saying, "Nyerere should be the last person to squeal and squeak. He began it. He provoked me last year by claiming part of our lake. Did he expect me to remain silent? What does he think I am, a jellyfish like himself? I am no jellyfish. In my back there is a bone."

Nyerere is said to believe that Tanzania's relations with Malawi are unlikely to improve very much as long as Banda is in power. In 1966, when the two countries were about to hold discussions over their mutual problems, Banda announced that the talks would deal primarily with Tanzania's surrender of the Malawian ministers who had taken refuge in Dar es Salaam. Nyerere is said to have cabled Banda: "There is no point holding discussions if you don't know what we're talking about."

Ever since the early TANU period, Nyerere had stressed the impor-tance of developing regional confederations as steps towards achiev-ing African unity. He disagreed, however, with Kwame Nkrumah's call for African Union because he believed it unrealistic at that stage and merely self-serving. He also disapproved of the widespread cor-ruption in Ghana; after Nkrumah's overthrow in 1966, Nyerere told friends, "He made the mistake of allowing corruption, and it has overwhelmed him."

Nonetheless, Nyerere was greatly distressed by Nkrumah's over-throw, and viewed it as a defeat for the African cause against Rhodesia and the white south. He was even more upset by the fall of Milton Obote five years later; at the time of the military coup in Uganda, Obote was in Singapore attending the Commonwealth Prime Ministers' Conference, at which he had joined Tanzania and Zambia in threatening to leave the Commonwealth if the British government proceeded with its plan to resume arms sales to South Africa.

In early 1971, following Obote's overthrow, Nyerere announced that Tanzania would train a "people's militia" or home guard to increase the national security. In his speech, he listed some of the events in which such militias might have been useful: the presumed murder of Patrice Lumumba in the Congo in 1961, the fall of Nkrumah in 1966 and of Obote in 1971, and the raid on Guinea in 1970 by a band of hostile forces which, the Guineans charged, were supported by the Portuguese and included some white mercenaries. Nyerere described the attack on Guinea as "a big lesson for us", especially since Tanzania, like Guinea, shared a hostile border with the Portuguese.

A few months after Nkrumah's fall, Nyerere had spoken of the military take-overs that were sweeping across Africa. "The soldiers are in," said Nyerere, "for the purpose of democracy, they say, and it could easily be true. But the method of establishing a government has its own logic. If they come in by the bullet, it will not be easy for them to withdraw from the bullet position."

Asked if he felt there was a way to protect Africa from internal coups, Nyerere replied, "How do you do it? Nkrumah used to talk of a High Command. I disagreed with him on this. Suppose it were like NATO, an alliance of governments organized for self-protection against an external enemy. But how would you use NATO to stop a coup in Britain? How does the outsider go in? I differed with Nkrumah on this because Africa is not going to be attacked from the outside. The answer is unity on the basis of the United States of America; this is the answer to our internal problems."

Only if there was "genuine subversion by an outside power," said Nyerere, would intervention by another African state be justified. "But if there is an internal uprising in Tanzania, what does Africa do? Invade Tanzania? And who invades?"

XII

GIVEN NYERERE'S PREOCCUPATION with the problems of developing a backward country, and given also his respect for spartan living and his abhorrence of luxury, his fascination with China was probably inevitable. The events of 1964 and 1965, especially including the union with Zanzibar, caused him to shift to a new political balance further to the left, and the Chinese became the chief foreign beneficiary.

The Peking government had already shown that it was seeking to strengthen its diplomatic presence in East Africa. In the weeks after the revolution, in January 1964, the Chinese had promised the Zanzibaris a £5-million interest-free loan and a shipment of arms. In June, about two months after Union, they offered an additional £10-million to mainland Tanzania. In August, Nyerere signed an agreement for a group of eleven Chinese military technicians, and reacted angrily to Western diplomatic pressure against the move; most of his officers were British-trained, he pointed out, and he had just signed an agreement with West Germany to train an air wing.

In February 1965, Nyerere made an eight-day state visit to China and was struck by the relevance of Chinese problems to those of his own country. He assured his Chinese hosts, "If it were possible for me to lift all the ten million Tanzanians and bring them to China to see what you have done since the liberation, I would do so." On his return to Dar es Salaam, he told a press conference, "At times I thought it was unfair that our country should be expecting economic assistance from a country like China, which is being extremely economical, while we are not." He said China's External Affairs Minister, Marshal Chen Yi, told him there were only about ten cars in his ministry, which employed three thousand people. "I passed this information to Oscar [who had been his own External Affairs Minister] immediately," Nyerere said.

In June 1965 he welcomed Chou En-lai, the Chinese Premier, to Dar es Salaam, where Chou repeated his famous remark of the previous year that "an excellent revolutionary situation exists in Africa". Kenya and a number of other African governments had objected to this ominous forecast, but Nyerere chose to interpret it as a call for social and economic revolution. "Africa is very much ripe for revolution," he said, "and I can assure you Chou En-lai is not responsible for this. If the revolution is not allowed to take place, Africa will not be Africa."

At a state banquet for Chou, Nyerere described how much the trip to China had meant to him: "The single-mindedness . . . and the conscious and deliberate frugality with which your people and your government are concentrating on development was the thing which most impressed me during my visit to your great country. It was a big lesson for me." As if to underscore his point, Nyerere announced four days later that the government thereafter would serve only beer, soft drinks, tea and coffee at its official receptions, and no more liquor. Except for four-wheel-drive bush vehicles, only automobiles that cost no more than £900 apiece would henceforth be bought for government officials.

Despite the warmth of the reception he gave Chou, Nyerere closed his speech with one of his characteristic warnings about Tanzania's independence: "From no quarter shall we accept direction or neo-colonialism, and at no time shall we lower our guard against the subversion of our government or our people. Neither our principles nor our country nor our freedom to determine our own future is for sale."

Neither then nor since have the Chinese made any serious mistakes in their dealings with the Tanzanians, although they soon demonstrated that they did not yet quite understand Nyerere. Shortly after Chou's visit to Dar es Salaam, Nyerere attended the Commonwealth Prime Ministers' Conference in London, the conference at which he dissociated Tanzania from the final communique on Vietnam and Rhodesia. At about the same time, President Ahmed Ben Bella, whom Nyerere respected immensely for his support of the liberation struggle against the white regimes in southern Africa, was overthrown in Algeria. The Chinese let it be known that they would recognize the new Algerian regime immediately in order to proceed as planned with the Afro-Asian summit conference in Algiers on June 29. Nyerere is said to have been appalled. "Can't they understand the meaning of friendship?" he asked. "Friendship cannot mean just because a friend is overthrown, you forget him. Now they want me to go to Algeria while Ben Bella is sitting in prison. That my friends can't understand this surprises me, and it surprises them that it surprises me."

He took the position that he wouldn't go to Algiers unless Ben

6

Bella was released, or put on trial and the charges proved. A few days later, Nyerere was also dismayed when the Algerian ambassador to Tanzania, who had previously been an ardent supporter of Ben Bella, returned from Algiers after the coup and, at the Dar es Salaam airport, denounced Ben Bella as a man who "played off one Algerian against another" to set himself up as dictator. "Everything is in good order and good hands," said the ambassador. Nyerere never received him at State House again.

The Chinese were already at work on a project that was intended to be a dramatic demonstration of their good will toward Africa. Kenneth Kaunda, the President of Zambia, had wanted a railway north to the Tanganyikan coast for years before his country became independent in 1964. Since Zambia had no access to the sea, its copper exports as well as its imports were shipped on rail lines that passed through Rhodesia and the Portuguese territories of Mozambique and Angola. After Rhodesia's unilateral declaration of independence in November 1965, the Zambians became determined that the northern rail line should be built; they felt, moreover, that if Britain and its allies were unwilling to bring the Rhodesian rebel regime to heel, they could at least build a railway that would decrease Zambia's dependence on the white south.

As early as 1963, Kaunda had discussed the plan with Nyerere, who sympathized with Kaunda's predicament and, in addition, wanted the railway as a means of developing south-western Tanganyika. Kaunda solicited the support of several Western countries —Britain, the United States, France and West Germany, as well as Japan—without success, but in 1964 the Chinese told him they might be willing to help. The following year, after Chou's visit to Dar es Salaam, the Chinese sent a twelve-man team to make a preliminary survey of the Tanzanian portion of the route.

Western reluctance was based on the cost of the project, which was originally estimated at £60 million and later increased to almost £150 million. The reluctance was strengthened by a World Bank report which concluded that a railway was not practical for the amount of traffic that would be involved, and instead recommended improvements to the highway between the Zambian Copperbelt and Dar es Salaam at a cost of only £11 million. At Kaunda's urging, the British and Canadians then sponsored another survey which, when finished in 1966, estimated the cost of the railway at £126 million, plus another £12 million for port improvements in Dar es Salaam. The

Anglo-Canadian report offered the view that the railway could be operated profitably if Zambia committed all or nearly all of its traffic to the route. But by the time the survey was completed, whatever slight Western interest that previously existed had vanished. The United States later agreed to rebuild the highway between Iringa and Tunduma, on the Zambian border, at a cost of about £10.7 million.

"I am determined that this railway should be built," Nyerere said in July 1965, "and I am prepared to accept money from whoever offers it to see that it is built." Two months later he confirmed that the Chinese had made an offer to build the railway: "At present we have only one definite offer, and that is from the Chinese." No other offers were ever received. The Tanzanians did not quarrel with the Western arguments that the eleven-hundred-mile rail line was too expensive, but they blamed the West for not placing a very high political priority on what was, after all, the most monumental development project that either the Zambians or the Tanzanians had ever contemplated. One day in late 1967 a Tanzanian cited to an American friend a London *Sunday Times* article which stated that the American involvement in Vietnam was costing the United States £23 million a day. "Our railway," he said, "could be built for what the Americans are spending in Vietnam *every seven days*."

The final agreement was not signed until 1970, following a two-year survey by the Chinese. The accord called for the Chinese to make a £168-million interest-free loan, which is repayable by Tanzania and Zambia equally over thirty years, beginning in 1983. All local costs, including the wages of as many as ten thousand Chinese workers to be sent to Tanzania and Zambia, would be covered by the sale of Chinese goods on credit to state-owned trading corporations in the two countries. Both countries accepted the risk that they might be saddled with some expensive or inferior goods that they might not have bought otherwise.

Among all foreign aid projects undertaken in Africa, the Tanzam railway will rank with the Soviet-built Aswan Dam in Egypt and Ghana's Volta River Dam, which was financed primarily by the World Bank, the United States and Britain. It will be the largest foreign aid project ever undertaken by the Peking government.

Apart from the railway, the list of other Chinese aid projects to Tanzania was already long. Since Tanganyikan independence, the Chinese had provided about £21 million in loans and grants. For the mainland, they built the £2.7 million Friendship textile mill near

Dar es Salaam, as well as a farm implement factory, an experimental farm, and a radio transmitter. They also started a Chinese-Tanzanian shipping line with two ships. On Zanzibar they built a rice farm, a cotton farm, a shoe factory, a water-pumping station and a tractor-repair plant. Their influence has increased steadily on Zanzibar, while that of another Communist nation, East Germany, has declined; the East Germans made a series of classic foreign aid blunders in Zanzibar, including the supplying of two fishing trawlers that were unsuitable for East African waters because they weren't equipped with refrigeration.

In addition to the technical aid, the Chinese now provide perhaps two hundred instructors for the mainland army and for several camps where black refugees from white-ruled southern African countries receive guerilla training under the auspices of their own exiled political parties. The Chinese also provide about four hundred instructors for one of the two army battalions on Zanzibar. They have supplied several patrol boats for the Tanzanian marine police, and are currently building a small naval base near Dar es Salaam for which they have promised to provide another six boats.

There are rumours that the Chinese have also offered to build the Tanzanians an air base and to supply them with jet fighters. For five years, Canada played an important role in training Tanzania's army and air wing. When the agreement for this programme expired, at the end of 1969, the Tanzanians decided not to renew it. One factor in the decision was Canada's membership in NATO, to which Portugal, the last colonial power of any significance in Africa, also belonged. It is doubtful that the Tanzanians really thought the Canadians would tell the Portuguese their military secrets, but they may have reasoned that in the event of a fight with the Portuguese, the position of the Canadians would be ambiguous, while that of the Chinese would not.

If Nyerere has any misgivings about the size of the growing Chinese presence in Tanzania, he doesn't admit it. "The West," he has said, "which doesn't want to build the railway, doesn't want the Chinese to build it either. So should we go without a railway?" But he added, "We are a stubborn people. The Chinese will learn that if they want to control us they will get into trouble."

Early in 1966, at a time when Tanzania, as a result of a series of foreign policy incidents, had lost most of the foreign aid it had been receiving from Britain, West Germany and the United States,

Nyerere was asked if he felt his policies had cost his country any aid unnecessarily.

"The current criticism is that I have tended to be rather over-principled," he said, "and that this has cost us development funds. But this is easier to say than prove. Yes, we have lost some aid—the seven-and-a-half-million-pound loan from the British, for instance. The difficulty, you know, is that a loan is often tied to procurement, and then there is the problem of local costs to go with the loan. But with this loan, the British were paying the local costs, too. It was one of the best we ever received.

"Another example. One country most interested in helping us, because of its history, was [West] Germany. Then we clashed—over German interpretations of Tanzanian unity. I believe this was inevitable. I was not elected to sell the blessed country to the highest bidder.

"The real source of money in the world is the West. The West is wealthy, it has the experience. At one time I was very popular with the Western world, a model of reasonableness during that period. But what development did we get? There is very little philanthropy in the kind of aid required for nation-building. Yes, there is a little. Scandinavia, led by Sweden, is one example. They feel an obligation of wealthy countries, an obligation to assist in development. And Canada too, to some extent, I think. In Sweden it's almost a national feeling. Of course it is present, in varying degrees, in all countries. But it does not dominate decision-making. In the United States, what dominates is: You have got to fight Communism! And particularly: A country must matter, politically, before it can be given aid."

Asked if he felt a country could attract more aid by being non-aligned than aligned to either East or West, Nyerere replied, "No. This is not true. It has got to be strategic. For example, the United Arab Republic. India, the same. The problem in giving aid to India is not the millions of needy, but the millions of Chinese [with whom the Indians had fought a few years earlier]. The Indians, after receiving the cheque [from either the Soviet Union or the United States] could easily thank the Chinese!

"We are living in a most unfortunate world. The struggle for power is global. If we were in the Middle Ages, you could ask the Pope to divide it, not between Spain and Portugal but between the United States and Russia. But this is changing too; China is around, and she cannot be ignored.

"Africa is Europe's sphere of influence. It was long an appendage of Europe. As far as Africa—the Congo, for example—goes, the world thinks, 'Ah, Communists against the West!' With Ghana, it thinks, 'Chinese and Russians asked to leave!' But this is an over-simplification.

"If it hadn't been for the Cold War, I think the struggle would have been between Europe and the United States. The struggle would have been America leading the fight for freedom, and Europe saying no, this we can't do. But the Cold War came along. And the United States became much more concerned about Russia than about freedom. So it became identified with Europe and with colonialism. And without a single inch of Africa of her own! We say to the United States, 'You are a revolutionary power!' But no. The United States must listen to its allies, and its allies are in Europe. The United States still shapes her policies in regard to Africa *through London!* On Nigeria, on Ghana, certainly on East Africa, the United States will never listen to us. It will listen to London but not directly to us.

"Well, Europe still wants to keep us as its sphere; and we want to be nobody's sphere. We are not fighting the United States; we want to establish a direct relationship. The assumption in the United States [in response to news of Tanzania] is: 'They want to be Chinese!' This shorthand is understood! Communists!" He threw up his hands in a gesture of frustration.

The discussion turned to Vietnam and, inevitably, to China and the United States. "How much are African countries really concerned about Vietnam?" he said. "They are focused mainly on African problems. They are concerned with their own freedom. And what mars their relationship with any country is its attitude towards Africa. I can hardly imagine violent demonstrations over Vietnam in any African capital. Diplomatic talking, yes. Africans may say, 'We do not understand what you are doing.' The maximum you can expect is suspicion.

"I have never felt, myself, that I could play any particular role on Vietnam. There are two aspects to it—the idea part and the hard fact. The idea part is: Have the Americans the right to be there? The practical part is: But they *are* there. So the search for a realistic solution ought to ignore the idea part; it should just recognize the fact that they are there, and find a solution. This can only be done by the big powers. The power of small powers is moral. We can argue morality; we have no other choice.

"I've taken an extremely keen interest [in Vietnam], especially since I got into trouble in London." He was referring, with an ironic shiver, to Harold Wilson's success in isolating him on the question of a Commonwealth peace mission to South-east Asia in 1965. "At the time I said I didn't understand Vietnam. I disagreed about sending the peace mission—it was wrong, it was a gimmick that wouldn't help much. But Vietnam is a problem of power, basically a problem of power. And in this, small nations suffer. Vietnam is just the line that has been chosen for the struggle. *It could have been Tanzania!*"

The American role in South-east Asia was based on a fallacy, Nyerere said, of using power to try to contain China. "I don't believe you can contain China. What is the meaning? But I understand power, and therefore I understand the United States as a power with global responsibilities and views; I understand that. But what I cannot understand is the policy—started long before Vietnam—based on the idea that one way of assuring world peace is to ostracize China. Use all power—military power, diplomatic power—to treat China as an international leper, make China the untouchable of the modern world! Be suspicious of countries that have dealings with China! This yellow disease! This I do not understand."

Recalling that a leading churchman had once questioned his support of the Chinese, Nyerere said, "I was tempted to quote Abraham Lincoln—I believe it was Lincoln—who said, 'God must have loved the common people, otherwise he would not have created so many of them.'" Then, with great feeling: "But these people are our brothers, seven hundred million of them, and they have a right to a share in both the fellowship and also the goods of this planet. But the United States says, 'You must spit in the face of China! You must vote every time in the UN against China!' This is rubbish, absolute rubbish! As a moral issue I don't understand it. I don't understand those Asian and African countries that, year after year, vote against China—against seven hundred million people. I don't understand it. How do you work for peace that way? The United States has a Christian ethic. It's bad enough when hate is preached in a Communist country; but when the song of hate is preached in a Christian country, hate hate hate seven hundred million people . . .!

"I think it's wrong. It's a pity I have to speak as a head of state. If I could speak as a newspaperman, I'd shout it from on top of Kilimanjaro: It's wrong!

"The Chinese [diplomats and technicians] here in Tanzania: their mere presence is a problem. In the beginning, when people asked me about the Chinese here, I would answer, 'They are not causing me trouble.' Now I am being asked, 'Why are they *not* causing trouble? Why are they so *tame* in Tanzania?' I even have a letter an American friend brought me, written to a newspaper, in answer to some bishops and archbishops who feel I'm too friendly to China. So I even have bishops and archbishops worrying about it. I assume the Holy Ghost is less concerned than the bishops; otherwise I'd be facing very serious consequences.

"The Americans are trying to adjust themselves to Russia, thanks to Kennedy. But they have failed to accept China, a proud people, a great people, with a history that goes back for centuries. The Chinese are very proud, they speak with one voice, they are no longer just a humiliated giant, they have a pride of achievement. If we are beginning to understand Russia, why not China?

"Kennedy—I have great respect for that man; he was a good man, a great man—one day he had to say to Russia, 'Get out of here', and the whole world said, 'My God, nuclear war', and Kennedy took the maximum risk and said, 'Get out of here.' Whatever we may say, it's just possible China is feeling the United States is too close to it—too strong to be so close.

"I don't see how the United States can in one voice argue the case of the reunification of Germany, and at the same time argue the rejection of China's case. I understand Germany; that's why we did not recognize East Germany. The Chinese themselves tell me it is not the same thing"—he laughed jubilantly—"but it *is* the same thing.

"That's my view on China. We must learn to co-exist with China."

Since Nyerere had so often objected to the tendency of the West, and particularly the United States, to judge Africa in terms of the Cold War, his visitor asked him if he felt that there was such a thing as an African Communist. "By definition there shouldn't be an *African* Communist, any more than an African Christian," he answered. "He would be a Communist, wherever you might find him. I don't know, there might be such a thing. Intellectual Communists, perhaps, who have been to Europe and have become intellectually convinced Communists. There might be a sprinkling of these. Highly intelligent people, who find it extremely appealing—and are often disillusioned.

"They come back from Europe, and they are confronted with *Africa*. What is the application of Communism to Africa? How do you begin applying the textbook of Communism to Africa? And it is textbook Communism they have learned in London and Paris. But how do you go and preach it in Sukumaland? How? In a peasant country without feudalism, how do you do it? How do you begin?

"An African Communist has a real problem. He may study it in London, but when he comes back to Africa, he finds that it's a tool he cannot apply, and then he realizes that he must become a pragmatist. From a distance, Africa may look like a classical Communist situation. But, in reality, it's a Sukumaland situation."

A few years later, pondering the same subject, he wrote: "The Communist theoretical stages are primitive communalism, slavery, feudalism, capitalism and *then* socialism, which follows the destruction of capitalism. China did not quite follow this orthodox path. But even in China they had a highly developed feudalism and some capitalism to destroy. In Africa generally, we have to begin our socialism from tribal communalism and a colonial legacy which did not build much capitalism. Only South Africa has a substantial proletariat on which you could base the application of orthodox Marxism. In Africa generally, in order to apply Marxism we would have to adapt it to a rural economy which is more primitive than that which confronted either the Russian or the Chinese revolutionaries. A good African Communist would be forced to be a revisionist."

XIII

ON THE THIRD DAY OF JANUARY 1967, Nyerere set off on his longest tour of the interior since independence, a four-week journey that took him to eight of mainland Tanzania's seventeen regions and ended with a three-day meeting of the TANU National Executive Committee in Arusha. There he announced the completion of a document that was to be called the Arusha Declaration, the most important of the dozens of major speeches and policy papers he had prepared since independence.

Many of Nyerere's formal speeches are polished and translated, usually from English into Swahili, by his State House staff, which includes Joan Wicken, an Englishwoman who serves as a personal assistant, and Paul Sozigwa, his press secretary. The six-thousand-word Arusha Declaration, however, was written in Nyerere's unmistakable style, blunt and vivid, and was less formal than many of his prepared speeches. It started with an affirmation of the TANU creed of building a democratic socialist state, and outlined the party's policies of socialism and self-reliance. Emphasizing how difficult it would be for the government to pay for development out of increased tax revenues, it asserted, "Knowing all the things which could be done with more milk does not alter the fact that the cow has no more milk." As for aid from overseas, said the Declaration, Tanzania simply could not count on it: "It is stupid to rely on money as the major instrument of development when we know only too well that our country is poor. It is equally stupid, indeed it is even more stupid, for us to imagine that we shall rid ourselves of our poverty through foreign financial assistance rather than our own financial resources. . . . Firstly, we shall not get the money. There is no country in the world which is prepared to give us gifts or loans, or establish industries, to the extent that we would be able to achieve all our development targets. . . . And even if all the prosperous nations were willing to help the needy countries, the assistance would still not suffice. But in any case the prosperous nations have not accepted a responsibility to fight world poverty." Besides, it continued, "Independence means self-reliance. Independence cannot be real if a nation depends upon gifts and loans from another for its development. How can we depend upon foreign governments and companies for the major part of our development without giving to those governments and countries a great part of our freedom to act as we please? The truth is that we cannot." The only answer, it concluded, was slower growth through self-reliance, and an emphasis on the development of the peasant agricultural economy.

Tacked on to the Declaration as a sort of appendix was a new code of conduct for TANU and government leaders. Among other things, it specified that no leader could hold directorates or shares in any private company, receive two or more salaries, or own any houses that he rented to others.

On the Sunday following his return to Dar es Salaam, Nyerere spoke about the Declaration for two and a half hours to a crowd at the Arnautoglu playing fields. "The important thing," he said, "is that we should not adopt an attitude that nothing can be done until someone else agrees to give us money. There are many things we can do by ourselves, and we must plan to do them." However, he added, "it is not being self-reliant to refuse to carry out the directions of a foreign engineer or a foreign manager; it is just being stupid."

The very next day, to the astonishment of his countrymen, Nyerere announced that the government was nationalizing all banks in Tanzania as the first step in implementing the Arusha Declaration. He promised full compensation for nationalized property, and emphasized that private accounts were not affected. "Fellow citizens," he told a gathering of soldiers and policemen in front of TANU headquarters in Dar es Salaam, "I myself have my money deposited in one of the nationalized banks. My money is safe. What has been taken over is the institution and not the customers' deposits." Several of his Cabinet ministers hugged each other in joy at this triumph over the imperialists, and soldiers shouted and waved banners in the February heat.

Within the next two or three days, the government announced plans to nationalize a number of insurance companies, import-export firms, mills and sisal estates, and to purchase a majority interest in seven other firms that made cement, cigarettes, shoes and beer. There were bitter prophecies from London and Nairobi that the Tanzanian government would be unable to pay for the nationalized properties and would have difficulty running them after the take-over; both fears, as it turned out, were unfounded. The value of the properties was first estimated at £100 million, but appeared by late 1967 to be closer to £15 million or £20 million. The government promoted junior employees to fill jobs vacated by expatriates and in a few cases imported specialists to run the companies until Tanzanians could be trained. At the end of the first year, Nyerere made a speech praising Tanzania's Indians, who had been exceedingly worried that year about their future in Tanzania and about new restrictions in Britain's immigration laws preventing them from emigrating to Britain even if they possessed British passports. The Indians, said Nyerere, had enabled the nationalization of the banks to work. "These people deserve the gratitude of our country. Yet now"—he used his own Zanaki tribesmen as the butt of the joke, as he often does—"if a Zanaki goes to the bank to borrow money, and is refused a loan because he does not have any security, he comes running to me, saying that the Indians favour each other and that we should make Zanaki managers of the banks. *Wananchi* [countrymen], I beg you to beware of this kind of thinking."

The government later entered into agreements to participate in the ownership of the Italian-built Tiper oil refinery near Dar es Salaam, and of the rest of the petroleum industry, and in early 1970 announced plans to take over the entire wholesaling system, which was controlled by Asians. The government also nationalized the Tanzania *Standard*, the country's only privately owned English-language daily newspaper. The British editors of the *Standard* had attempted to adopt a sympathetic editorial position in the years after independence; but the sale of the newspaper chain to which the *Standard* belonged to Lonrho, the British conglomerate that had extensive holdings in white-ruled southern Africa, made the paper more suspect than ever in the Tanzanians' eyes. As an official paper responsible directly to Nyerere, the *Standard* was supposed to adopt a semi-independent policy; in one of its first issues it published a report that led to the release of twenty-six foreigners who had been jailed without charge. At this stage of Tanzanian history, however, the level of tolerance of published dissent is fairly low; this fact affected the *Standard's* reporting long before the government took it over.

In early 1971, in what Nyerere described as a "mopping-up" measure, the National Assembly passed a bill authorizing the nationalization of all commercial buildings, apartments and even houses—except those lived in by their owners—that were worth more than 100,000 Tanzanian shillings (about £5,900). The act required that compensation be paid only to owners of buildings that were less than ten years old, apparently on the theory that owners of older buildings had already received an adequate return on their investments. The measure was inspired by socialist motives—and by a fear of the kind of real estate profiteering that had afflicted so many African states in the years after independence. But, since a large share of the property involved was owned by Asians, it had the effect of further reducing the wealth of the Asian community.

The Arusha Declaration was followed by two supplementary papers, "Education for Self-Reliance" and "Socialism and Rural Development". The first was a plan for re-directing the country's school system, placing a new emphasis on training the majority of students who would return to the land rather than go on to higher education. The second outlined a three-step process for establishing *ujamaa* ("familyhood") co-operative villages. First, said the paper, a group of peasant farmers should be persuaded to move their houses to a single village, preferably near a water source, and plant their crops in the vicinity. They should then be persuaded to establish small communal plots, perhaps with ten family groups working together and sharing the proceeds at harvest time. Finally, if the second phase succeeded, the project should be turned into a community farm. The paper emphasized that the process was to be a gradual one and that the final stage represented an ideal to be strived for. "We would not automatically become wealthy," it said, "although we could all become a little richer than we are now." A few co-operative farms had existed in Tanzania for a long time, such as the women's farm at Kazima that Nyerere had visited during his Tabora trip in 1966. By the end of 1970, there were said to be as many as a thousand villages throughout the country that were at least calling themselves *ujamaa* co-operatives.

The nationalization programme was the only aspect of the Arusha Declaration that was discussed extensively by the press overseas. The discussion consisted largely of renewed comment that Tanzania was going communist, and Nyerere's joke to the effect that the TANU youth league members were the "Green Guards" of Tanzania was taken as the latest bit of bizarre evidence that Nyerere, in his "Chinese pyjama suit," had fallen under the Maoist shadow.

The most important part of the Declaration from the Tanzanian point of view, however, was the code of conduct it imposed on the political leadership. In June 1967, Bibi Titi Mohamed resigned from the presidency of the national women's organization and from the TANU Central Committee. She was ill, she said, and planned to go "back to the kitchen"; but it was understood in Dar es Salaam that she had had to choose between her public career and her rental property and had, as one observer put it, "opted for capitalism". Nyerere told the National Executive committee in March that he himself complied with the new rules. He said that his wife had formerly kept a poultry farm at Mji Mwema, near Dar es Salaam, and had now given it to the Mji Mwema co-operative village. He had sold his old house in the Magomeni section of Dar es Salaam, he said, and was living at Msasani Bay in the new house that he had built with a bank loan. He said he had no other source of income except a small sum in royalties from the first published volume of his speeches and papers, *Freedom and Unity*.

The months following the issuance of the Declaration were a period of political tension, during which government leaders tried to decide how to comply with the code. A leadership bill, as passed by Parliament in October, called for Members to submit to the Speaker a statement of their income and assets and those of their wives; the Speaker, in turn, was directed to submit his statement to the President. When a friend asked Nyerere if there couldn't be a transition period, to soften the blow to the leaders affected, Nyerere snapped, "No! It would only give people time for loopholes. We must do it now. You're talking about, at most, a thousand people; I'm talking about thirteen million." The bill did, however, give leaders a year in which to "purify" themselves, and it allowed persons who inherited property three months in which to sell it or give it away, or to resign. By mid-September, some thirty MPs who had outside incomes had surrendered their monthly parliamentary salaries of £53 6s. in order to retain their seats.

The Declaration was widely interpreted as a result of Nyerere's disappointment over the state of the country's development. He had spent a full month in the interior, it was said, visiting peasants whose lives had barely changed since independence. He was conscious of a slight tendency toward corruption by the privileged—a very modest level of corruption compared to that of such countries as Nigeria and Ghana and even Kenya, where the greater wealth and higher state of development had caused more money to filter into the hands of leadership. But he was sickened by it, nonetheless, and believed it could destroy the meaning of African freedom.

Nyerere rejected the notion, however, that the Declaration was the direct result of such influences. "If you knew the whole truth," he told a visitor a few months later, "it would not be as exciting." In 1962, he noted, he had written a pamphlet on TANU in

Swahili which contained many of the points that were made in the Arusha Declaration. "The most important element, the part dealing with self-reliance, is found in the 1962 paper. About development through the work of the people. It must be clear, it said, that the benefits go to the people themselves, and not to their leaders.

"Last December [1966], I had a draft of the pamphlet. We had already discontinued giving loans to civil servants to build houses to live in, because it turned out that, in some cases, they were renting the houses. We said we were stopping this, and Rashid [Kawawa] said in Parliament that we were stopping it. There were also to be no such loans made to political people like regional and area commissioners."

He kept pondering over how best to present the problem to the National Executive committee, he said, until he realized: "We can't merely talk about houses, we must talk about leadership in relation to property. The responsibility of leadership in terms of property. The best way was to argue socialism, and to define socialism as a lack of exploitation, and then draw up a list of what this is. So it struck me: instead of a pamphlet I issue out of the blue, this should be the theme of the meeting, and this is how it came about. No"—he grinned—"it wasn't so much out of frustration as inspiration. It was a confirmation of what we ought to be doing. The Declaration says two things: that there is not enough aid for developing countries. But even if there were enough aid to handle all our development, it says no, that would be wrong."

Nyerere was asked if he were not actually making an attack on all the privileged groups in his society at once. "Yes," he said. "This is the intention. If we say we have to develop, it must be very clear to the people that the benefits are going to the people themselves. So you might say, 'Fine, we'll tackle one group now and another later on.' You could say, 'We'll tackle just the Indians. Use the African to help fight the Indian, and the African will help because he can replace the Indian. Tackle your immigrants.' You could do that. But you would just be postponing the problem. We had set a socialist goal for ourselves, and really we had no choice. How could we allow exploitation by the indigenous few? So we took them all together—foreign investors, local capitalists, our own political leaders. In a sense, we tackled the masses at the same time. We took on everybody.

"How do we engage the people in pursuing objectives that are not understood? The definition of objectives had to be total—and uncompromising. Once the decision is taken that the banks should be in the hands of the government, it's worse for the economy of the country to delay. The speed of our progress will depend on the realities of the country. But as a nation we ought to know what we are trying to do."

Suddenly—or so it seemed to anyone reading *The Nationalist*, the TANU-sponsored daily paper in Dar es Salaam—the whole country was caught up in a frenzy of marching in support of the Arusha Declaration. "Tempered and remoulded by the flames of the Spirit of Arusha," began a *Nationalist* news story in early September, "nine gallant youths from Singida have advanced their column on the longest march of all—through eight regions—in support of the Arusha Declaration, the President and the party. A long revolutionary column of one hundred and six people, of all ages, is advancing south toward the capital where the gallant marchers will make revolutionary contacts with party leaders, and pledge their support for the Arusha Declaration. . . . The gallant marchers will present *Mwalimu* with a total of three hundred and thirty shillings, being their contribution of aid for the bereaved parents of the youth hero, the late Seti Benjamin." Seti Benjamin was a twenty-year-old from Arusha who had collapsed and died at Moshi while marching to Dar es Salaam.

September 26: "A column of seventy-four gallant youths, of an average age between four and six years, has marched into Moshi town from the Kindergarten School at the Police Training School."

September 27: "The column of the gallant youth hero and martyr, Seti Benjamin Mpinga, is now heading south to the capital where they will pledge before *Mwalimu* their unswerving support for the Arusha Declaration."

October 9: "A group of sixteen TANU Youth League members marching thirty-five miles from Ngare Nanyuki to Arusha in support of the Arusha Declaration and the President's move to place under detention traitors of the nation, found themselves joined by a herd of elephants marching peacefully ahead of their column along the way. . . . After leading the column for some time, the loyal Tanzanian elephants changed the route. . . ."

And then, suddenly, Julius Nyerere was marching too. On October 3rd, he had started what seemed to be an ordinary tour of the interior in Mara region, his home territory. In one village he warned townspeople against two dangers—domination of Tanzania by foreign powers, and excessive drinking of *pombe*, the local brew.

Then, quite unexpectedly, he and his party walked twelve miles from Butiama, Nyerere's birthplace, to the village of Kiabakari, and the next day they walked twenty-two miles to Bunda. "President Nyerere moved the revolutionary Presidential column further deep into Mwanza region," *The Nationalist* reported a few days later, "covering a distance of fifteen miles from Chamgasa to Nyakaboja where the revolutionary marchers rested." At Nyakaboja, it added, "the entire village was seething with revolutionary enthusiasm emitted by the Spirit of Arusha."

The President's party was tired and hot by the time it reached Bunda on the second day. Everybody sat exhausted in the shade of a green-and-white house trailer that the government had recently purchased for journeys in the interior. Somebody asked Bhoke Munanka, the Minister of State, how the march was going. "Terrible," he groaned. Nyerere, his feet covered with talcum powder, was resting in a canvas chair tilted back against the trailer. Ackland Mhina, his former secretary, who had recently been named commissioner of Mara region, complained that his legs were chafed, and added that he had just learned from Brigadier Sarakikya that a marcher was supposed to reverse his socks every ten miles. "'You mean I must change my tyres every ten miles?' I asked him, and he said yes. I must tell my son. He is leaving on a march of his own in two days' time." The most accomplished marcher in Nyerere's party turned out to be Hashim Mbita, the President's former press secretary, who had been transferred to TANU headquarters and was later to become the party's executive secretary. Mbita had flown from Dar es Salaam to Mwanza the day before, and then took the long bus ride from Mwanza to Butiama—a distance of 138 miles. Learning that the party had already left Butiama, Hashim ran twelve miles to catch up with it.

Late in the afternoon, when the sun had faded, Nyerere addressed a rally at Bunda. He had changed from his khaki trousers and shirt and cap into a Tanzanian suit. He spoke about the need to use cattle for working the land instead of keeping them as a mere symbol of wealth. "We are sleeping while the Americans are going to the moon!" And he spoke of Africa's shame that it could not control its own affairs. His eyes bulged; he was animated, as usual, and the crowd laughed with him as he joked in a high, staccato voice. He hadn't wanted to give a speech that day, presumably preferring that the march be allowed to speak for itself. The next day, when the regional commissioner asked him to speak at another stop, he refused. He seemed determined to avoid routine political gestures. Many villagers, consequently, seemed quite bewildered as he passed. In the group of marchers, his head lowered and covered with a floppy canvas hat, he was unrecognizable.

The country was magnificent, the rim of Lake Victoria gleaming on the horizon. Beside the road were rock outcroppings and anthills as tall as a man. The earth was dry and dusty because the rains were late. "If you want my legs," complained Joseph Namata to nobody in particular, "you can have them." Like Ackland Mhina, Namata was a former member of Nyerere's staff who had recently become a regional commissioner.

That night at Bunda the three beer shops and the tea-house were filled with people, the most exciting occasion since independence. The walls of the Heshima bar had four pictures of Mao Tse-tung on the wall, and one of Nyerere. Had the Chinese ambassador passed through town and given a hundred pounds for a new community centre? Had the bar owner received the pictures in the mail and put them on the wall because he had nothing else?

After four or five hours of sleep in Bunda, the party was awakened at two and soon was on the road again, everyone groggy, flashlights pointing the way. Nyerere walked on the left, behind Brigadier Sarakikya, who was still as lithe as a runner; at Nyerere's side were two security men. Everyone tried to walk in the deep tyre tracks to avoid the loose gravel. Suddenly two men jumped aside to avoid a snake coiled in the roadway; a soldier kicked it to death expertly.

At last the President called a ten-minute halt. "Well fellows, we've done two and a half hours." Hashim Mbita emptied the sand from his shoes. Nyerere noticed the shoes worn by Joseph Namata, now the commissioner of Mwanza region—brown suede with pointed toes. "Ah, Manhattan," Nyerere said, feigning scorn. "Not so good." Nyerere had been appealing to Tanzanian women that year to discard "illusions of glamour" and the "Manhattan way of life". After crossing a bridge, the group stopped again, beside a rural police station house, for tea and bread, and later, hard-boiled eggs. "We should start again now, before our muscles grow stiff," said one of the soldiers, but instead the party tarried for eight hours until the heat of the day was past. The President retired into his trailer, which was being pulled along the route by an army lorry, Munanka and Namata drove away, probably to the mission on the road ahead, to get some rest. The others lay on the hoods of Land-Rovers or threw

heir bedrolls on the concrete floor of the station house. When a
:urry lunch was served, Mbita looked for a spoon for a Western
visitor; the others, in the tribal African manner, used their fingers.
'Take a banana," Hashim said, a gruff good host. "Now! Take
more!"

Two of the security men, leaning against a Land-Rover, spoke of
ı visit to New York. "Do you suppose we'll ever be like that?" one
ısked. At the remark that Tanzania had changed a great deal in the
last five years, they agreed, yes, a bit sceptically; it was changing,
yes, but very slowly. Sarakikya spoke of his mountain climbing. He
had climbed Kilimanjaro eight times, he said. He had made a vow
to climb it every January. But he couldn't get away in 1964 and 1965,
he said, when he was very busy.

At five-thirty in the afternoon, Munanka, Namata and the others
returned. "The *Wabenzi!*" somebody gibed, using Africa's derisive
term for the new "tribe" of affluent politicians who drive Mercedes
Benzes. Then the President emerged from his trailer, and the march
resumed. This time the villagers along the road had been forewarned;
drummers and flag carriers and dozens of children joined the march.
The children kept crowding in front of the party, and some of the
marchers kept pushing them out of the way. It was after dark by the
time the party reached a roadside police camp. Then, in the warm
evening, everyone sat around in front of the trailer and drank beer
or orange Fanta. The President was jovial. He pointed to an older
man, barefoot, who had just joined the party—clearly an uneducated
man. "This is the fellow," Nyerere said slyly, "who made history by
defeating my Minister of Finance." Hashim Mbita, reading a copy
of the *Standard* that had just arrived from Dar es Salaam, announced
excitedly that Chief Lugusha had been elected a local TANU chairman for the Tabora rural district, defeating seven contestants.
"Chief Lugusha?" cried Nyerere, seemingly taking a sort of fatalistic
delight in the bizarre report that Lugusha, who had been placed in
preventive detention for about three years following the 1964 army
mutiny, had now been elected, as if nothing had happened, to a
minor party post.

The food was late. "We must eat," said Namata. "We should all
be in bed by now," said Sarakikya. Finally, at nine-thirty, a dozen
members of the party drove to the comfortable house of two
American Maryknoll priests. The priests greeted the group with
elaborate hospitality, painstakingly filling orders for drinks, but the
marchers were almost paralyzed with fatigue. Someone complained

about how hard it had been to sleep at Bunda the night before with the music playing. "You just make up your mind to sleep," Hashim said, "and you sleep."

They awoke at three, an hour late already. What had happened to the driver? Later, as they marched past the mission at four-thirty, one of the priests was standing waiting, and joined in the march. "Which one is the President?" he asked. They marched for three hours and a half, with no breaks at all, and by the time they finally stopped they had gone fifteen miles. Then they sat down around the trailer, the President's informal court assembled, everyone listening and contributing an occasional quip to the conversation. The young priest lingered in the background until Munanka said, "Ah, here is the poor fellow whom we moved in on last night. Where did you sleep finally?" "In the car," said the priest happily. "Ah," said Nyerere, allowing the invisible barrier to be broken, "so you have been marching too? Ah, good. Good." Then the police served tea with milk and sugar, and hard-boiled eggs.

The marchers continued for eight days, covering one hundred and thirty-eight miles in all, until they reached Mwanza, where they were to attend the TANU National Conference. Three miles out of Mwanza, they were met by half the population of the town. As *The Nationalist* described it: "Heralded by peasants' war cries, strains of brass-band tunes, and a din of women's ululation, the President, beaming with revolutionary confidence, steered the Presidential column into the streets of the summit town hedged with crowds of cheering masses. . . . *Mwalimu's* brisk march into the town stunned the masses who on seeing him in sound health were driven wild with admiration and excitement to the borders of near frenzy. The entire town was gripped with the revolutionary fervour of the Spirit of Arusha." And so it was. Nyerere's driver, Christopher Kabaka, announced that he had been ashamed to watch the President walk one hundred and thirty-eight miles in front of him, while he himself was forced to drive his car, and that he was giving up his fourteen-day leave in support of the Arusha Declaration. The members of the late Seti Benjamin's group, having walked four hundred and fifty miles to Dar es Salaam, then travelled on to Mwanza by train, their odyssey at an end.

"I had been thinking of it for several weeks," Nyerere said later, explaining why he had decided to make the march. "I kept saying to the boys [who marched to Dar es Salaam], 'Don't listen to those people' "—the ones who had questioned the usefulness of the marching and suggested that the energy could be better spent by working in the fields. "After all," Nyerere continued, with a grin, "it's not as if these boys had been building bridges! The marching is a symbol of the acceptance of the challenges ahead of them.

"I thought the only way I could encourage them was to join the youth movement. Also, I felt the time would come when we would have to say, 'Now stop.' But how would you say 'Now stop'? And who would say 'Now stop'? So, after this march, *I* could say, 'Now stop.' But after the third day of the march, I thought, 'This is very good. Why say stop? If it's good for me, it's good for them.' So they're still marching.

"And also," he said, with a motion towards his new press secretary, Paul Sozigwa, "my fellows; I knew them better than I had ever known them before."

But finally, when eight youths from St Andrew's College reached Arusha, after walking four hundred and thirteen miles from Dar es Salaam, Nyerere told them, "The rains are pouring. Therefore the marches should be abandoned, and people should start their farm work."

XIV

IN LATE 1966, Julius Nyerere was asked how it had happened that there had been no angry fights or schisms within his government during the first five years of independence, no ministers who had fled into exile or been placed behind bars. "It is true," he said. "We have not had violent dismissals or violent resignations. There is an objective reason for this: I've been lucky. I've been one of the luckiest Presidents in Africa. My colleagues are very loyal to me. It is true that people try to imagine cliques working against me; but this is not true.

"You shift responsibilities, of course; I often do that. There are only one or two men who have held the same positions for a long time; there's [Solomon] Eliufoo [the Minister of Education, who later resigned because of illness], who holds his like a sultan. I have dropped a few ministers by giving them other jobs. I appointed two as ambassadors. But why should I shake the damned system? It suits a young country very well.

"It is also true, I think, that it is in my character. Partly, at least. This has weaknesses; you can maintain too many incompetents because you don't want to shake them up. If someone else had been President, I don't know, he might have shaken it up, for the sake of competence. It's possible.

"My colleagues know they are my colleagues. Many are from the party, such as Rashidi, Oscar, Bhoke. These are the political group, the party veterans. Jamal, too, although he didn't actually join the party at the beginning, because of the rules; but he is a virtual founder. Derek Bryceson, somewhat later. So this political group, in a sense, has *been* the party. It has given character to the country. I would need the strongest reason for destroying this unity. And even when it is necessary to remove someone, you do not humiliate him, you give him a job he can do better. In any case, we are building institutions, and habits of government."

Why was it that Oscar Kambona was disliked or distrusted by so many foreigners?

"Oscar is a shy man," Nyerere answered. "In the West you speak of open societies and closed societies. When you have a closed individual, people don't know him too well. When they have got to know him, they say, 'Ah, I see; the image is quite wrong.' But it creates a mystery. Secondly, he is not particularly articulate. So, even if you have an opportunity to talk with him, he does not express himself well—maybe even in terms of slogans. So outsiders build up a mystery.

"It is never fair, but it is true that my character gives an impression of openness. Well, you can't change this. But it is never fair. Oscar is a man of the people. So is Rashidi, but Rashidi is not a mystery. Rashidi has a detachment; he is not a *personal* sort of person. Oscar feels very strongly. Like all people of feeling, he creates strong attachments. He is a barometer of feeling. Rashidi is an administrator, a doer; he is unemotional. Oscar *feels* for people. When outsiders misjudge Oscar, they are very wrong. They do a disloyalty to Oscar. He is extremely loyal—to the party, to me, to the people. With the others, it is 'the correct thing to do'. With Oscar, it's strong feeling.

"He is very human, very kind. Let me put it this way." A broad grin. "He has some of the faults and qualities of the United States of America. Your country has been accused of having this as one of its faults—I myself have accused it of this. It's a very human fault, but a fault nonetheless. Because you love strongly, you want to be loved strongly. You want to be loved by all! You feel strongly. And when you are accused of something, or misunderstood, you say, '*Me*? Why? I do this and this and this—and get misunderstood!' A very human thing. And there are others, like Rashidi Kawawa, who are very British. If you love them, fine. But if not, it won't stop them from doing their work. And they'll certainly shed no tears. No!"

Many of Oscar Kambona's friends in Dar es Salaam would agree with Nyerere's description. Kambona is a sentimentalist, a man who remembers his old friends and sometimes gets into trouble because of it, a man who was always surrounded by a swarm of hangers-on, job seekers, relatives, cronies; a man who spent a good deal of money, at least by Tanzanian standards, on his friends and extended family.

Almost anyone who talked with Kambona at length during those years would have recognized him as a flawed man, easily wounded, who seemed to have believed from childhood that powerful people whose affection he sought—notably white schoolmasters and later all sorts of foreigners—misunderstood him and disliked him. He once said with self-deprecating humour that he was off to London to let the Commonwealth Office "have a look at this dreadful fellow". The inevitable consequence was that most influential Europeans in Tanganyika in the years before independence did in fact misunderstand and dislike him. He seemed to have an absolute gift for annoying governors by arriving an hour late for dinner parties, and offending sympathetic whites at the beginning of the TANU period by insisting that they must leave party meetings. After independence he was blamed by Europeans for having a hand in almost every act that frightened or angered them or seemed to have racialist connotations. Sometimes the blame was ascribed to deviousness, other times to inefficiency, for he was, by all accounts, one of the government's worst administrators. He was blamed for the Preventive Detention Act, and for the early rash of deportations of Europeans. He was accused of Africanizing the police too quickly. He was held partly responsible for the 1964 army mutiny; at the very least he was said to have contributed to a breakdown in army discipline by talking with the enlisted men directly and inviting them to voice their grievances; at the worst he was whispered to have played a mysterious role in the mutiny itself—a rumour for which there is no evidence whatever.

He was blamed for several of the anti-American incidents, notably the 1965 case of the "documents" that alleged a Western conspiracy against his country. Europeans in East Africa tended to like Nyerere and to exonerate him from responsibility for governmental actions they didn't approve of. Even today, many British residents of Kenya who disapprove of Tanzania's socialist policies speak of "Julius" with a grudging affection and a respect for his integrity and some of his actions—his fight against corruption, for example. Kambona always deflected the criticism from Nyerere. As a British journalist once observed, "Nyerere always comes out of it pure; nobody ever blames him. Isn't this the essence of a good politician? You let others do the hatchet work."

There is no proof that Kambona was ever disloyal to Nyerere in the years before 1967, but there is ample reason to believe he was increasingly dissatisfied. Until January 1962, Nyerere had no clearly designated deputy or heir apparent; when he resigned as prime minister, he could have chosen any of at least four of his colleagues —Kambona, Kawawa, Paul Bomani, and perhaps George Kahama, his Home Affairs Minister at the time—to succeed him; he chose

Kawawa. Kambona's influence probably reached its peak just before the 1964 mutiny, when he served as minister for both external affairs and defence. In the Cabinet reshuffle that followed, Nyerere gave the defence portfolio to Kawawa, took external affairs himself, and assigned Kambona to regional administration. This, it was said, was a more logical extension of Kambona's duties as secretary-general of TANU, a post that he continued to hold until 1967. Kambona seemed unwilling to accept the fact that, since 1962, Kawawa had been Nyerere's probable successor. At one point in 1964, when Nyerere's colleagues advised him against making a trip that was deemed risky, Kambona spoke with genuine concern about Nyerere's safety, and added, "What would we do without him? Who would take over ?" The remark seemed curious, since everyone else assumed Kawawa would take over. (Following the union with Zanzibar, however, the constitution specified that, in the event of the President's death in office, he would be succeeded by the First Vice-President, Abeid Karume, until a special election could be held; Karume himself was killed in April 1972.) Another time, when Kambona apparently felt or at least wondered if he were not being shunted aside, he remarked ruefully to a friend that Nyerere "gives you a lot of rope". Occasionally he seemed to betray a jealousy of other people's relationships with the President; after Nyerere's disappearance in the 1964 mutiny, Kambona said to State House aides who had stayed behind, "But you must know where he is. You can get one of his European friends to put him on a boat. . . ." Nonetheless, Kambona's colleagues never questioned his loyalty or doubted that he cared passionately about the problems of Africa; he could speak with great feeling about the plight of bright youngsters who would never have the chance to fulfil themselves, and about the freedom struggles in the south.

In 1966 Kambona spent several months in the Netherlands resting and recuperating from what was said to be high blood pressure. By the time he came home to Dar es Salaam, he had lost at least thirty pounds and seemed more relaxed than he had been for years. The following May, Kambona flew to East Germany for a few days; he needed a routine medical check-up, he said. Then, on June 10, he resigned quite suddenly from both his government and party posts because of "circulation troubles". The resignation occurred during a Cabinet reshuffle in which Kambona was being transferred from regional administration to local government and rural development. Tanzanians were particularly surprised that he was leaving not only his new Cabinet post but the secretary-generalship of TANU, which he had held for thirteen years.

In mid-July, the government arrested Eli Anangisye, a former leader of the TANU youth league, who had lost his position in March after leading a youth league attack on the Netherlands Bank in Dar es Salaam following the bank nationalization. As an MP, he had criticized Tanzania's acceptance of military assistance from Canada because of Canada's NATO ties with Portugal. A few days after that, the government announced that it had foiled a plot to subvert the government through the armed forces. Two men were detained: Anangisye and Hamisi Salumu, a one-time bodyguard of Kassim Hanga, the Zanzibari—an old friend of Oscar Kambona's —whom Nyerere had dropped the previous month as his Minister of State for Union Affairs.

On the same day, July 22, the Tanzanian Parliament passed a private motion asking Oscar Kambona to state the true reasons for his resignation. Nyerere charged in a speech that Tanzania had a few "madmen" and a few politicians who were "prostitutes" who valued money more than their personal dignity. The government knew who the "mercenary" politicians were, he said, and would pick them up one by one. After that, three intermediate-level civil servants were placed in detention, and were held until February 1968.

Kambona never appeared in Parliament to clear up the rumours about his resignation. On July 31, it was learned in Dar es Salaam that Kambona and his family had slipped away to Europe; after cancelling a reservation to fly to Nairobi by private plane, Kambona had driven from Dar es Salaam to Nairobi, and flown from there to London. Even after the news of Kambona's sudden departure had spread through the capital, someone was still answering the phone at his new Msasani Bay home by saying that Mr Kambona had merely gone to town.

The Tanzanian police might well have arrested Kambona if he had flown to Nairobi by private plane as planned; whether he took them by surprise when he left by car, or whether he was actually allowed to escape, is still unclear. The government is said to have been split over how to proceed against him; some members felt he should be arrested, while others believed he should not be turned into a martyr but should be permitted to get away.

The defection of Kambona, who had long been one of the three or four best-known politicians in the country, produced an atmosphere of stress. It came during the period, moreover, when the leadership was trying to adjust to the rigid requirements of the Arusha Declaration. Several diplomatic observers in Dar es Salaam believed that, to some extent, the feverish wave of marching in support of the Declaration was sponsored by the TANU organization in order to demonstrate to the full leadership that the people were behind the President.

More than a week after his arrival in London, Kambona declared that he was the victim of a plot to overthrow the President. In a jumble of charges of plots and mischief-making he claimed that there was "no friction at all between the President and myself. The President's enemies know full well that to get rid of him they must first get rid of me." An undercover power struggle had broken out in Tanzania, he charged, led by a small but influential group that opposed the Arusha Declaration and had found loopholes in the law by which to transfer their property to their children and families. This group, said Kambona, controlled "the intelligence service, the police, army and other key positions," and had been trying to frame him and assassinate him. As for the peculiar way in which he had left East Africa, Kambona explained that he had wanted to drive through Moshi en route to Nairobi so that he could say goodbye to his wife's family. "As soon as my health is restored," he said, "I shall go home. I have no intention of deserting my constituents."

Some of Kambona's friends thought that, by his curious statement, he was hoping Nyerere would invite him to return. Instead Nyerere, very angry, told a group of visitors from Morogoro, Kambona's constituency, that Kambona should be stripped of his seat in Parliament. Nyerere called on Kambona to come home, resign his seat and seek re-election, and promised that he would be renominated by the National Executive. "He deceived Tanzania and Africa as a whole," Nyerere said. "I trusted him and all of you trusted him too. When he came to me to say that he wanted to resign because of failing health, I trusted him, because it is true that his health is not good." Now Kambona was saying in London, said Nyerere, that "he and Kassim Hanga were the founders of the Union. He said in London that there will be a revolution in Tanzania within three months."

The argument continued for several months; in a sense, in fact, it has never ended. Kambona offered to come home and resign if Nyerere would resign; then he threatened to hold a press conference at which he would "lift the lid off politics in Tanzania". *The Nationalist* answered him: "Say what you have to say, or be branded a coward and a traitor to Tanzania and to Africa."

In September, both Kassim Hanga and Denis Phombeah, another friend of Kambona's, left Tanzania for London. Hanga had recently been dropped as Vice-President of Zanzibar as well as minister for Union affairs in Nyerere's Cabinet; Phombeah had been removed as commissioner of commerce and marketing and subsequently from a post in the foreign ministry. Three months later, Hanga returned to Dar es Salaam and almost immediately was placed in preventive detention, as were two of Oscar Kambona's brothers, Otini and Mattiya. *Ulimwengu*, a Swahili paper that Otini Kambona edited, was closed down.

In January 1968, making his full-scale attack at last, Kambona declared that Nyerere was "making himself a dictator", and condemned the recent arrest of Hanga as "a bleak chapter for Tanzania". Kambona claimed that the Tanzanians had given assurances to Sékou Touré, the President of Guinea, that Hanga would not be arrested. So how, asked Kambona, could he himself go home?

One day in mid-January a very tense scene took place before twenty thousand people at a Zanzibar Day rally in Dar es Salaam. Nyerere denounced Kambona and Kassim Hanga, and, ordering that Hanga be brought before the crowd, Nyerere said to him, "I don't know what you told Sékou Touré." To the crowd he said, "After his return, I did not intend to detain him. But he started saying he had been called back by the army in Zanzibar, which was a lie." To Hanga: "That's why I detained you."

After his return from London, Hanga had told a Zanzibari friend in Dar es Salaam that Zanzibar authorities were locking up his friends and relatives on the island. Even more imprudently, he had implied to someone else, who was in fact a police agent, that he was waiting in Dar es Salaam for a move by the military authorities on Zanzibar against Abeid Karume. In December 1968 Hanga was released from detention on Nyerere's order. It was eight months later that Nyerere, convinced that Hanga was involved in further conspiracy, made the mistake of turning him—as well as Othman Shariff—over to Zanzibari authorities for questioning. Both men were apparently executed, on Karume's orders, following a secret trial.

In November 1967, more than three months after Kambona had fled to London, Nyerere was reminded of how he had described Kambona in conversation a year earlier. "Yes, I remember," he said, "And did I tell you what a professor of mine once said? 'A dictator is like all of us. A person with a strong desire to be loved. And where he goes wrong is, he says, "I love being loved, so love me —or else!" '

"Well, I can tell you what I understand about my friend. Last year Oscar had very bad health. That's absolutely genuine. He had gone to Addis Ababa, and they had a silly row over whether to accept the Ghana delegation [to an OAU conference]. And afterwards he came to me and said, 'My doctor says I should go for treatment.' I said, 'Of course, go. Go to Holland immediately.' I gave him a letter to Prince Bernhard's doctor, who had treated two of my colleagues.

"Well, he was away quite a few months. When he came back, he was much better. He had lost a lot of weight. This year—in April, I think—he said his doctor had said he should get a medical check-up. I said, 'Yes, please go.' So he went—this time to East Germany, for a 'second opinion'. In a few weeks he wrote and said, 'I'm worried, I think I may have to resign.' Sometime after this, a Dutch friend of mine said, 'I think Oscar will resign, and he has asked me to inquire about a job with the World Council of Churches.' He said, 'I think you will find him a very changed man.' "

Kambona returned in time for the meeting of the National Executive committee in Iringa, Nyerere continued, where Kambona spoke frankly of his ill health and confided, "One day I may ask you to let me go." "So," noted Nyerere, "this was the third reference to his health." In early June, Nyerere announced a Cabinet reshuffle. "And on the eighth, twenty minutes before the ministers were due to take the oath, he came to me and said, 'Look, *Mwalimu*, if you had told me about this, I would have said I should resign.' I argued with him upstairs; I said, 'Let's reach no conclusion. You come in the evening and we will discuss it.' We came down together. He said, 'I must go this time.' He gets these feelings of despondency. I told him, 'I can't stop you, but have you considered the timing?' "—the fact that the resignation would coincide with the Cabinet reshuffle. "He said, 'Look, *Mwalimu*, I'm always misunderstood. If I resign now, I'll be misunderstood. If I wait, I'll be misunderstood.' Well, this sounded quite all right to me. But he said he would wait before resigning the secretary-generalship.

"And," Nyerere continued, "trouble began almost immediately. Hashim [Mbita] told me, 'But he has also resigned as secretary-general!' I thought, 'Well, he will explain later.' Then Ben Mkapa, of *The Nationalist*, said, 'But what is the real story?' I said, 'He resigned for his health, as he said.' 'But,' Mkapa said, 'he *came* [to the press conference] *with Hanga!*' " Nyerere threw up his hands in confusion.

"The following Saturday—we hold a Central Committee meeting every Saturday—I had expected him to come and explain. I told them the real reason was his health, but many didn't accept this. That evening, an elder of TANU came to see me. I said, 'He resigned because of his health. If you don't believe me, go and ask him.' The elder said, 'I've just come from his house. He says he resigned because of Hanga.' I said, 'Good heavens!' I said, 'But this is rubbish! An intelligent person doesn't resign because of another person, he resigns on principle!' "

During the negotiations that followed, Nyerere told intermediaries, "I'm not taking back Hanga, *I* form this government." Finally Kambona appeared before the Central Committee. "He said some things that shocked me a little bit," Nyerere said. "I felt he was mentally tired. He said, 'I'm frightened, I have my brother staying with me to protect me.' I told him, 'Rest, take leave.' He came to my house. He said yes, he would go to Morogoro. Well! That's not my idea of a rest—Morogoro was his constituency!

"In the meantime," continued Nyerere, referring to the five men who were put in preventive detention, "we rounded up these clots, really they were clots. And he panicked and left the country. We had asked for his diplomatic passport. Hanga had submitted his. I think this may be the thing that did it; I think he thought we would stop him from leaving the country."

He spoke again of Oscar in an earlier time. "His sense of insecurity was always sufficient to me to explain his every foible. I could explain everything because of this.

"He loves the myths. We took Oscar on in early 1955, and he left for London in 1956." Why? "As a result of insecurity—because he was not loved by every member of the Central Committee. And he stayed in London until 1959. Finally Oscar told me, 'All right, I'll come back. But what about those fellows in the Central Committee who never write to me?' I said, 'Look, Oscar, I can't promise that every member of the Central Committee is going to love you.' And he returned to find that the party had been built by others— and by confident people. We did all sorts of things to rehabilitate him."

Reflecting on the number of important events in which Kambona had played an ambiguous role, Nyerere insisted that he himself, and not Kambona, was responsible for the American "documents" case of 1965. And yet, said Nyerere, yes, it was true that he was looking back on earlier events in the light of what he had learned in recent months. "If there is something I don't understand," he said, "I begin to read history backwards."

In October 1969, Bibi Titi Mohamed, the former head of the national women's organization, and Michael Kamaliza, the former Labour Minister and former Secretary-General of the National Union of Tanganyika Workers, were placed in preventive detention, along with four army officers, for activities "not conducive to good law and order". A day later, a former news editor of *The Nationalist*, Gray Mattaka, was arrested at the Nairobi airport and turned over to Tanzanian authorities; he was said to have been acting as an emissary for Oscar Kambona. In the ensuing treason trial, Mrs Mohamed, Mattaka and two other defendants were convicted of plotting to overthrow the government and assassinate the President, and were sentenced to life imprisonment. Kamaliza and an army officer received ten-year terms.

Oscar Kambona has since remained in London. Very little is known of his recent life; once, late in 1968, he was fined £25 for illegal possession of a firearm. His attacks on Nyerere have subsided, but he has apparently retained an avid interest in Tanzanian politics; occasionally, it is said in Dar es Salaam, he sends Christmas cards to members of the Tanzanian Parliament and letters of sympathy to persons who have been dismissed by the Tanzanian government.

XV

MAN-EATER AT SINGIDA IS GENUINE LION. A police spokesman at Singida yesterday denied reports that the famed killer lionmen were operating again following the deaths of six children in the Mtipa division this year. It is not the lionmen, but a man-eater that has killed the children. A game scout, assisted by villagers, is hunting it.'

The lionmen of Singida terrorized the region some years ago. Witchdoctors enslaved people who, dressed in lion skins, killed a number of people in the area.

—The Standard, *March 1966*

An MP asked in the National Assembly yesterday if there was a fish which had the form of a woman.

The Minister for Lands, Settlement and Water Development, Mr Maswanya, told the member, Mr Saileni (Kilosa West) that mermaids do not exist.

Replying on behalf of the Minister for Agriculture, Forests and Wild Life, Mr Maswanya added that sea cows, mostly seen around Mafia and Kilwa, were most probably mistaken for mermaids. Sea cows preferred to live near river mouths and fed on sea weed, and were hunted for their meat and fat. In Tanzania they were preserved by law.

Stories of mermaids were heard as far back as the ancient times, and they were probably spread by sailors who wanted to impress others.

The Standard, *October 1966*

The contrast between the primitive and the modern is something that the visitor to Tanzania never quite comes to terms with. On the one hand, Tanzania has had for at least fifteen years the best organized political party in eastern Africa; on the other hand, many Tanzanians still feel a far deeper sense of identification with their tribe than with their country. Tanzania is a land in which a foreign tourist can travel widely without encountering danger or hostility—curiosity and suspicion, perhaps, but rarely hostility. It can therefore come as quite a jolt to be reminded—as on an evening flight between Dar es Salaam and Nairobi—that Tanzania by night is still a world of blackness pierced only by the orange dots of occasional village fires. Julius Nyerere travels among his people almost constantly, sometimes for weeks at a time without a rest; he has probably spoken directly to as large a percentage of his countrymen as any head of state on earth. Yet, when he visited the remote village of Mbulu three or four years ago, a tribal elder greeted him with incredulity, saying, "Are you the *Mwalimu*? We thought the *Mwalimu* was a white man."

In December 1967 the government announced the results of a new census, the first since 1957. The census revealed that the population had reached 12,125,000, had increased by almost 35 per cent in the previous decade, and would double by the year 1992. More important, the census showed that the population was higher by 1,700,000 than the latest estimate published only three months earlier by the Government Statistical Department; the population, it turned out, was increasing at a rate of two and seven-tenths of one per cent rather than the two and two-tenths of one per cent that the government had estimated. This dismaying information showed that the country's economic progress since independence had been even more modest than the Tanzanians had realized. In 1964, based on a population estimate of 10,500,000, the government had calculated the per capita income at about £19. In actuality, the population at that time was approaching 12,000,000, so the true per capita income was considerably lower.

In his 1969 speech to the TANU National Executive committee, Nyerere recalled his government's progress in expending secondary education: 7,100 children would enter secondary school that year, as compared with some 5,200 in 1964 at the beginning of the previous five-year plan. But in consequence, he added, the expansion of the primary school system had necessarily been neglected. "Indeed the census has revealed," he told the committee, "that the chances of a seven-year-old Tanzanian going to school are worse now than we thought they were when we drew up the first plan. At that time we used to say that about fifty per cent of our children went to school. The much larger population of the country, which was revealed in the census figures, showed us that the actual percentage in 1964 was nearer forty-six per cent, and even now, at the end of the plan period, only about forty-seven per cent of our children can find a primary school place."

7

Moreover, said Nyerere, a large number of primary school children were leaving school after only four years, and would probably forget most of what they had learned; so the government had decided to remove the Standard IV examination and increase the number of classes at Standards V, VI and VII to enable virtually every child who entered primary school to get a full seven years' primary education.

The delegates cheered, but Nyerere quickly told them the price of this decision: the futher postponement of one of the country's most cherished goals. "The effect of giving priority to eliminating the Standard Four examination," he said, "is that by the end of the second five-year plan we will still only have places for about fifty-two per cent of our eligible children in Standard One. But no child who enters primary school this year or afterwards will have to take that examination; they will go straight to Standard Seven. It will, however, now be 1989 before we are able to introduce universal primary education in Tanzania."

Later in the same speech, he turned to some of his favourite criticisms of the Tanzanian diet. "Those who have seen the Chinese working on the railway survey," he said, "or the Americans building the road to Zambia, will have noticed how our people get tired very quickly in comparison with the Chinese and the Americans. The reason is not that our people are lazy. It is that they do not get enough meat, eggs, fish and milk, or other protein foods even to feed their bodies properly. But, although this is well-known, if you suggest to our citizens that they should keep chickens, they will ask, 'Where shall we sell them?' Or: 'Where shall we sell the eggs?' These are very stupid questions. . . . And what of fruit? We act as if fruit is only good for Europeans or for children. . . ."

In 1968, for the first time, the Tanzanian Parliament refused to pass a bill that the Nyerere government had sponsored. The bill was a proposal to grant gratuities—which could be used as retirement income—for ministers, regional commissioners and area commissioners. Nyerere, for whom the law already provided a pension, had recently been shocked by the illness of Solomon Eliufoo, his long-time Minister of Education, who had been paralyzed by a stroke; and this may have induced him to recommend the gratuities bill at that time. In any event, the proposal was angrily denounced by MPs as contrary to the spirit of the Arusha Declaration, and was soundly defeated.

When asked about it the following year, Nyerere said he had
decided not to press the matter. "Parliament had a point. In the
atmosphere of the Arusha Declaration, perhaps my timing was
wrong. I had to bow to Parliament. But this matter can't be elevated
to a principle. A person can work at developing the state for five or
ten years; and when the time comes, he just goes. I don't see how
we can justify this. The manager of the National Development
Corporation can have a pension or a gratuity when he goes, but not
a minister." Besides, he added, "it's not a principle in Tanzania,
because *I* have a pension. I'm not a king, I'm paid in recognition
of services. So how do you distinguish between me and the
ministers?"

On that same day in late 1969, Nyerere commented on the government's proposals for a new marriage bill—a measure that was already being described in Nairobi and overseas as a "two wives for
every Christian" bill. "As of now—to use an American expression—
we recognize Christian marriages, Moslem marriages, tribal
marriages, Hindu marriages. We have always accepted that Moslems
can have four wives, and tribalists can have ten or twenty. Tribal
polygamy, Christian monogamy, both are recognized by the law
as it is.

"Now we are saying, We are a secular state. Certain laws can be
regarded as laws of the state, or of God, or the church. 'Thou shalt
not kill' is also a law of the state, and we would take a man who
violates it to court. But some church laws are not laws of the state.
'Thou shalt not eat meat on Fridays,' for example. Moslems don't
take pork. But the state doesn't get involved in this. In Tanzania,
marriage falls into this category. Islam says, 'You may have no more
than four wives.' Christians can have only one wife. If a Moslem
takes a fifth wife, we don't prosecute him. If a Christian takes
two wives, we prosecute him. Why? The British introduced the
system."

Under the existing laws, Nyerere continued, "if I [as a Christian]
take a second wife, I can be prosecuted. How do we explain this?
We accept that Moslems can have four wives, and tribalists can have
ten or twenty. The police constable who arrests me may be a
polygamist himself. The prosecutor may be a polygamist, as well as
the magistrate who sentences me to four years at hard labour. This
is ridiculous."

Under the new law, he explained, "we are abolishing the law of
bigamy. Then the position will be exactly the same for everybody.

Legally, a man may not take another wife; but we won't prosecute him if he does. It will be between himself and his wife and his God. We are not legislating morality. When two marry, it will be a monogamous marriage. But we are saying they can choose—they can agree—to change their status to polygamy."

The bill also provided that henceforth the traditional bride-price could be paid on a sort of instalment plan. "We are saying," Nyerere explained, "that bride-price should not delay marriage. If it is not paid, this will not invalidate the marriage. It can be paid later. We hope the custom of bride-price will die. But no, we are not making it illegal." Implying that the tradition was still deeply rooted in tribal tradition, he added with a shiver, "After all, we have elections next year."

The elections of 1970 proved to be a reprise of the 1965 voting. Nyerere, again unopposed, was overwhelmingly re-elected—this time by 97 per cent of the vote—to another five-year term. Two ministers, two junior ministers and a dozen backbenchers were defeated. Once again, parliamentary elections on Zanzibar were postponed.

Probably Nyerere's most controversial initiative in African affairs was his support of the Biafran rebel regime against the Nigerian government. Tanzania was the first African country to grant diplomatic recognition to Biafra; three others followed. Nyerere's position surprised many of his friends because it seemed to mark a break with the majority of orthodox African nationalists; it also seemed inconsistent with his customary support of the concept of national unity, whether it had been the unity of the Congo, Germany or Vietnam. In November 1969, a few months before the collapse of the Biafran rebellion, Nyerere explained why he had felt it necessary to side with the Ibo tribesmen against Nigeria.

"It was the Ibos who said, 'We can't have independence for Eastern Nigeria alone,' when they had been virtually offered it by the British in 1956. Now, the Ibos are not a bunch of damned fools. They're not socialists, but they are dynamic, intelligent and hard-working. They decided to co-operate with federation. They said, 'We can't have a Nigeria without the north.' The north, meanwhile, worked hard to control the west; the area that was raped was the west.

"The first coup was directed at the central government. Abubakar [Balewa] was a very good man, but it was a corrupt government.

And when the West used to put up Nigeria as an example of African democracy, I was sick. *Every job had a price*.

"The first coup was an Ibo coup. I don't like this, but it happened. They killed, but very selectively; I think [General Yakubu] Gowon says twelve were killed. The second coup was anti-Ibo. Ibos were virtually expelled from the Federation. Thirty thousand were massacred, and two million became refugees from Nigeria. A Tanzanian landing at Lagos was asked, 'Are you an Ibo?' But the Ibos continued to search for a formula for a united Nigeria. Even after massacre and expulsion from the rest of Nigeria, they were still working for a united Nigeria. Even if no one else could see it, Africa should have seen it. Africa should have said to Nigeria, 'Look, what are you asking?'

"Africa didn't. Because the idea had been drummed into us that every African state has its own Biafra. This is stupid nonsense. It confuses the weakness of African governments with the weakness of African states, which is a very different thing; governments have fallen, but the states have remained. There is a desire to be together. I know there is a desire in Tanzania to create an East African nation. Are the Sukuma determined to establish a Sukuma nation? No. Or my little tribe of forty thousand, is it determined? No. I have said it before [to Africa]: You are learning the wrong lesson from Nigeria.

"After all, nations do break up. Senegal and Mali broke up. One of the touching moments of the 1963 OAU conference was when [Presidents Leopold] Senghor and Modibo Keita embraced. They can still become one; but they didn't kill one another."

It was then that he added his view of his own troubled Union: "If the Zanzibaris felt the Union was of no use to them, and broke away, and this was the genuine feeling of the Zanzibaris, I could not possibly kill Zanzibaris. If they came in freely, they can leave freely, we did not conquer Zanzibar. And if they remain, this must be borne of their own free choice."

Tanzanians sometimes complain that they are badly misreported by the overseas press, and often they are right. Only one Western news organization, Reuters, maintains a staff correspondent in Dar es Salaam; the others cover Tanzania from Nairobi, Kenya, if not from Europe. The Tanzanians are sensitive to the fact that, as a rule, the Nairobi-based correspondents visit their country only once or twice a year; they also suspect that the correspondents are overly influenced by the Kenyans and particularly by the British community of Kenya, which tends to regard Tanzania as socialist, pro-Chinese, hot-headed and somehow a bit threatening.

The problem is complicated by the situation on Zanzibar. Western readers find it hard to comprehend that when, for instance, Abeid Karume declared that there should be no elections on Zanzibar for fifty years, his statement had no relation to the policies of the Union government to which he theoretically owed allegiance. There is, however, another news problem, perhaps common to every neglected country in the world but particularly severe in the case of Tanzania. What is important about Tanzania is the imaginative and often experimental way in which Nyerere's government is trying to solve African problems—a difficult subject to explain in a newspaper or television report.

On the other hand, a land where human beings pretend to be lionmen and MPs at Question Time ask whether mermaids exist is obviously full of oddities that make extraordinary stories. Sometimes a minister or a regional commissioner or some lesser official will launch a campaign, often on his own initiative—and suddenly, from reading the overseas papers, it seems as if the whole of Tanzania is engaged in a frenzy of fighting mini-skirts, hair straighteners, bleaches and other threats to "Tanzania's culture and the aims of the Arusha Declaration"; or forcing the noble Masai to discard their blankets and ochre and nakedness in favour of khaki trousers and shirts.

A more legitimate but greatly exaggerated story dealt with the 1967 deportation drive by Home Affairs Minister Lawi Sijaona against the country's Indian aliens, which coincided with similar but more serious anti-Asian compaigns in Kenya and Uganda. Some three hundred Asian residents were ordered to leave the country, but most of the deportation orders were later cancelled. Often Nyerere contributes to the ambiguity by remaining aloof— as in the case of the youth league's campaign against mini-skirts— until the phenomenon plays itself out.

A further reason for misunderstanding is that, even at close range, Tanzanian politics remain ultimately incomprehensible to outsiders. Decisions are made in the secrecy of party councils; disagreements become publicly known months or even years after the fact. One reason for the secrecy may be racial pride: to keep family quarrels obscured from a hostile world. Certainly there is a racial undertone to all sorts of undertakings. A European acquaintance once suggested to Nyerere that he should switch the job assignments of two British employees of the Tanzanian government. Nyerere stared in mocking disbelief. "A *white face* for a *white face?*" he demanded jubilantly, rolling his eyes in wonder. "Ahhh, my friend, how little you understand African politics."

The British relationship with Tanzania underwent another crisis in late 1970 when the Conservative government of Prime Minister Edward Heath appeared to have decided to resume arms sales to South Africa. Along with Zambia and Uganda, Tanzania threatened to leave the Commonwealth if the sales took place. After talking with Heath in London, Nyerere described the British attitude as "almost a psychological desire to defy; it's the nearest thing you can think of to the Suez mood." Back in Dar es Salaam, he gibed at the British by attributing to them the sort of thin-skinned protests often associated with young African states: " 'Why can't we make decisions for ourselves? Are we not independent like anyone else? Do we have to be pushed around by little countries like Tanzania?' " At the Commonwealth Prime Ministers' Conference in Singapore in January 1971, the question of arms sales was referred to a special eight-nation committee for further study, thereby postponing but hardly settling the Commonwealth dispute.

The United States' relations with Tanzania are in an even worse state of disrepair. Despite the fact that American tourism in East Africa is increasing sharply, the American public accords to Tanzania about as much attention as it gives to any other subject that must be both defined and pronounced. The indifference derives in part, no doubt, from a disenchantment with African politics since 1960—the spawning of so many truculent and unviable little states, and the ravaging civil wars of the Congo and Nigeria. But it has served to accentuate the disadvantage that the United States already suffers in its relations with independent Africa—or at least with those governments that are not prepared to accept for ever the white domination of southern Africa. In its relations with these countries, the United States has several handicaps: its substantial private investment in South Africa; its NATO connection with Portugal, and its close ties with the former colonial powers; its own race problem; and—increasingly, in the late sixties—its disastrous adventure in Vietnam. None of these factors, however, quite explains the degree to which African problems have been ignored by both the Johnson and Nixon administrations. Late in 1971, for example, the United States Congress voted, despite a United Nations embargo on important Rhodesian products, to remove the ban on the importation of Rhodesian chrome—thereby strengthening a white-minority regime in Salisbury that is outnumbered by Rhodesia's black majority by twenty-two to one. If there is any prospect for a significant change in American attitudes toward African affairs, it may lie in the possibility that the American black community may some day exercise the sort of influence on United States policy in Africa that American Jews exert at present on Middle East policy; but that day is by no means imminent.

The Chinese, on the other hand, have steadily strengthened their position in Tanzania since 1965. The primary reason for their huge aid commitment to Tanzania and Zambia remains somewhat uncertain. Some Western observers have suggested that the Chinese have an eye on Zambia's copper; and that they would like to acquire down-range facilities for the testing of intercontinental ballistic missiles launched from the Asian mainland. Many of Nyerere's Western friends believe, however, that if he has demonstrated anything at all during Tanzania's first decade of independence, it is that neither his country's non-alignment policy nor anything else is for sale, not even for the price of a railway; and that the Chinese must, to some extent, realize this.

It has also been pointed out by Westerners that if a military build-up in Tanzania should lead eventually to serious fighting with the Portuguese along the southern border with Mozambique, and particularly if the Portuguese were backed by the South African Army, Tanzania could find itself dangerously dependent upon the Chinese and could be forced to accept whatever terms the Chinese might choose to offer.

However that may be, it seems clear that the Chinese are in the process of making a long-range commitment to Africa. Through the Tanzam railway, the Chinese are seeking to demonstrate not only the quality of their technology but their willingness to build a large development project that the rich Western countries refused to undertake. Presumably the Chinese are also calculating that the Western nations will continue to withdraw their aid and abdicate their influence; that the white countries will draw together when the crisis comes in southern Africa, as it surely will; and that the countless individual relationships that bind the men and institutions of Tanzania and its neighbours with those of Britain and, to a lesser extent, America will not survive beyond the next twenty or thirty years. And indeed, if the Western nations continue to deal half-heartedly and unresponsively with the problems of African development, there may be a terrible inevitability about such a calculation.

At the time of Tanganyika's independence, in 1961, Nyerere used to say to friends, "If only I can have three years"; "If I can have just five years." In 1969, he told a journalist that he was torn between staying in office to carry out his own ideas and retiring in order to encourage new leadership. In 1970, during a visit to one of the hundreds of new *ujamaa* co-operative villages, he promised the local farmers that he would retire to such a settlement some day to live in peace and to write his memoirs.

Part of the burden that Nyerere carries—it is one that he shares with the continent's other leaders—is that he has seen so many of Africa's best men assassinated, either by their countries' enemies or their own. Among the ones he knew and respected were Sylvanus Olympio, the President of Togo and Sir Abubakar Balewa, the Prime Minister of Nigeria. Another was Tom Mboya, Kenya's Minister of Planning and Development, who was shot to death in a Nairobi street in 1969 under circumstances that have never been fully explained; Nyerere trusted him and counted on his wisdom and co-operation in every round of conferences concerning the East African Community. Still another was Eduardo Mondlane, the president of the Mozambican Liberation Front, who was killed in Dar es Salaam in early 1969. To be an African leader in this era is to be reminded again and again of one's vulnerability.

Those who believe that Nyerere would genuinely like to retire point out that he once resigned as prime minister without warning because he wanted to rebuild the party. But his continued presence, for the immediate future, may well be essential to the survival of his troubled Union. Troublesome as he was, the late Abeid Karume sometimes paid a grudging heed to Nyerere's counsel. Under Aboud Jumbe, a relatively well-educated member of the Revolutionary Council whom Nyerere appointed to succeed Karume, there is at least a slim chance that the situation on Zanzibar will gradually improve.

When an assistant or an institution falters, Nyerere's solution is to step up his own dialogue with the people: as if, by travelling more and more, he could inspire more and more *ujamaa* communities and self-help projects, higher and higher cotton and tobacco yields, and could fire the people's enthusiasm all by himself—and to a great extent he has done just that. His aim, often expressed, is to block somehow the rapid rise of the elite—the ambitious politicians, the university graduates returning from overseas, the prosperous men of the towns—and to address his government to the primary task of advancing the lives of the peasant majority.

About this rigidly idealistic scheme, some observers believe, there is a suggestion of futility. It is hard to believe that the fight against the growth of the elite will not be lost; that there will not be, in the end, a privileged class of university graduates who earn twenty or thirty times as much as peasant farmers. Nyerere presumably disagrees; in any case he perseveres. Years ago, he gave an eloquent talk to the schoolchildren of Tabora, in central Tanzania in which he said, again and again, "We must run while they walk," meaning that Africa must run as fast as it can to catch up with the modern world. He knew full well—and his Arusha Declaration underscored the knowledge—that the race was anything but a fair contest, and was in fact already lost: the developed world was running faster and faster, while the developing world fell further and further behind. No matter, Nyerere says today, in a thousand variations; we must move on as best we can.

At the end of a long visit to Dar es Salaam, a foreign visitor once asked Nyerere what sort of country he would want Tanzania to be in twenty years' time. Both he and his press secretary of that period, George Rockey, burst out laughing; in terms of the crisis of the moment, whatever it may have been, the question seemed impossibly theoretical. Nevertheless, as usual, he tried to answer. "Twenty years from now, I hope there won't be a Tanzania," he said. "If there is not an *Africa*, then at least I hope there will be an East Africa. But if we have failed to use African nationalism to destroy our nationalism; if we have failed to take another step toward Pan-Africanism during that period; we should at least have a Tanzania that is very committed to Pan-Africanism itself. And by that time we should have a society of which the people are very proud; we should really have built a classless society. So, if there should still be a Tanzania twenty years from now, I hope it will be a classless society very committed to an African goal."

Several years later, toward the end of 1969, the visitor asked Nyerere the same question, and this time he answered it somewhat differently. "I still believe history has assigned Tanzania to us," he said. "This is our piece, a piece we do for Africa. The future of the

African is in Africa. We could get so bogged down in Tanzania that we lose sight of Africa. But even now, we are already more identified with Africa than with Tanzania. This is truer of Africa than of any other continent—African problems are really very African. We can only join this march of humanity as Africans; we have no other choice.

"Recently, I visited Canada and Sweden. Well, the more knowledgeable people I met knew I was from Tanzania. But really, even to them I was just an African. And rightly so. The real revolution we have to work out is African."

XVI

A FEW WEEKS AFTER his Tabora trip in 1966, Julius Nyerere paid a five-day visit to Kilimanjaro region, in the north-east of Tanzania. During the earlier trip he had often praised the hard-working Chagga who had got rich by growing coffee on the slopes of Mount Kilimanjaro, and he had urged the people of Tabora to emulate them. Now, in Chaggaland, he took a different tack. "Ah, the Chagga are *verrry* conservative," he said, jubilantly chiding Miss Lucy Lameck, who represented the region in Parliament and was a junior minister in his government. "The Chagga want us to expand the mountain," he continued, "and expanding the mountain is very expensive." "They *have* been conservative, *Mwalimu*," Miss Lameck replied defensively, "but they are changing." Nyerere's point, which was reasonable but perhaps not realistic, was that the Chagga should begin to move from their over-populated mountain to less thickly settled places in Tanzania. "I leave you with two ideas," he said at one stop. "Kilimanjaro region has a big population —five hundred thousand, the size of Gabon—and it is growing by ten thousand a year. If we want to maintain this population, we must increase the yields per acre. Secondly, Tanzania is a big country. Everybody can move. The Rufiji basin, for instance, is as large as Great Britain, and very fertile. Our country is different from most others: the land belongs to all the people. Any Tanzanian can live anywhere in Tanzania."

One morning as his procession drove through the cool, lush, incredibly green countryside, with the great mountain looming above, the Chagga turned out by the tens of thousands to cheer him and toss flowers. "Well, you have seen our population explosion," Nyerere told a visitor, laughing. "I never saw so many Chagga babies in my life." When he stopped at a mission station, the people gave him two sheep, one for himself and one for his wife. "*Mwalimu*, you are the shepherd," said one, "and we give you the sheep." As Nyerere was about to return to his car, a young man stepped forward and, like a cheerleader in a frenzy, stood directly in front of the President and began to shout, "Secondary school! Secondary school! If you will allow us, sir, we shall build a secondary school!"

This, it soon became clear, was the main concern of all the Chagga.

"You see," Ackland Mhina, the President's secretary, explained to a foreign visitor, "the problem of this region is the problem of progress. In the Central region, an area secretary would have to convince a parent to send a child to school. But here the parent has already sent his children to school, and wants higher schooling for them."

Over and over, at every meeting, a local TANU official would lead the crowd in a litany of Tanzanian politics.

Chairman: *Uhuru!*

Crowd: *Uhuru!*

Chairman: *Uhuru na* Nyerere!

Crowd: *Uhuru na* Nyerere!

Chairman: *Uhuru na* TANU!

Crowd: *Uhuru na* TANU!

And so on. As each visitor from Dar es Salaam was introduced, he would greet the crowd by shouting, "*Uhuru na* Nyerere" or "*Uhuru na kazi,*" freedom and work, the TANU motto. At such meetings, Nyerere made it clear that the villagers could not hope for any more secondary schools in the near future. "It is a dream," he would say, "to think that all children who have attained Standard Seven can expect to have a secondary education. We could build more schools if we could produce more, but we can't produce more if we all stay in Kilimanjaro."

Then he would tell the people about his stop at Vudee village two days earlier. Vudee lies in the Usambara mountains, and for three years the villagers of Vudee had been engaged in the arduous and painfully slow task of chipping a road to their village out of rock. "They get firewood," Ackland Mhina explained. "They light a fire, and when the rock becomes hot, they pour buckets of cold water, and this makes the rock break." Nyerere urged the Chagga to work as hard as the people of Vudee; at Vudee he had asked the villagers to work as hard as the Chinese and had promised to send one of them, a Mr Marigani, to China to see how hard the Chinese worked to improve their lives.

In the evening, at the presidential lodge in Moshi, Nyerere remarked, "What they need here is piped water and electricity. Right now many could afford to buy electricity if it were available." When asked how long it would take to provide it, he replied, "Maybe eternity," with that ironic shiver of his. "We have no money." Grinning, he added, "If it wasn't for Vietnam, maybe I could ask for a Marshall plan."

The following morning Nyerere answered questions at two separate meetings at the Kawenzi secondary school. He sat perched on a sort of throne chair, leaning his chin on his ebony stick. The first meeting was for adults and, like the one at Tabora a few weeks earlier, it dealt with purely practical matters. "Why did the government put a duty on copper spray?" a farmer asked. Nyerere said he didn't know but would look into it.

An hour later Nyerere spoke to the students of the Kawenzi school, and the meeting was very lively. "Shouldn't the people of Rhodesia try the passive-resistance techniques of Gandhi?" a girl asked. Nyerere said he doubted it. "Whether these techniques will work or not depends on the situation. Suppose my father was a doctor, and he refused to treat a patient, and in protest I refused to eat. Then it might work. On the second or third day, my father might agree to treat the patient. But in Rhodesia, [Ian] Smith might be happy to have the African population reduced."

"Sir," a boy asked, "it sometimes happens that you recognize new governments and you don't tell us whether you have recognized them. For example, the Congo. We do not know your stand on the Congo, and yet I understand you have visited there recently."

"What further proof do you want," Nyerere said, "that I recognize the Congolese government?"

"Why is it that in Britain there are no African Members of Parliament," asked another, "while in Tanzania we have Europeans in Parliament? Why shouldn't we do away with the white members and give their seats to the people of Tanzania?" Nyerere answered angrily, "One of the reasons for rejecting the British system is their discrimination, and one of the rules of TANU is that all men are our brothers, regardless of colour. That is what we have been fighting for."

One boy asked, "What happens to us, with our education, when we go back to our home areas?" Nyerere replied sharply, "What do you expect is going to happen to you? In Tanzania, ninety-six per cent of the people live on the land and farm it. Therefore, ninety-six per cent must go to the land where the people are, and four per cent can go to the cities. In America it is almost exactly the opposite, so in America most graduates can expect to go to the cities."

At the presidential lodge that night, Nyerere was visited by a United Nations agricultural expert, a heavy-set Swede, who invited him to visit the UN's ten-thousand-acre experimental farm that might some day accommodate ten thousand cotton growers. "Fine," Nyerere said. "I am a very big cotton man. When can I see it? Tomorrow?" He turned to his secretary. "No? Tomorrow is too full? When must I be back in Dar es Salaam? When am I going to Nachingwea?" Turning back to his visitor, Nyerere said, "No. Look, brother. Friday. Tomorrow they will rush us too much."

On Friday morning, a few hours after he had planned to fly back to Dar es Salaam, Nyerere was met at the cotton farm by the UN man, who introduced him to an aide. "Did you meet Mohamed Abdul, from the UAR?" "I met Mohamed," Nyerere said. "Mohamed, we should trade. Half a million of our people for half a million of yours who know about irrigating. That would do it, eh?"

As he walked through the irrigation scheme, Nyerere seemed preoccupied and said little. At one point, when someone mentioned the shortness of time, he murmured, almost to himself, "Plenty of time. Time is no problem. Money is the problem." At the end of the tour, the UN man told him, "When you come back in October, it will all be green. Thank you for encouraging us, sir."

"I'll be back, I'll be back," Nyerere said. "I don't know who is encouraging who."

Published by Transafrica Publishers Ltd., Kenwood House, Kimathi Street, P.O. Box 42990, Nairobi and printed by General Printers Ltd., Dar es Salaam Road, P.O. Box 18001, Nairobi, Kenya.